ULTIMATUM

ULTIMATE X-MEN

FANTASTIC FOUR

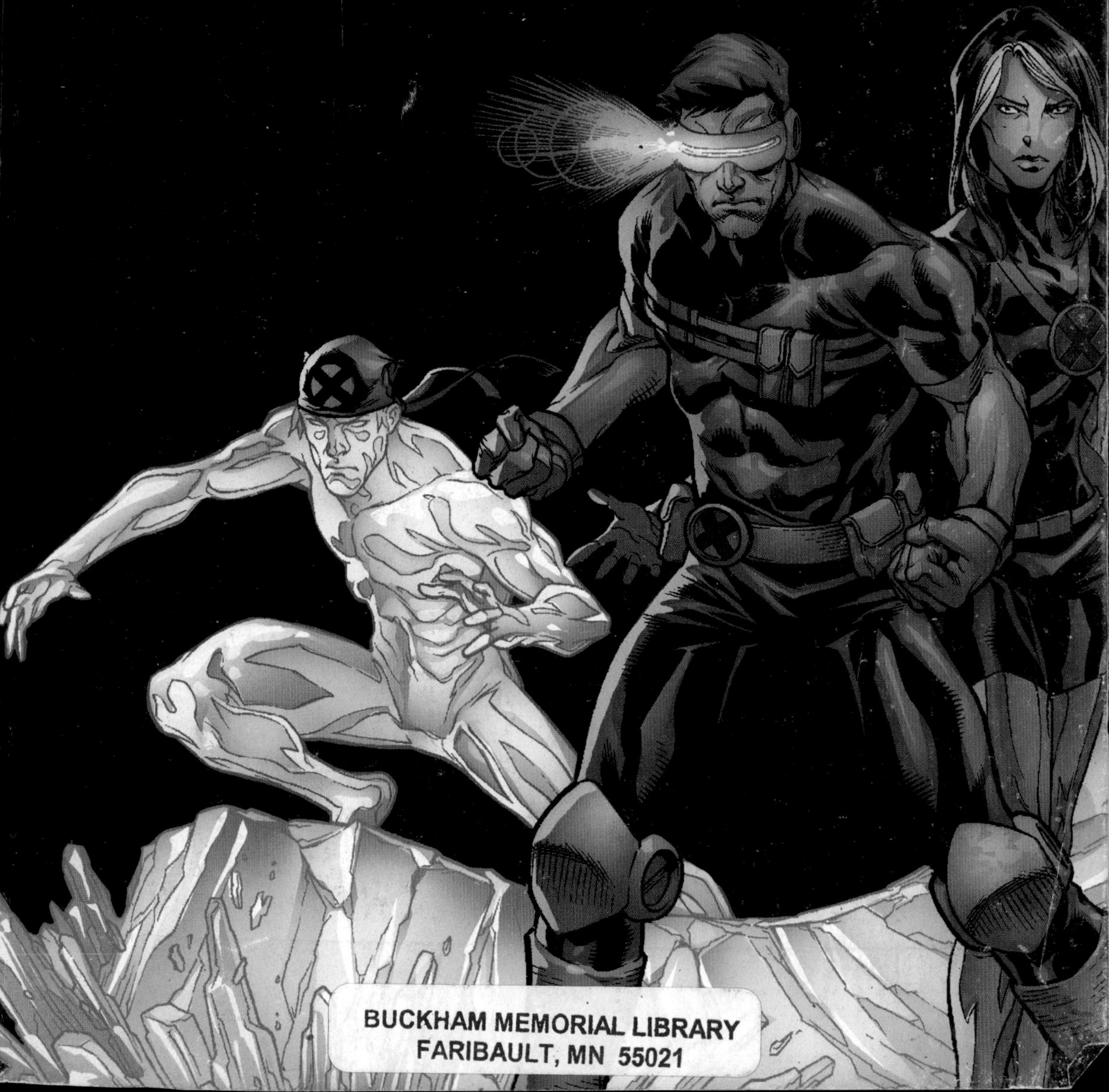

ULTIMATUM

ULTIMATE X-MEN ULTIMATE FANTASTIC FOUR

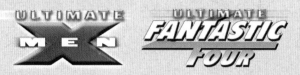

ULTIMATE X-MEN #98-100

Writer: Aron E. Coleite
Pencilers: Mark Brooks with Dan Panosian (Issue #99)
Inkers: Karl Story with Danny Miki & Victor Olazaba (Issue #99)
Colors: Edgar Delgado
Letters: Comicraft's Albert Deschesne
Cover Art: Mark Brooks (Issues #98-99) and Ed McGuinness, Karl Story & Justin Ponsor (Issue #100)

UTLIMATE FANTASTIC FOUR #58-60

Writer: Joe Pokaski
Art by Top Cow Productions, Inc.
Penciler: Tyler Kirkham
Inkers: Ryan Winn & Jason Gorder with Rick Basaldua, Joe Weems & Sal Regla
Colorist: Blond with Larry Molinar (Issue #59)
Letters: Virtual Calligraphy's Rus Wooton
Cover Art: Pasqual Ferry & Dave McCaig (Issues #58-59) and Ed McGuinness, Karl Story & Justin Ponsor (Issue #60)

Assistant Editor: Lauren Sankovitch
Senior Editor: Mark Paniccia

Special thanks to Michael Horwitz, Rob Levin & Filip Sablik

Collection Editor: Jennifer Grünwald
Assistant Editors: Alex Starbuck & John Denning
Editor, Special Projects: Mark D. Beazley
Senior Editor, Special Projects: Jeff Youngquist
Senior Vice President of Sales: David Gabriel
Book Design: Spring Hoteling

Editor in Chief: Joe Quesada
Publisher: Dan Buckley
Executive Producer: Alan Fine

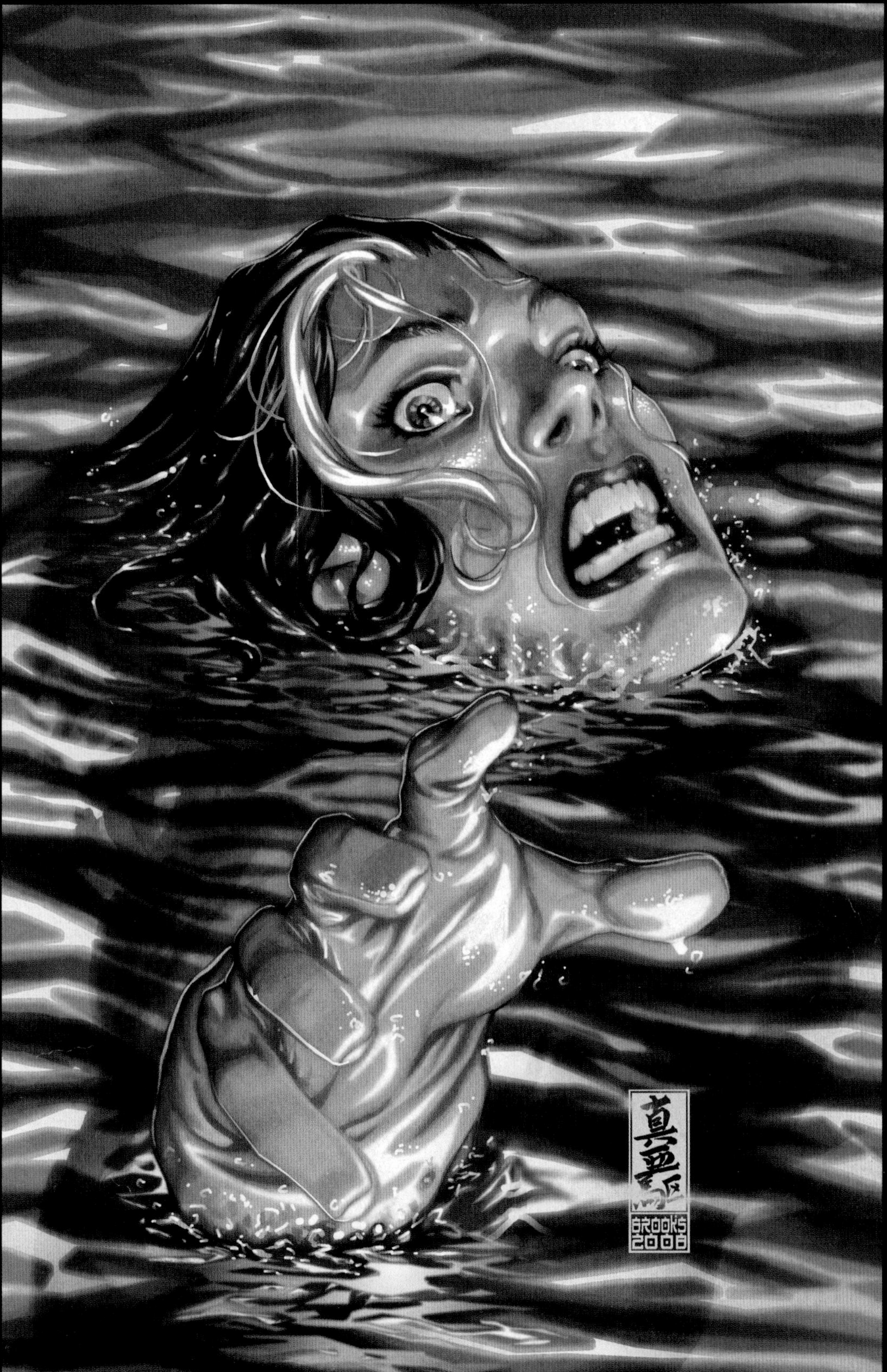
BROOKS
2008

Ultimate X-Men #98

Born with strange powers and amazing abilities, the X-Men are young mutant heroes, sworn to protect a world that fears and hates them.

PREVIOUSLY IN ULTIMATE X-MEN:

After a series of traumatic events involving the defeat of the power-mad mutant Apocalypse and the unexpected return of their mentor, Charles Xavier, the X-Men have been battered both physically and emotionally. Nothing could have prepared them for Alpha Flight, a drug-enhanced squad of mutants who attacked the team's home searching for Northstar, the boyfriend of Colossus. When the dust settled, Alpha Flight had kidnapped Northstar and what ensued tore the team apart...

Colossus was revealed to be using Banshee, the same mutant power-amplifying drug that allowed Alpha Flight to take down the X-Men...a drug Jean Grey discovered was created from Wolverine's DNA! Colossus led a group of Banshee – injected X-Men on a rescue mission to save his boyfriend, but the teens were so overwhelmed by its effects they were unable to save Northstar from overdosing on the drug.

In the end, it was Jean Grey – now inexplicably more powerful than ever after her battle with Apocalypse – who saved the team from falling apart. But with half of its members trying to kick a deadly habit and the others unsure if there's a dream worth fighting for, the X-Men are due for some much needed R&R...

...and that's when the Ultimatum Wave hits...

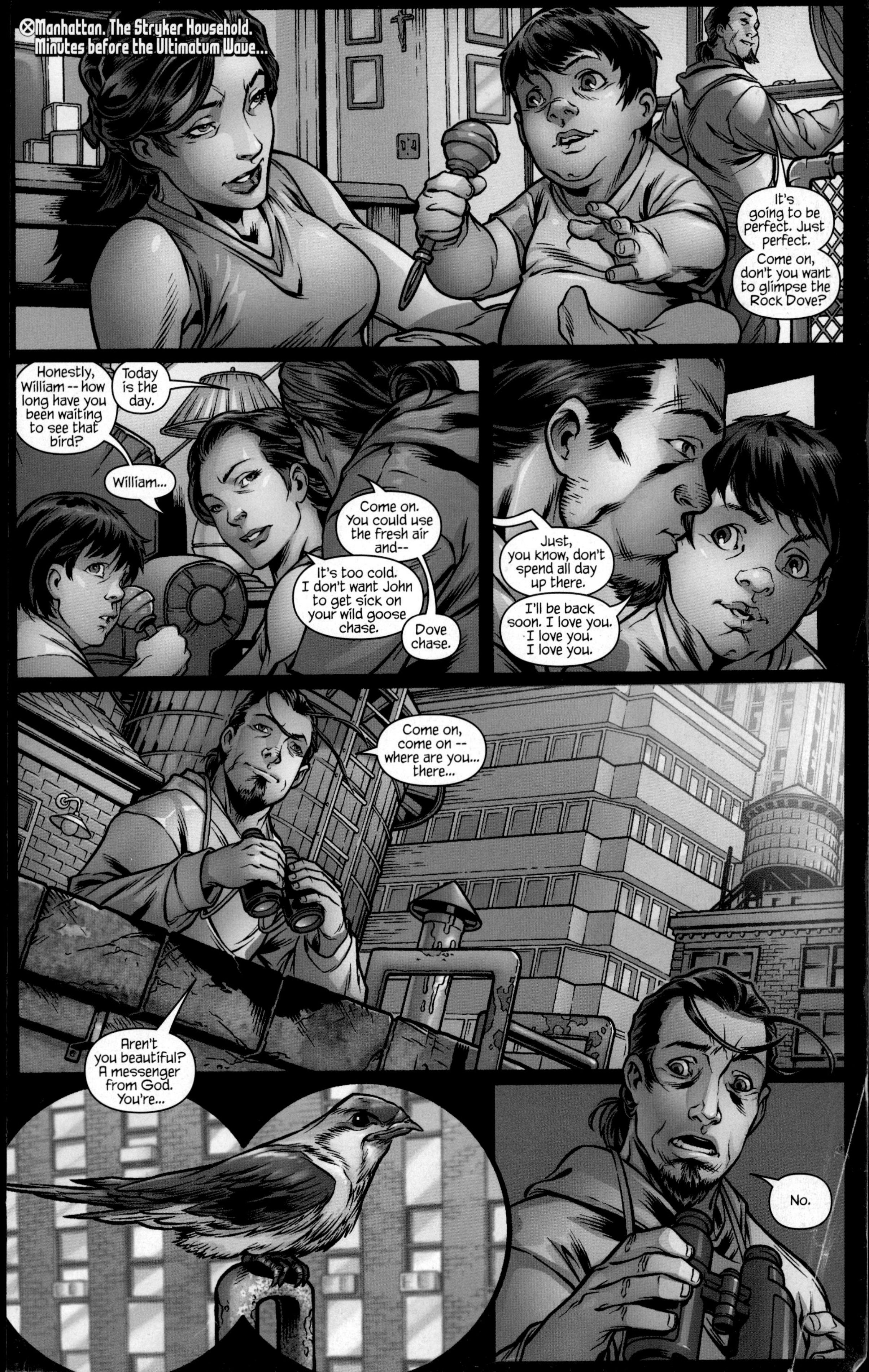
Manhattan. The Stryker Household. Minutes before the Ultimatum Wave...
It's going to be perfect. Just perfect.
Come on, don't you want to glimpse the Rock Dove?
Honestly, William -- how long have you been waiting to see that bird?
Today is the day.
William...
Come on. You could use the fresh air and--
It's too cold. I don't want John to get sick on your wild goose chase.
Dove chase.
Just, you know, don't spend all day up there.
I'll be back soon. I love you. I love you. I love you.
Come on, come on -- where are you... there...
Aren't you beautiful? A messenger from God. You're...
No.

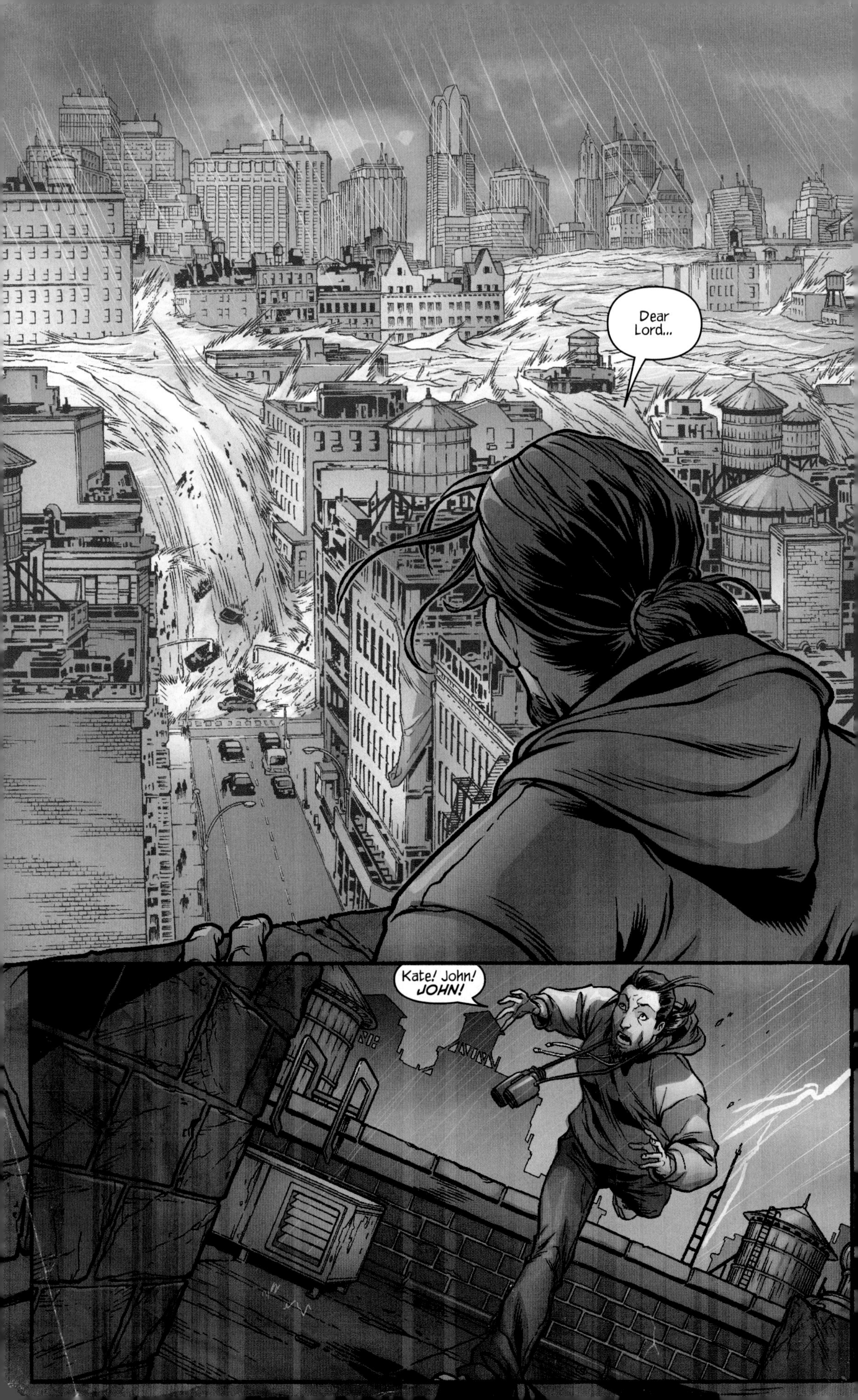
Dear Lord...
Kate! John! JOHN!

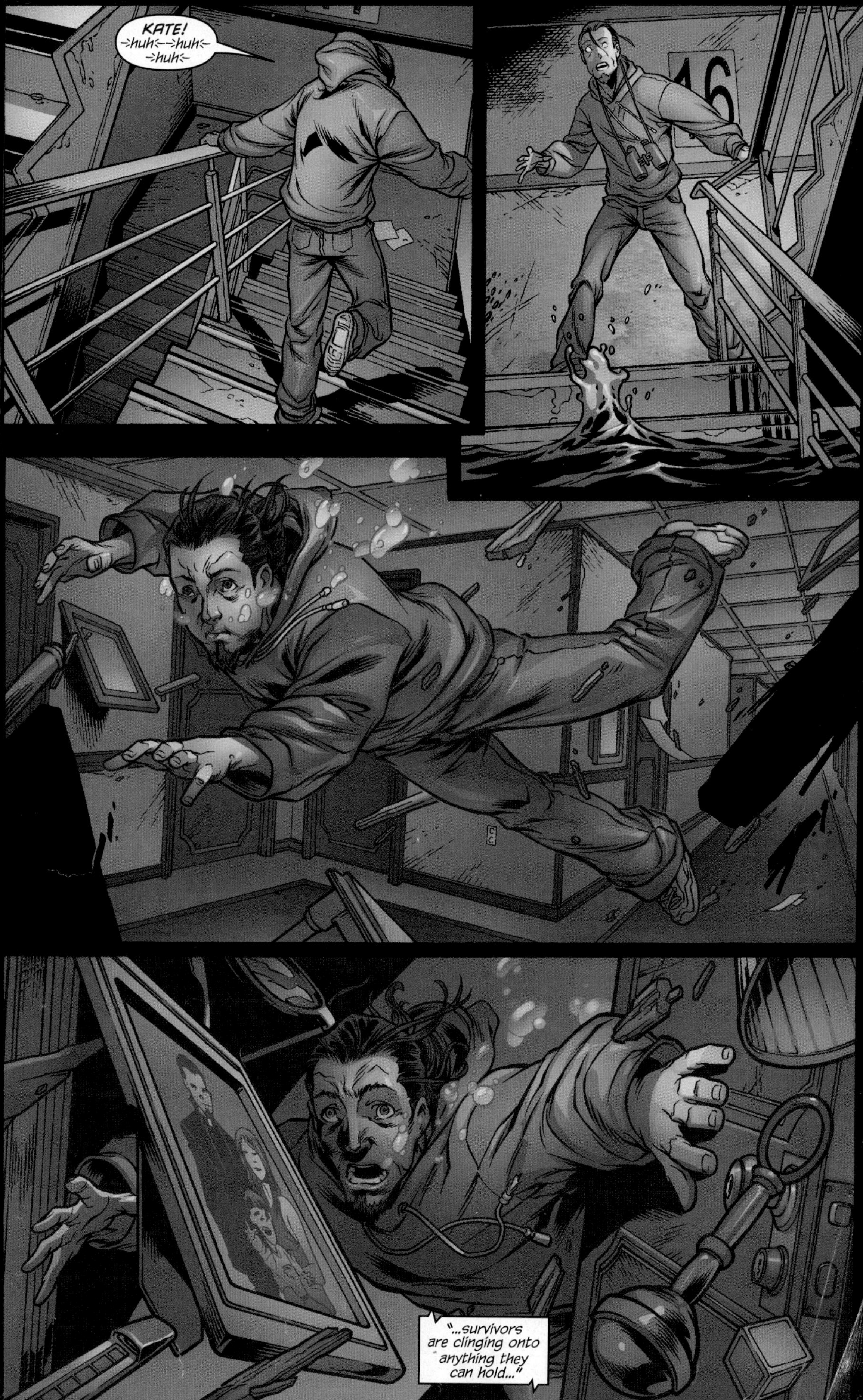
KATE!
-huh- -huh- -huh-
16
"...survivors are clinging onto anything they can hold..."

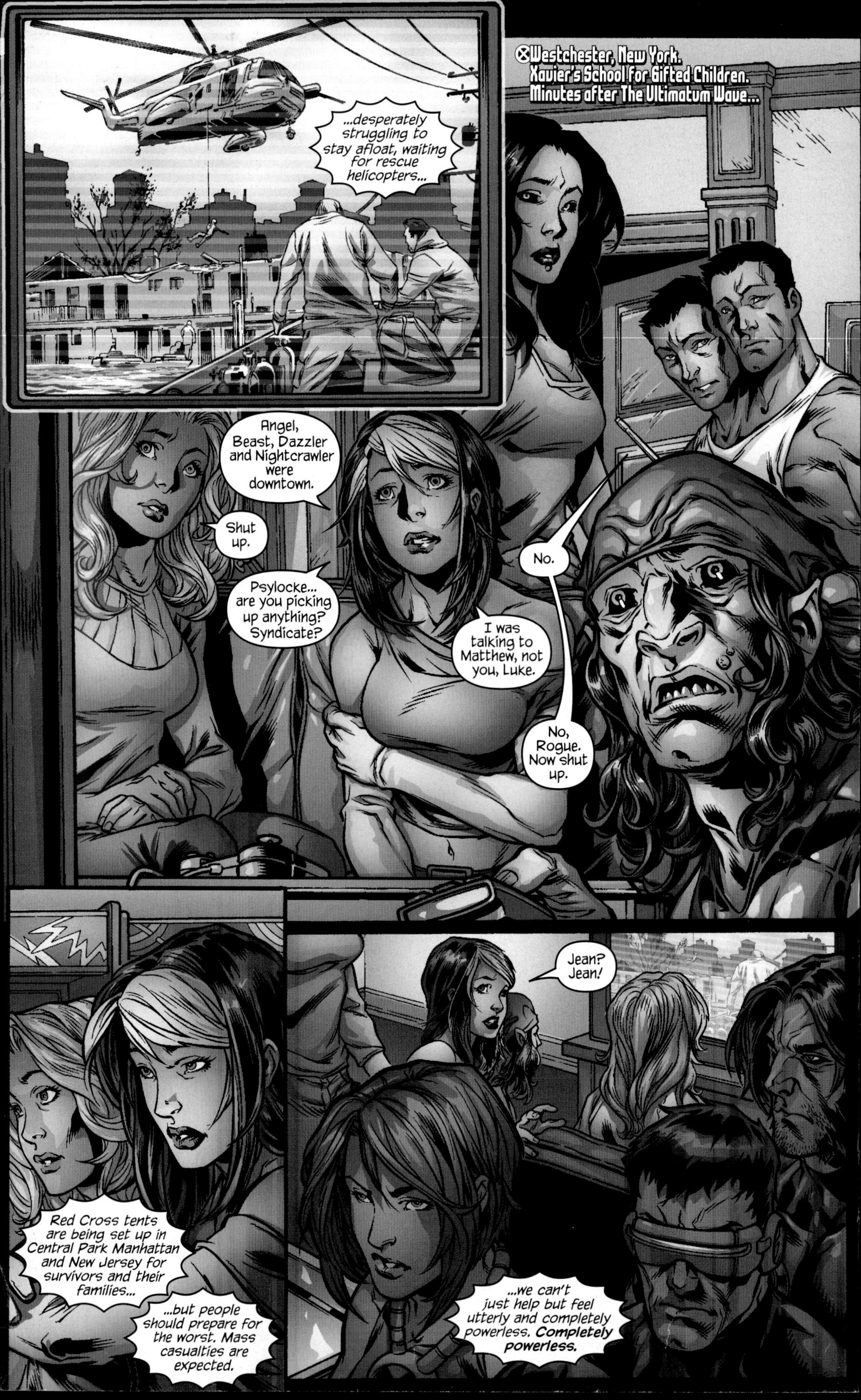

...desperately struggling to stay afloat, waiting for rescue helicopters...
Westchester, New York. Xavier's School for Gifted Children. Minutes after The Ultimatum Wave...
Angel, Beast, Dazzler and Nightcrawler were downtown.
Shut up.
Psylocke... are you picking up anything? Syndicate?
I was talking to Matthew, not you, Luke.
No.
No, Rogue. Now shut up.
Red Cross tents are being set up in Central Park Manhattan and New Jersey for survivors and their families...
...but people should prepare for the worst. Mass casualties are expected.
Jean? Jean!
...we can't just help but feel utterly and completely powerless. **Completely powerless.**

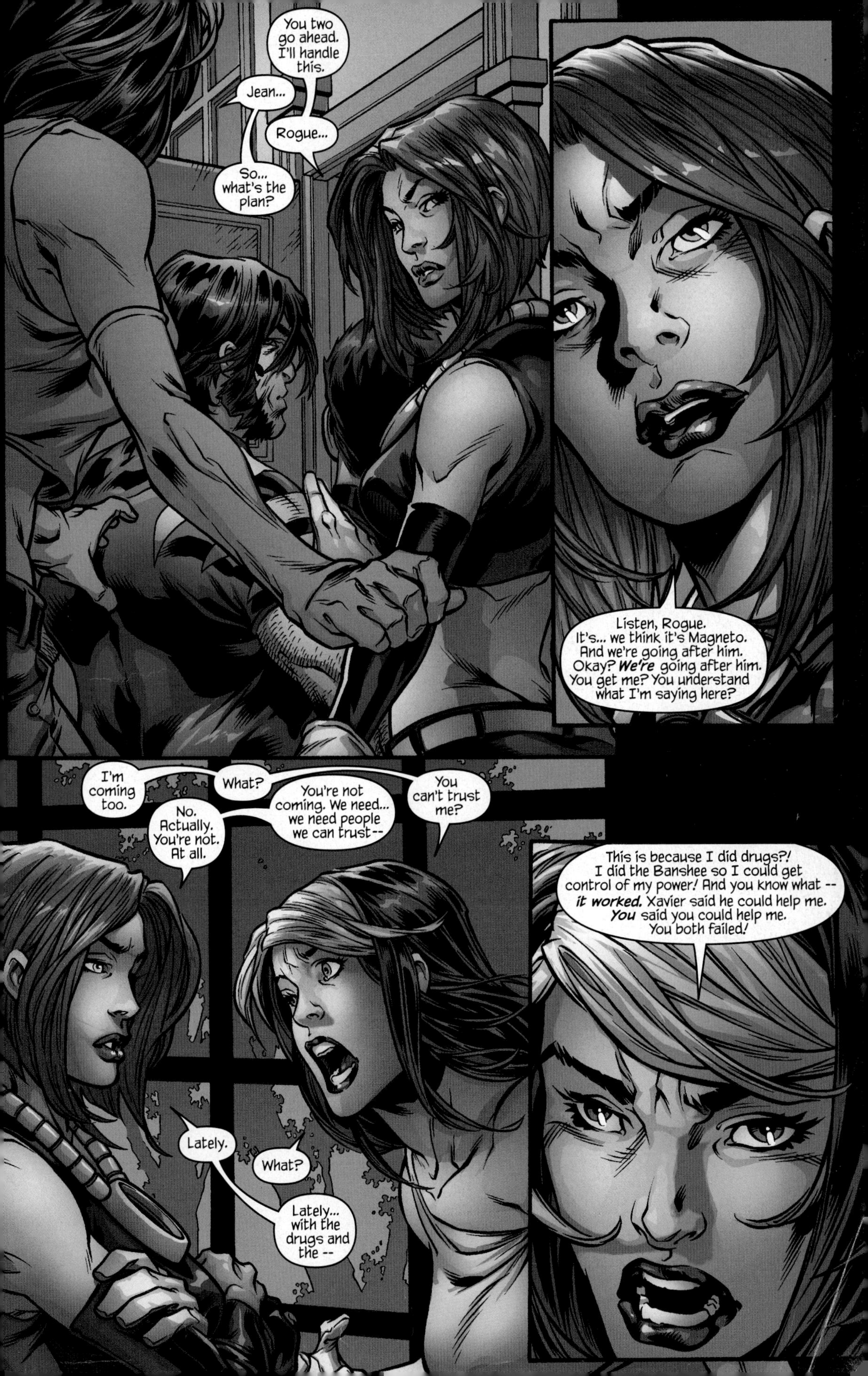

Jean...
You two go ahead. I'll handle this.
Rogue...
So... what's the plan?
Listen, Rogue. It's... we think it's Magneto. And we're going after him. Okay? ***We're*** going after him. You get me? You understand what I'm saying here?
I'm coming too.
What?
No. Actually. You're not. At all.
You're not coming. We need... we need people we can trust--
You can't trust me?
Lately.
What?
Lately... with the drugs and the --
This is because I did drugs?! I did the Banshee so I could get control of my power! And you know what -- ***it worked.*** Xavier said he could help me. ***You*** said you could help me. You both failed!

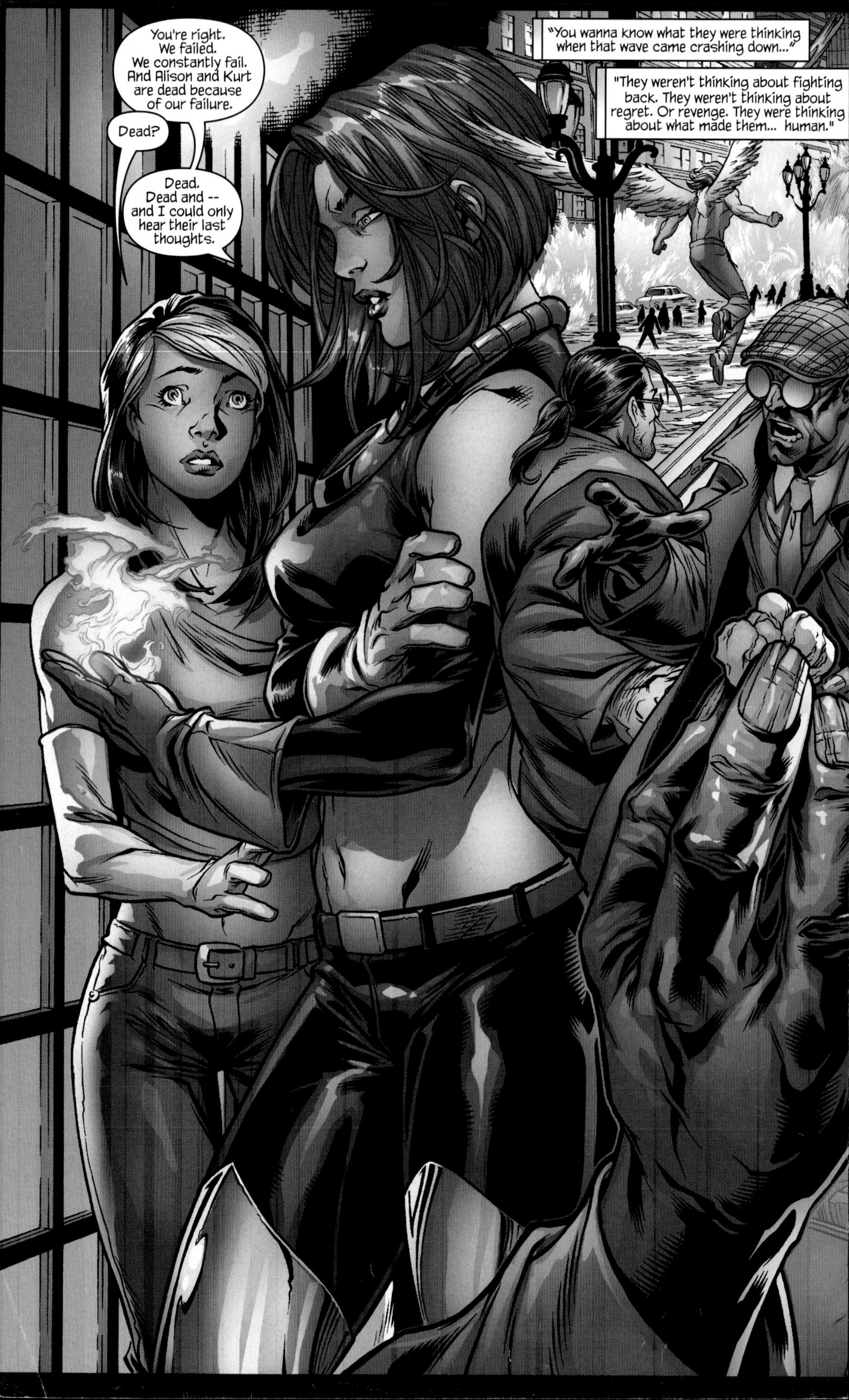
You're right. We failed. We constantly fail. And Alison and Kurt are dead because of our failure.
Dead?
Dead. Dead and -- and I could only hear their last thoughts.
"You wanna know what they were thinking when that wave came crashing down..."
"They weren't thinking about fighting back. They weren't thinking about regret. Or revenge. They were thinking about what made them... human."

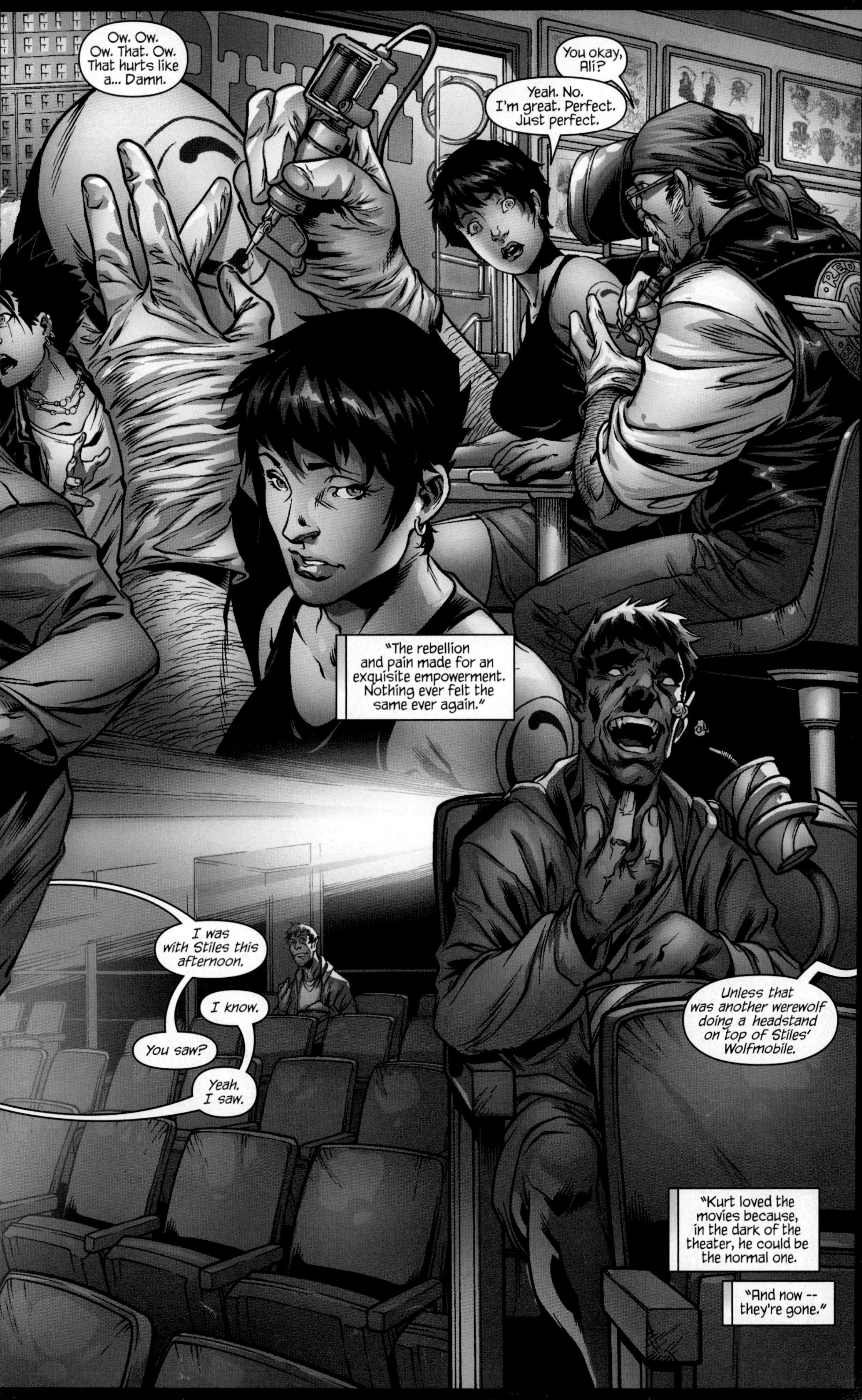
Ow. Ow. Ow. That. Ow. That hurts like a... Damn.
You okay, Ali?
Yeah. No. I'm great. Perfect. Just perfect.
"The rebellion and pain made for an exquisite empowerment. Nothing ever felt the same ever again."
I was with Stiles this afternoon.
I know.
You saw?
Yeah. I saw.
Unless that was another werewolf doing a headstand on top of Stiles' Wolfmobile.
"Kurt loved the movies because, in the dark of the theater, he could be the normal one.
"And now -- they're gone."

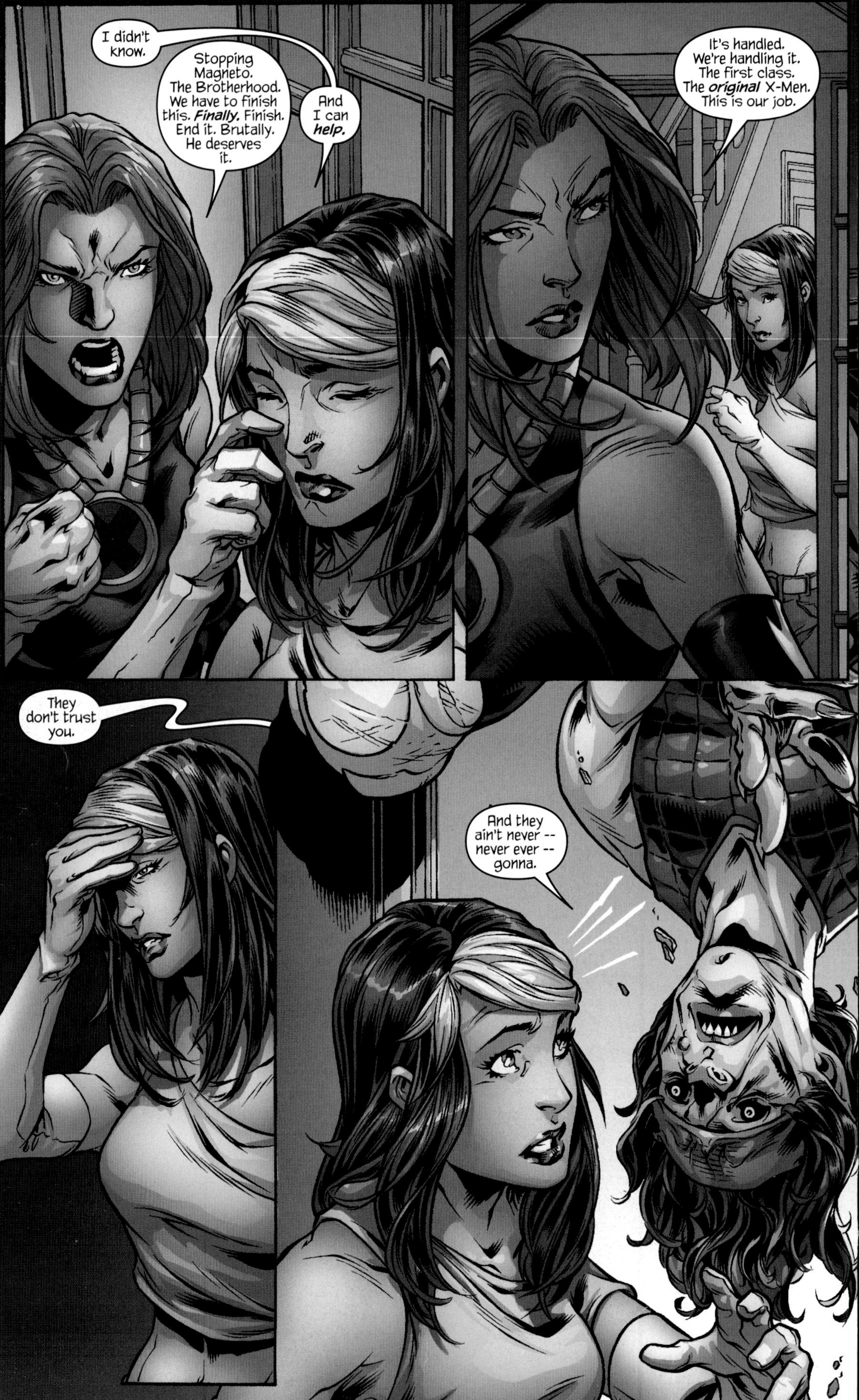
I didn't know.
Stopping Magneto. The Brotherhood. We have to finish this. *Finally.* Finish. End it. Brutally. He deserves it.
And I can *help.*
It's handled. We're handling it. The first class. The *original* X-Men. This is our job.
They don't trust you.
And they ain't never -- never ever -- gonna.

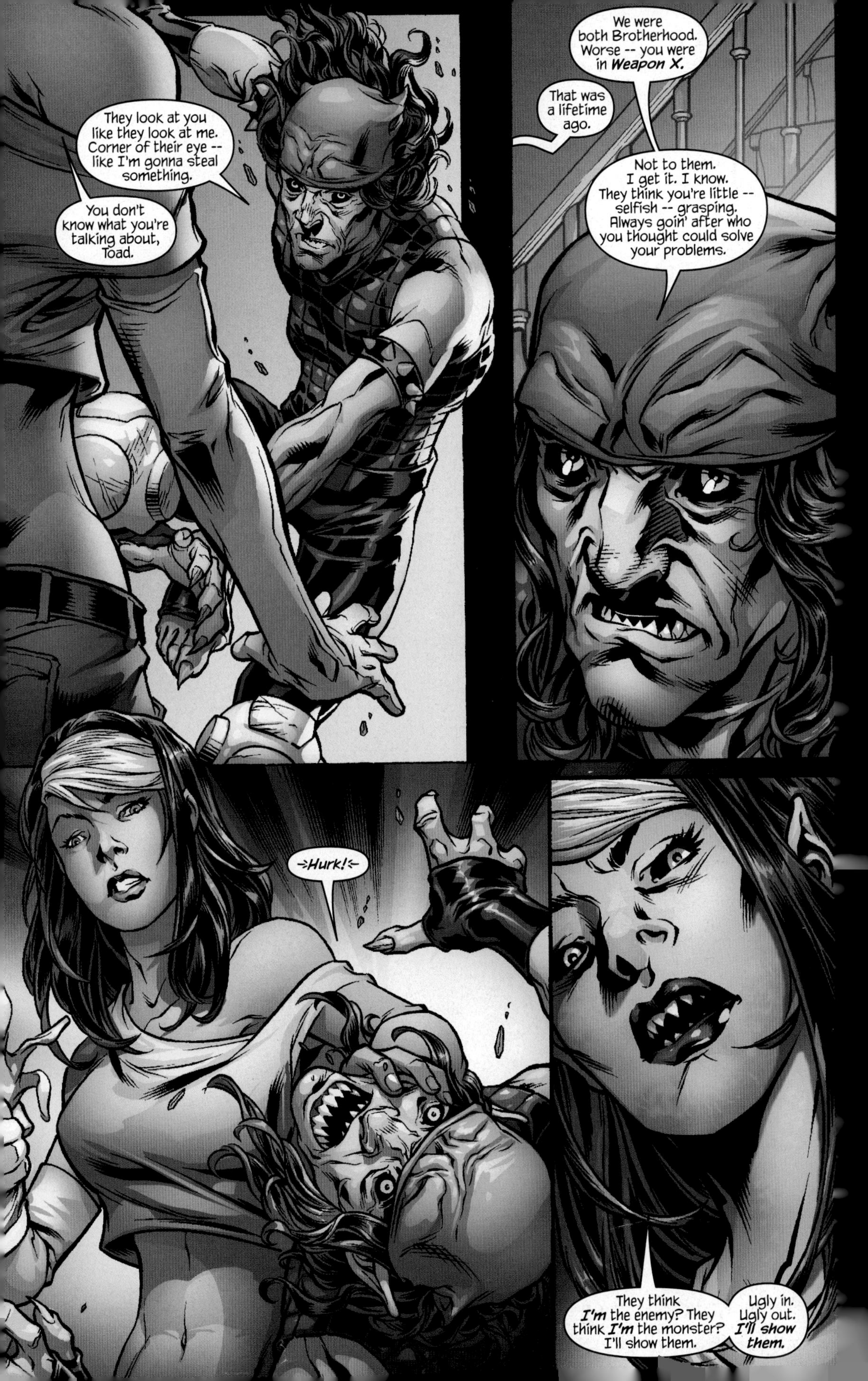

They look at you like they look at me. Corner of their eye -- like I'm gonna steal something.
You don't know what you're talking about, Toad.
We were both Brotherhood. Worse -- you were in *Weapon X.*
That was a lifetime ago.
Not to them. I get it. I know. They think you're little -- selfish -- grasping. Always goin' after who you thought could solve your problems.
-Hurk!-
They think *I'm* the enemy? They think *I'm* the monster? I'll show them.
Ugly in. Ugly out. *I'll show them.*

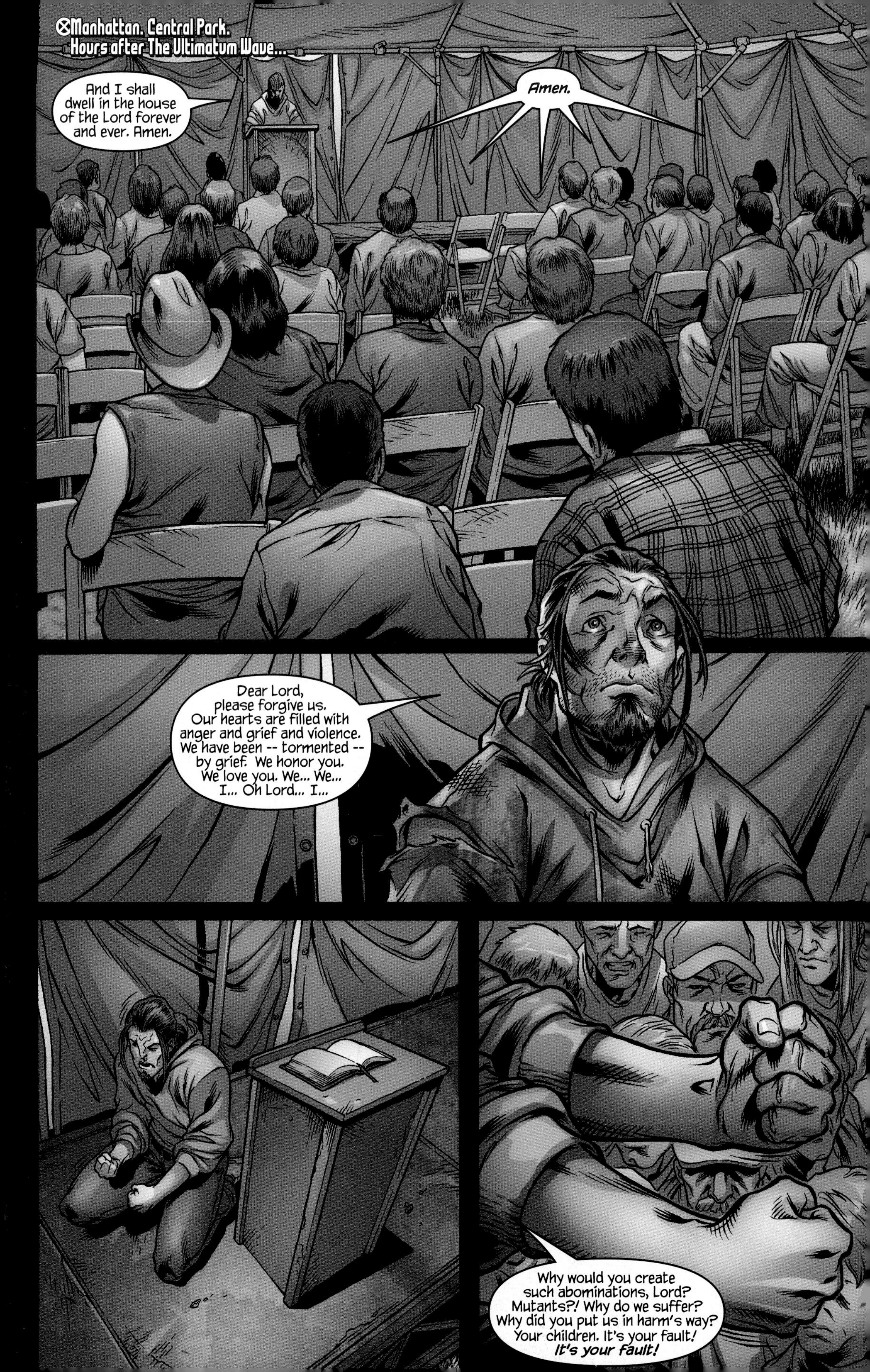
Manhattan. Central Park.
Hours after The Ultimatum Wave...
And I shall dwell in the house of the Lord forever and ever. Amen.
Amen.
Dear Lord, please forgive us. Our hearts are filled with anger and grief and violence. We have been -- tormented -- by grief. We honor you. We love you. We... We... I... Oh Lord... I...
Why would you create such abominations, Lord? Mutants?! Why do we suffer? Why did you put us in harm's way? Your children. It's your fault! It's your fault!

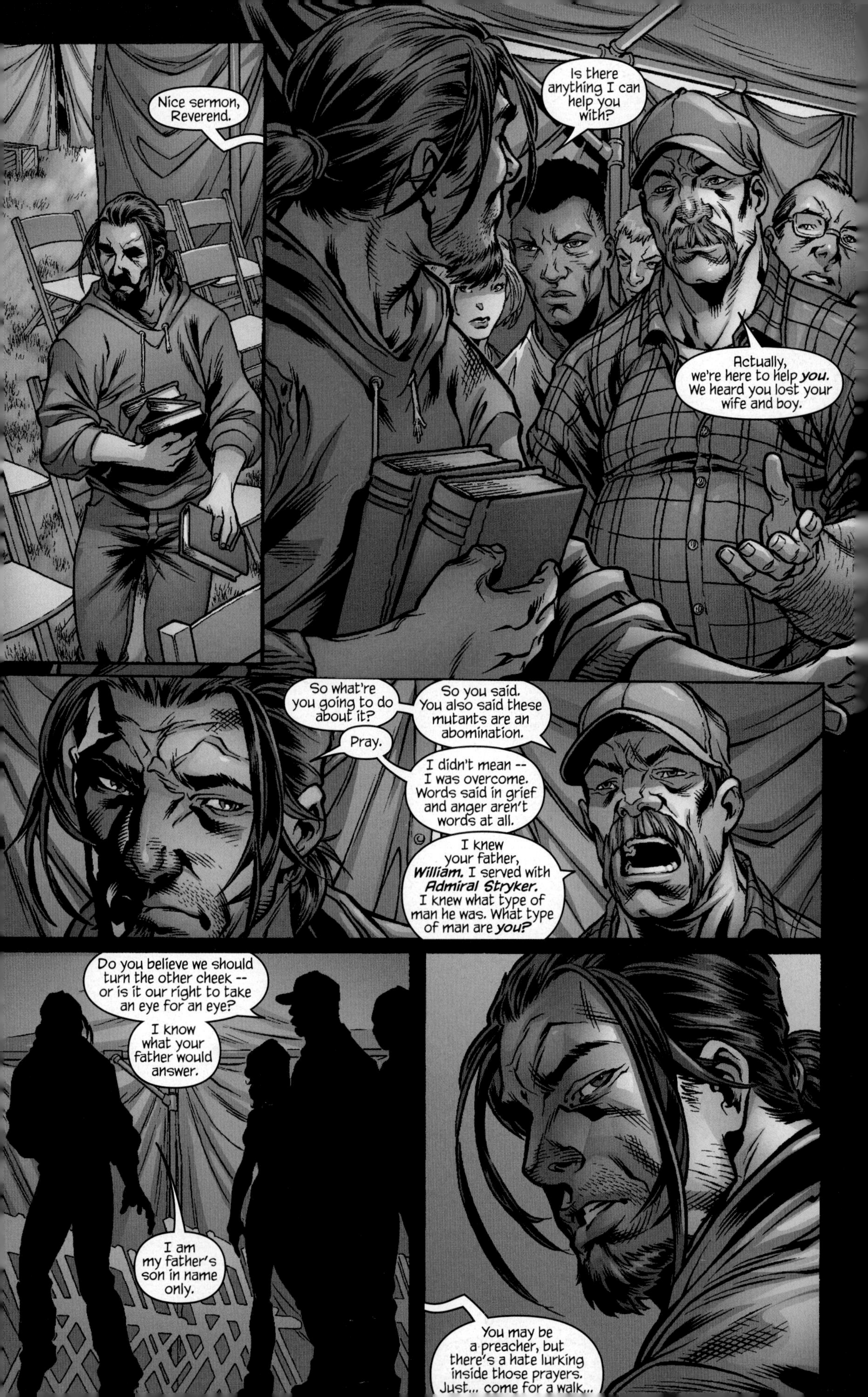
Nice sermon, Reverend.
Is there anything I can help you with?
Actually, we're here to help *you*. We heard you lost your wife and boy.
So what're you going to do about it?
Pray.
So you said. You also said these mutants are an abomination.
I didn't mean -- I was overcome. Words said in grief and anger aren't words at all.
I knew your father, *William*. I served with *Admiral Stryker*. I knew what type of man he was. What type of man are *you?*
Do you believe we should turn the other cheek -- or is it our right to take an eye for an eye?
I know what your father would answer.
I am my father's son in name only.
You may be a preacher, but there's a hate lurking inside those prayers. Just... come for a walk...

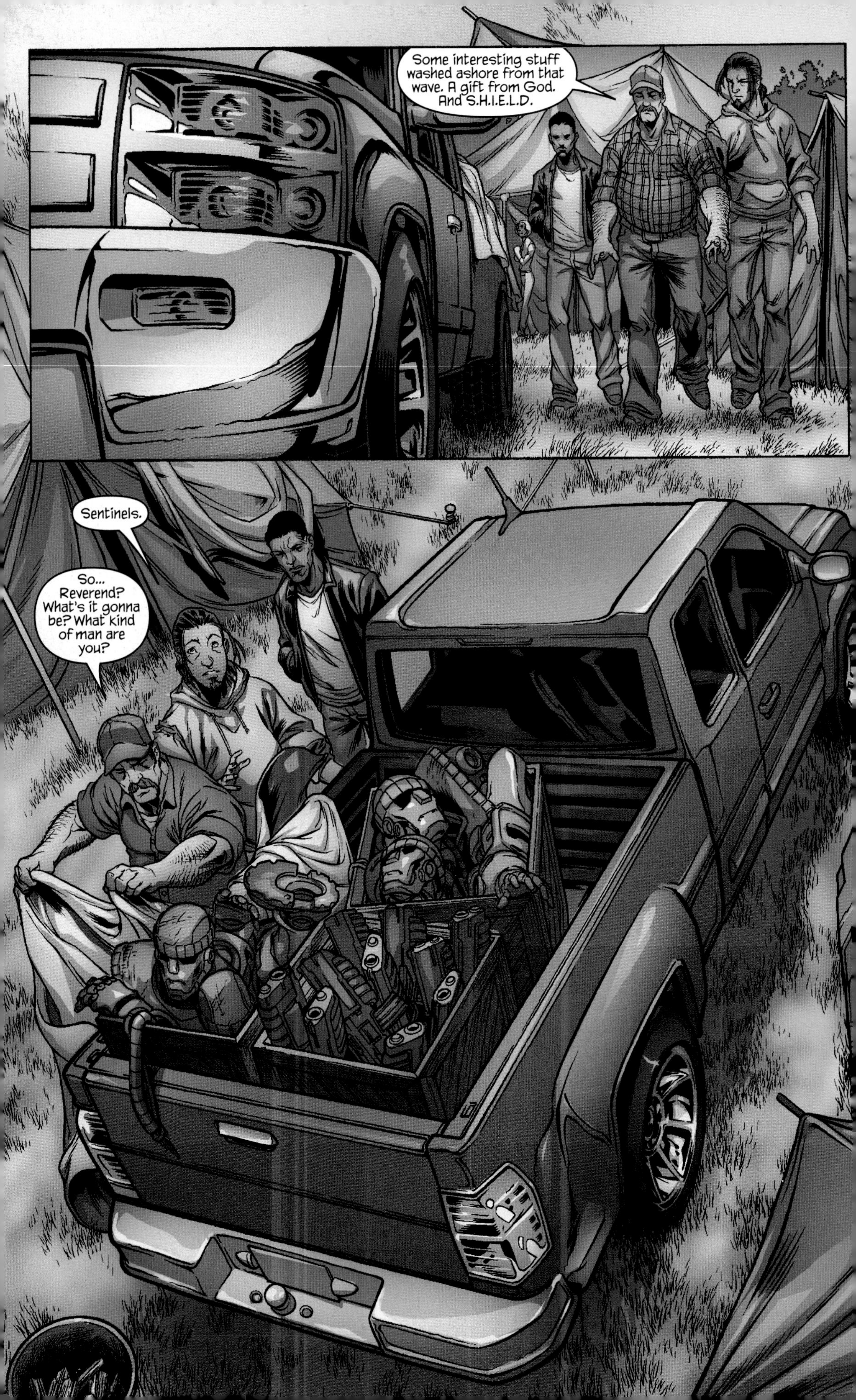
Some interesting stuff washed ashore from that wave. A gift from God. And S.H.I.E.L.D.
Sentinels.
So... Reverend? What's it gonna be? What kind of man are you?

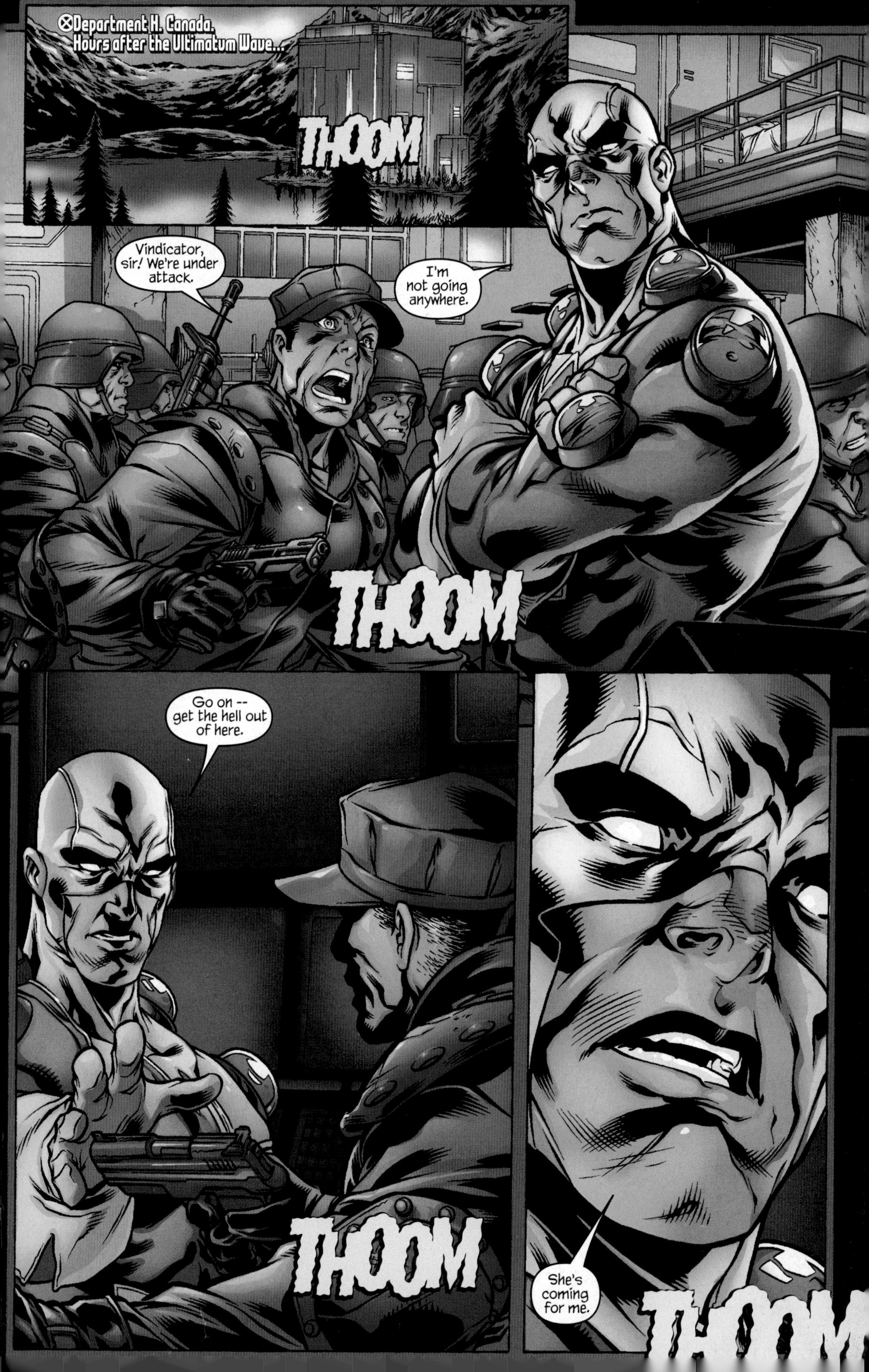
Department H. Canada.
Hours after the Ultimatum Wave...
THOOM
Vindicator, sir! We're under attack.
I'm not going anywhere.
THOOM
Go on -- get the hell out of here.
THOOM
She's coming for me.
THOOM

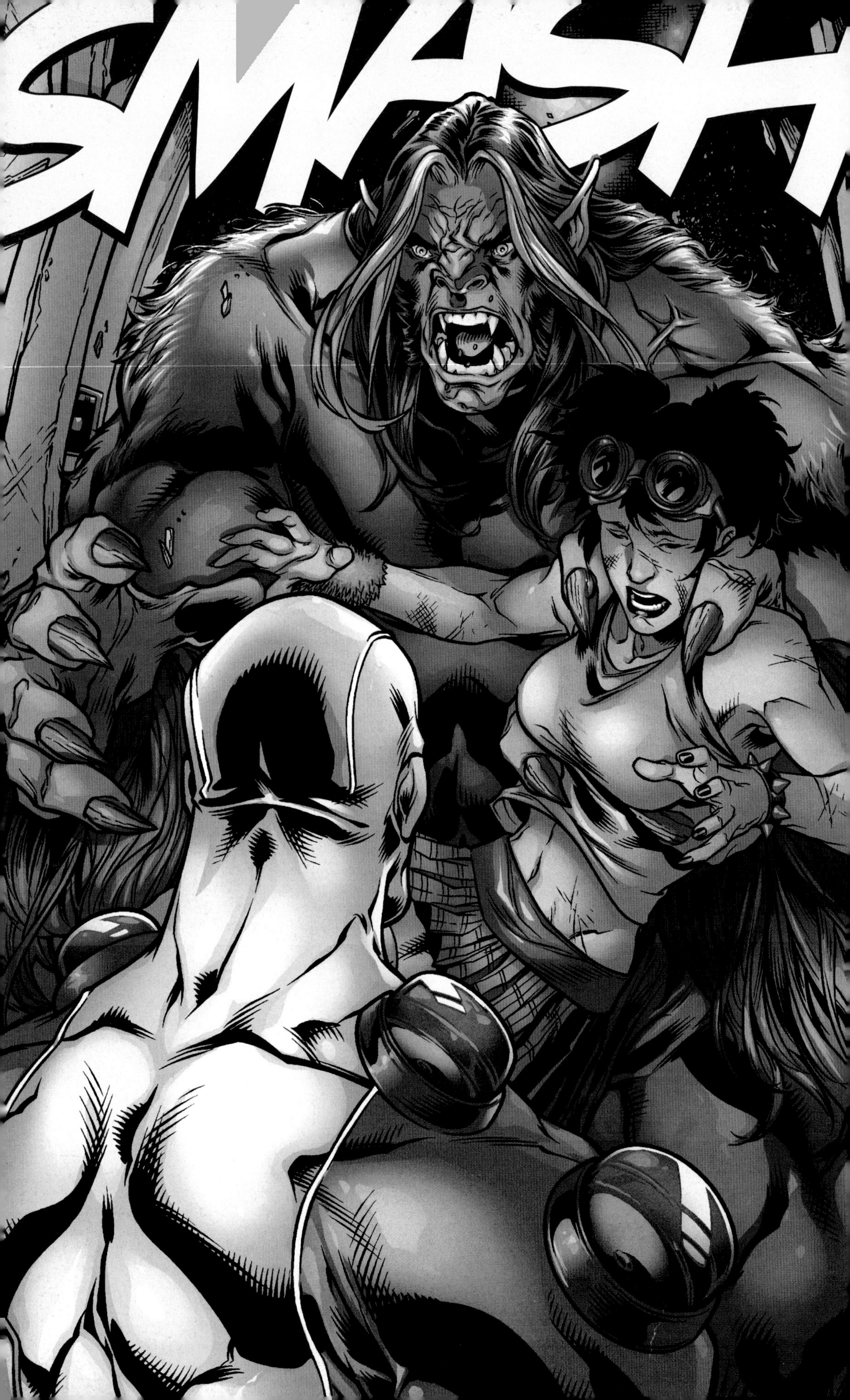
SMASH

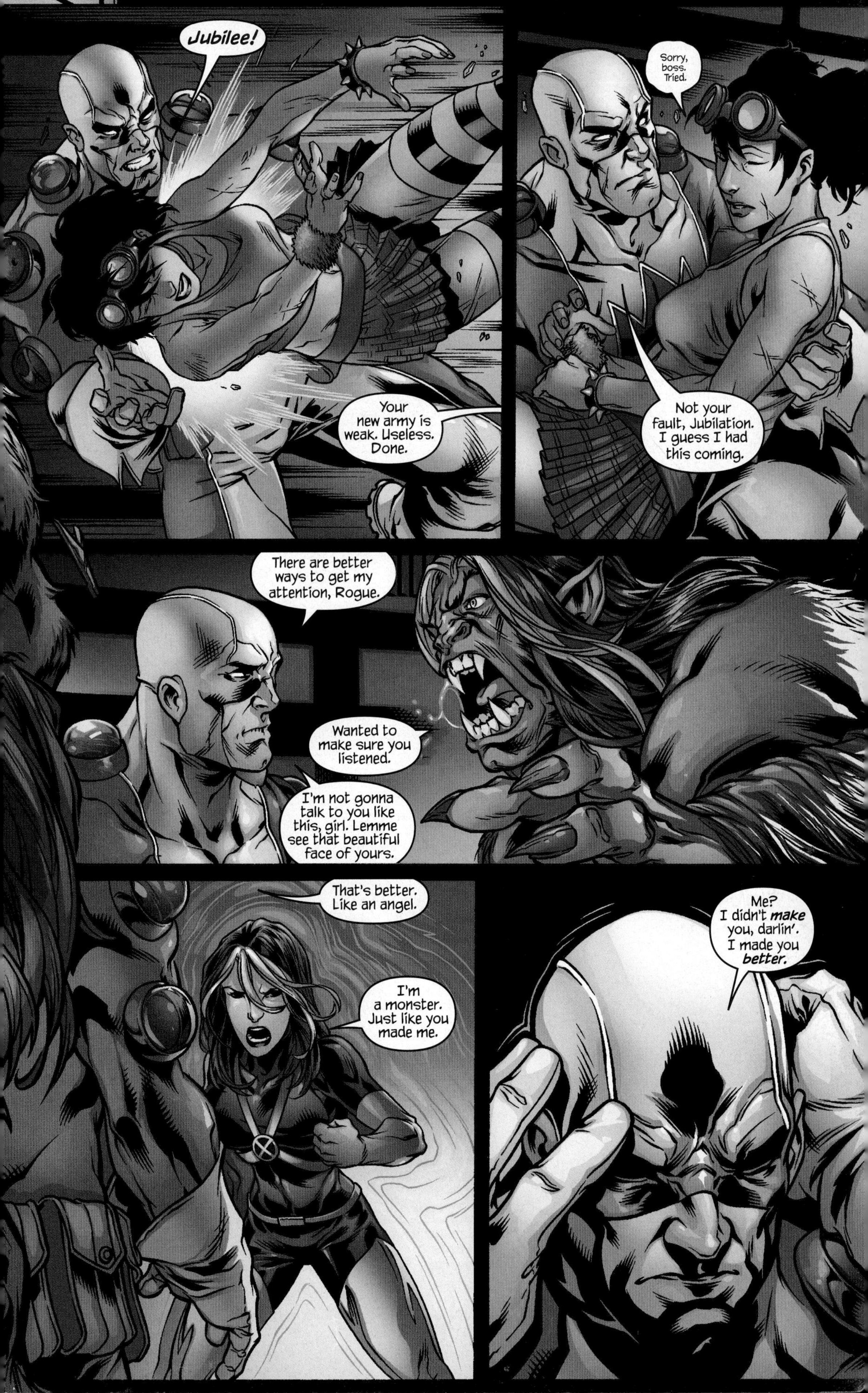
Jubilee!
Your new army is weak. Useless. Done.
Sorry, boss. Tried.
Not your fault, Jubilation. I guess I had this coming.
There are better ways to get my attention, Rogue.
Wanted to make sure you listened.
I'm not gonna talk to you like this, girl. Lemme see that beautiful face of yours.
That's better. Like an angel.
I'm a monster. Just like you made me.
Me? I didn't *make* you, darlin'. I made you *better*.

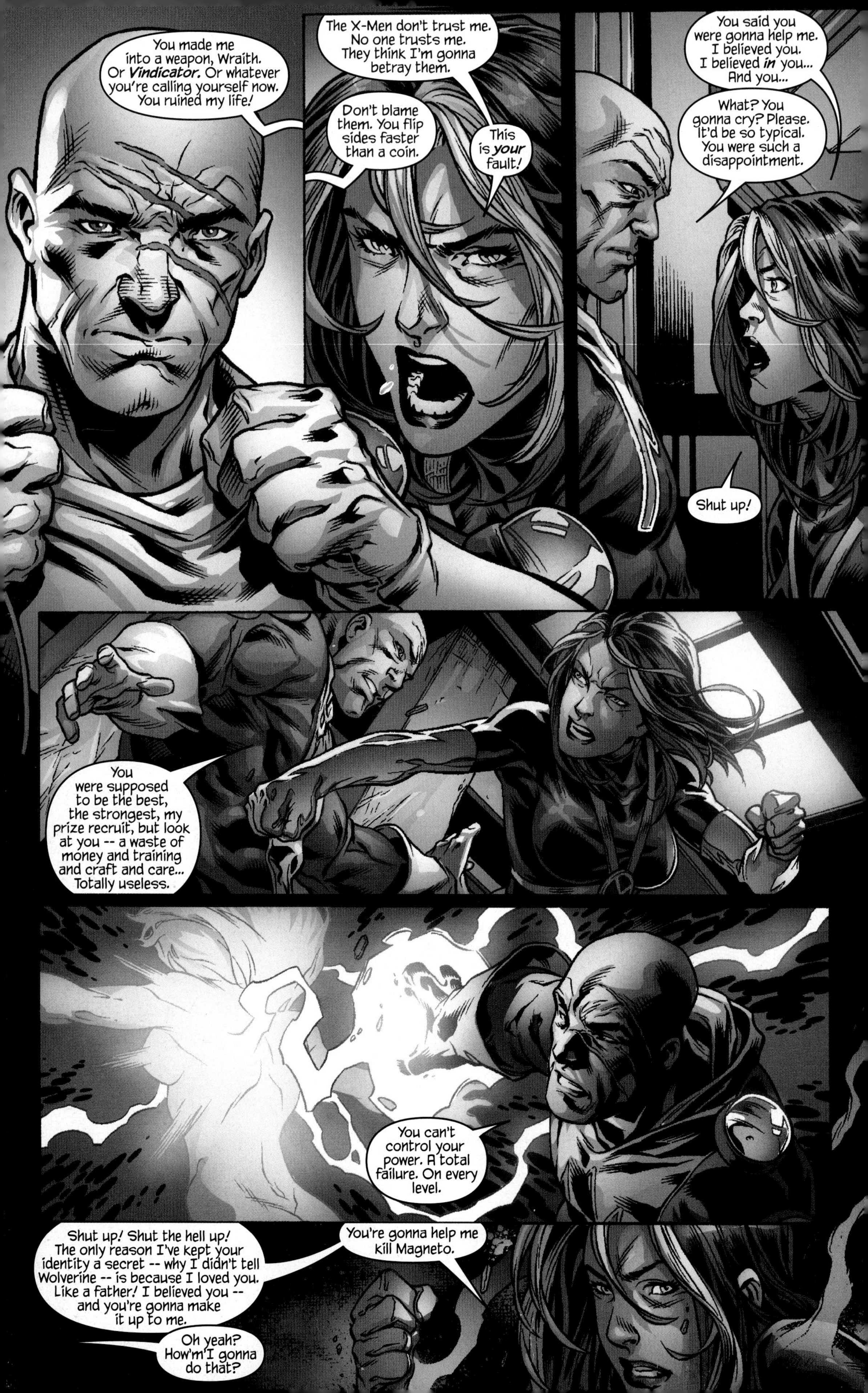

You made me into a weapon, Wraith. Or *Vindicator.* Or whatever you're calling yourself now. You ruined my life!
The X-Men don't trust me. No one trusts me. They think I'm gonna betray them.
Don't blame them. You flip sides faster than a coin.
This is *your* fault!
You said you were gonna help me. I believed you. I believed *in* you... And you...
What? You gonna cry? Please. It'd be so typical. You were such a disappointment.
Shut up!
You were supposed to be the best, the strongest, my prize recruit, but look at you -- a waste of money and training and craft and care... Totally useless.
You can't control your power. A total failure. On every level.
Shut up! Shut the hell up! The only reason I've kept your identity a secret -- why I didn't tell Wolverine -- is because I loved you. Like a father! I believed you -- and you're gonna make it up to me.
Oh yeah? How'm I gonna do that?
You're gonna help me kill Magneto.

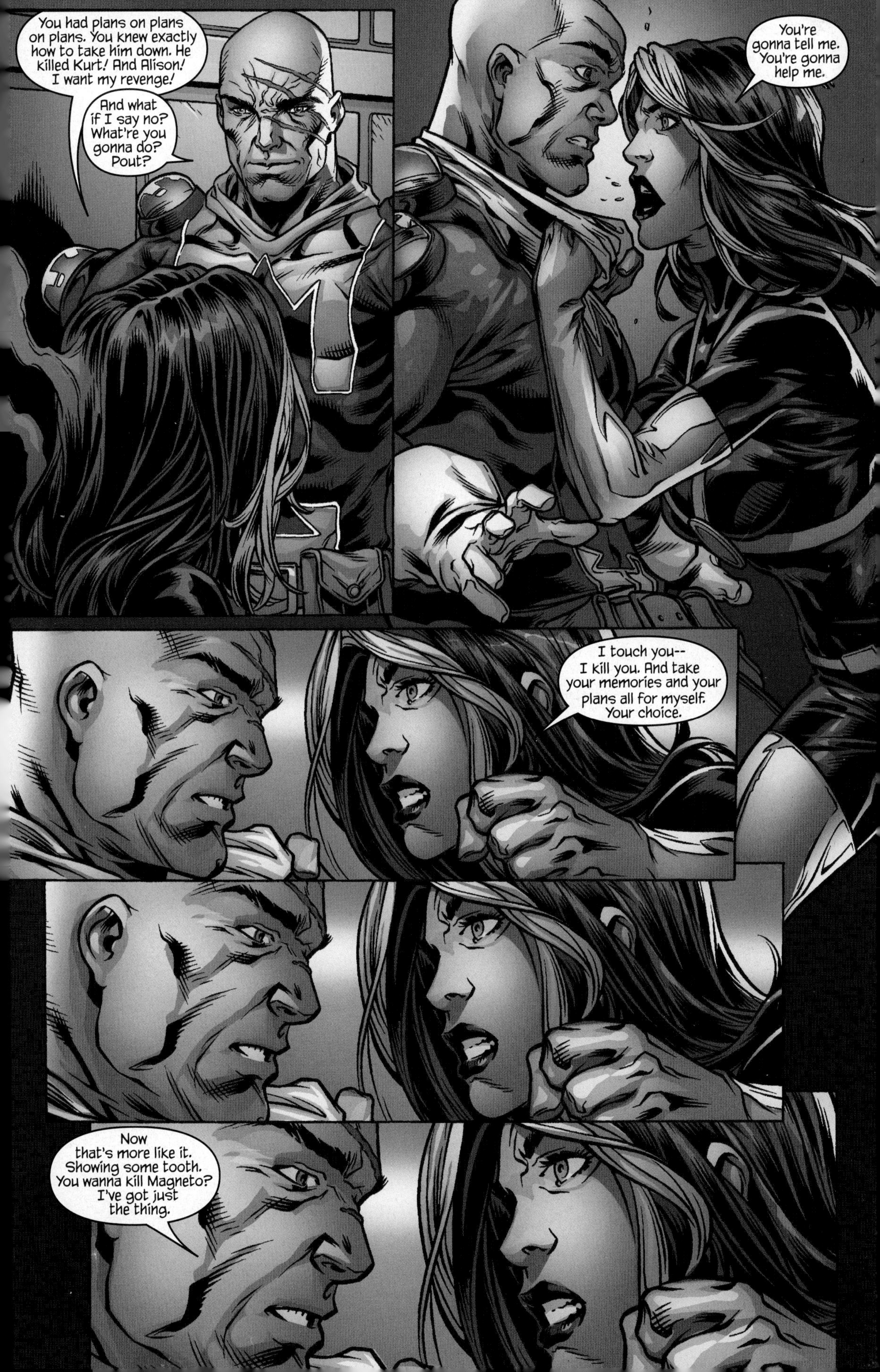
You had plans on plans on plans. You knew exactly how to take him down. He killed Kurt! And Alison! I want my revenge!
And what if I say no? What're you gonna do? Pout?
You're gonna tell me. You're gonna help me.
I touch you-- I kill you. And take your memories and your plans all for myself. Your choice.
Now that's more like it. Showing some tooth. You wanna kill Magneto? I've got just the thing.

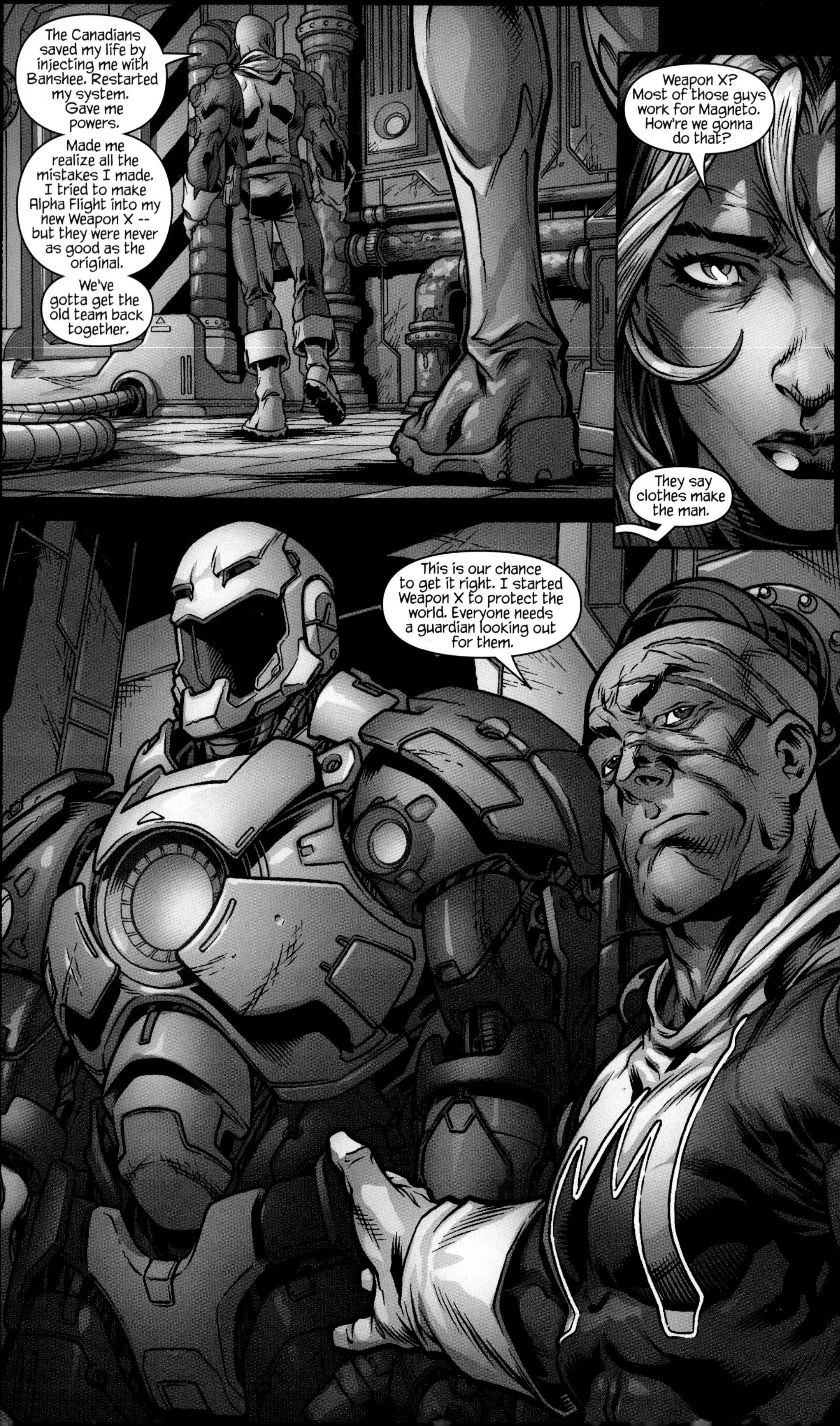
The Canadians saved my life by injecting me with Banshee. Restarted my system. Gave me powers.
Made me realize all the mistakes I made. I tried to make Alpha Flight into my new Weapon X -- but they were never as good as the original.
We've gotta get the old team back together.
Weapon X? Most of those guys work for Magneto. How're we gonna do that?
They say clothes make the man.
This is our chance to get it right. I started Weapon X to protect the world. Everyone needs a guardian looking out for them.

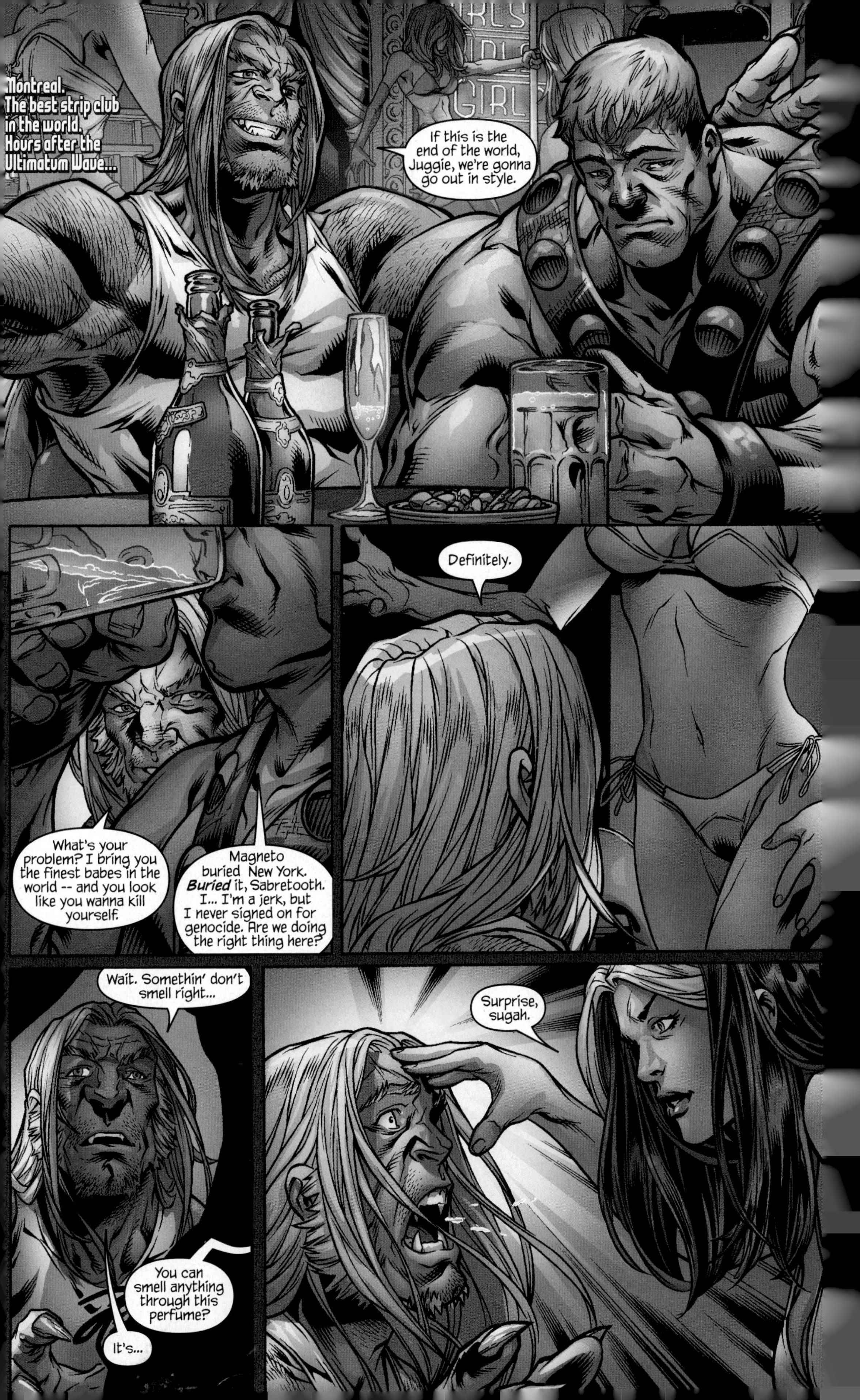

Montreal. The best strip club in the world. Hours after the Ultimatum Wave...
If this is the end of the world, Juggie, we're gonna go out in style.
What's your problem? I bring you the finest babes in the world -- and you look like you wanna kill yourself.
Magneto buried New York. *Buried* it, Sabretooth. I... I'm a jerk, but I never signed on for genocide. Are we doing the right thing here?
Definitely.
Wait. Somethin' don't smell right...
You can smell anything through this perfume?
It's...
Surprise, sugah.

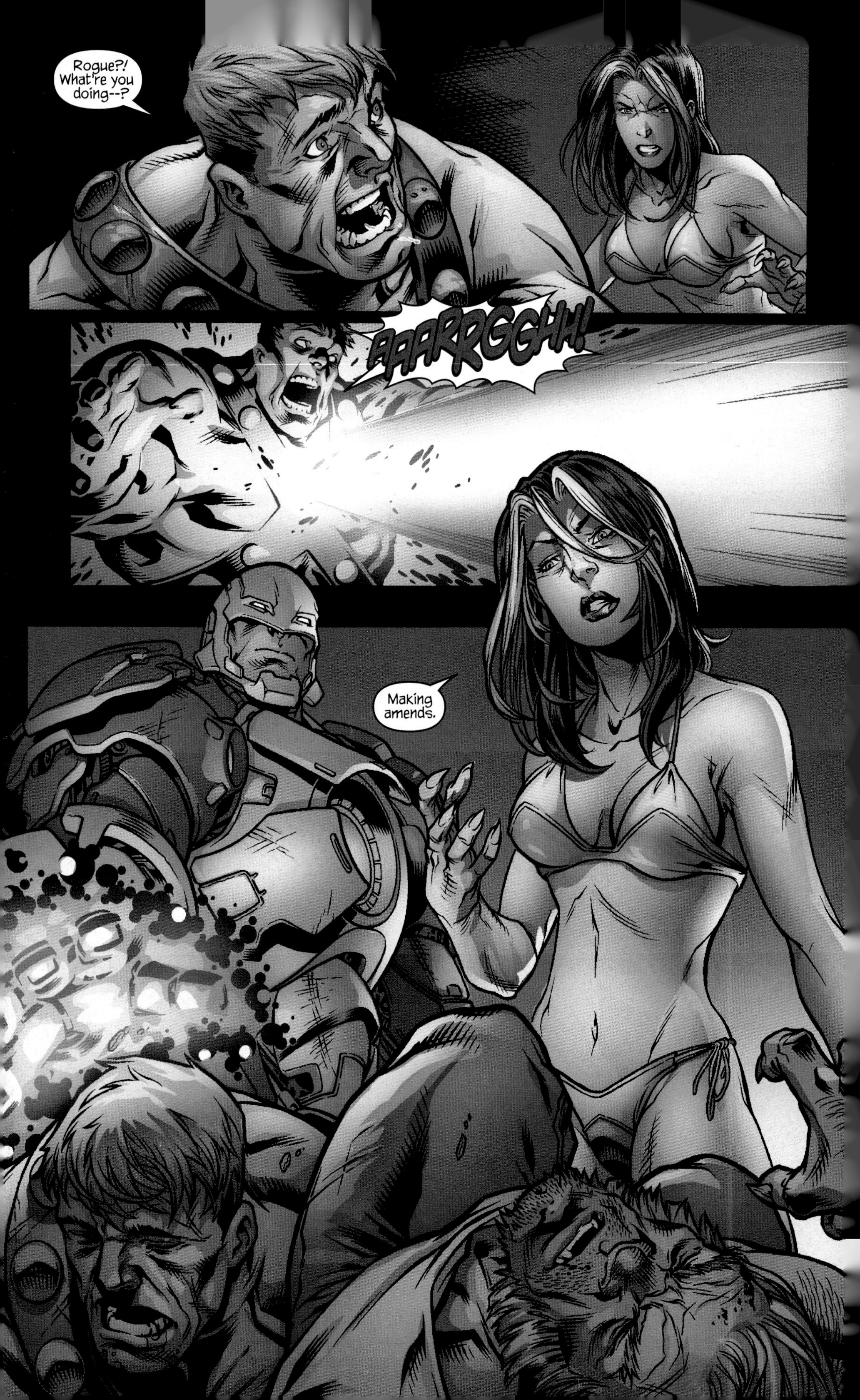
Rogue?! What're you doing--?
AAARRGGHH!
Making amends.

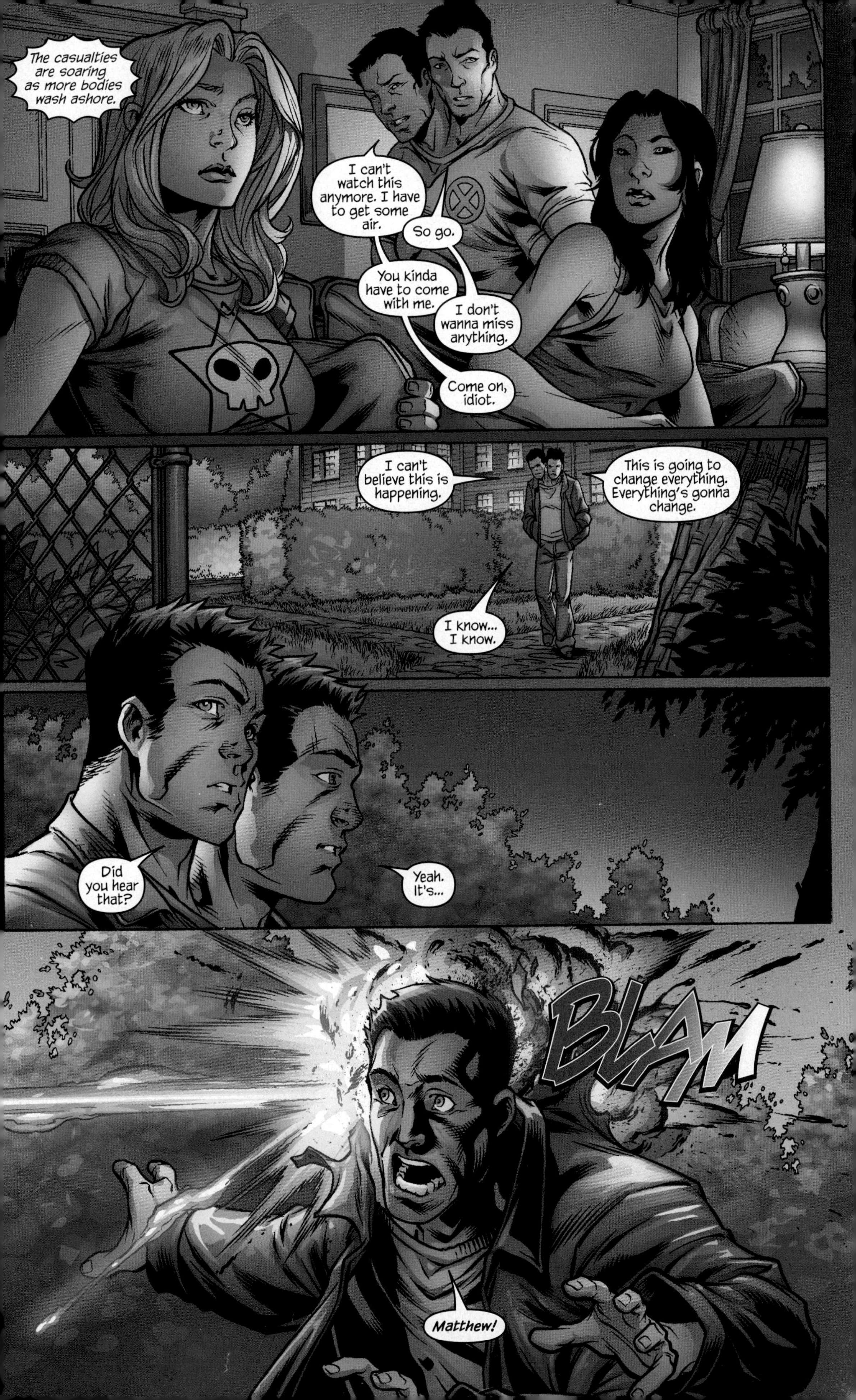
The casualties are soaring as more bodies wash ashore.
I can't watch this anymore. I have to get some air.
So go.
You kinda have to come with me.
I don't wanna miss anything.
Come on, idiot.
I can't believe this is happening.
This is going to change everything. Everything's gonna change.
I know... I know.
Did you hear that?
Yeah. It's...
BLAM
Matthew!

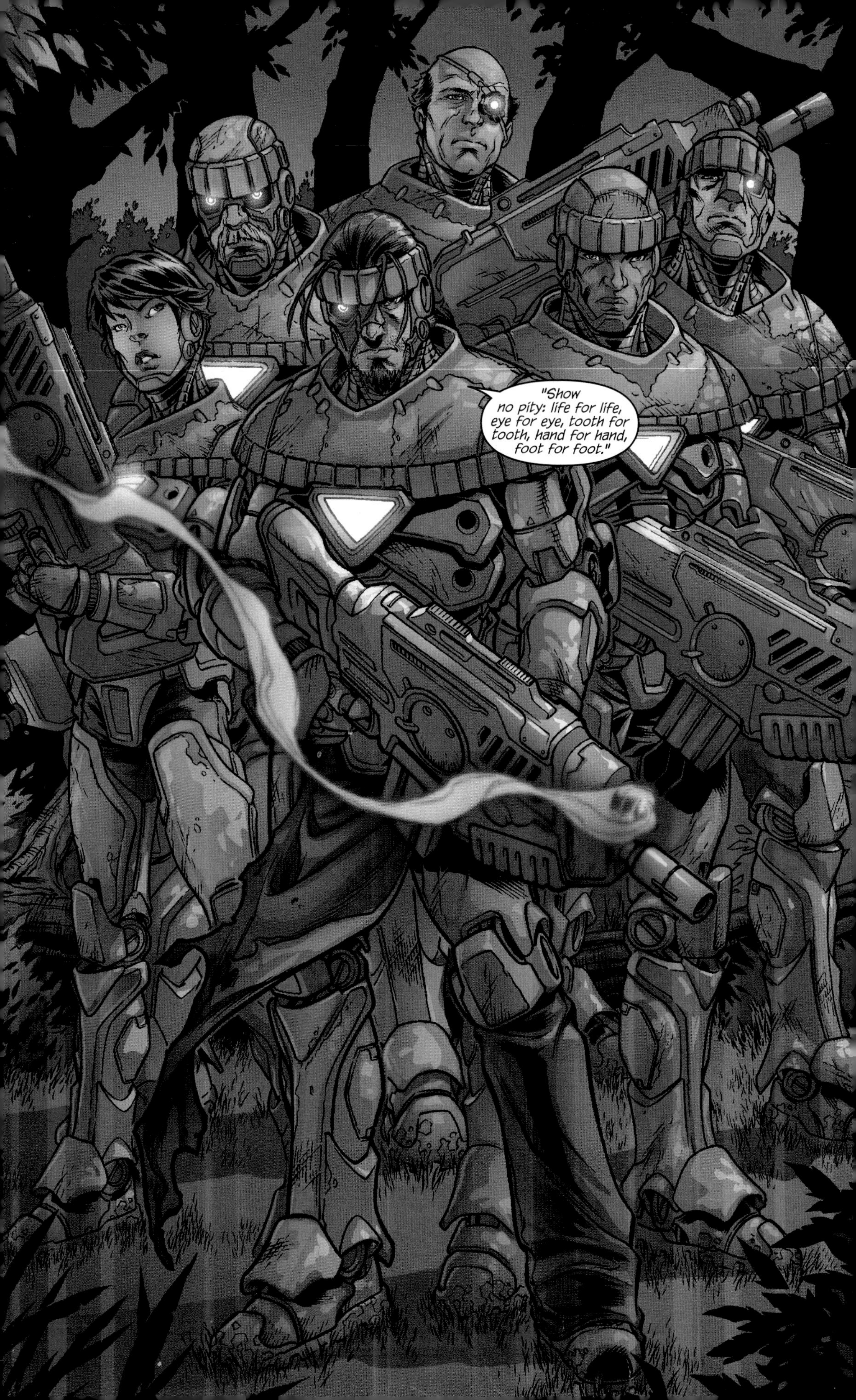
"Show no pity: life for life, eye for eye, tooth for tooth, hand for hand, foot for foot."

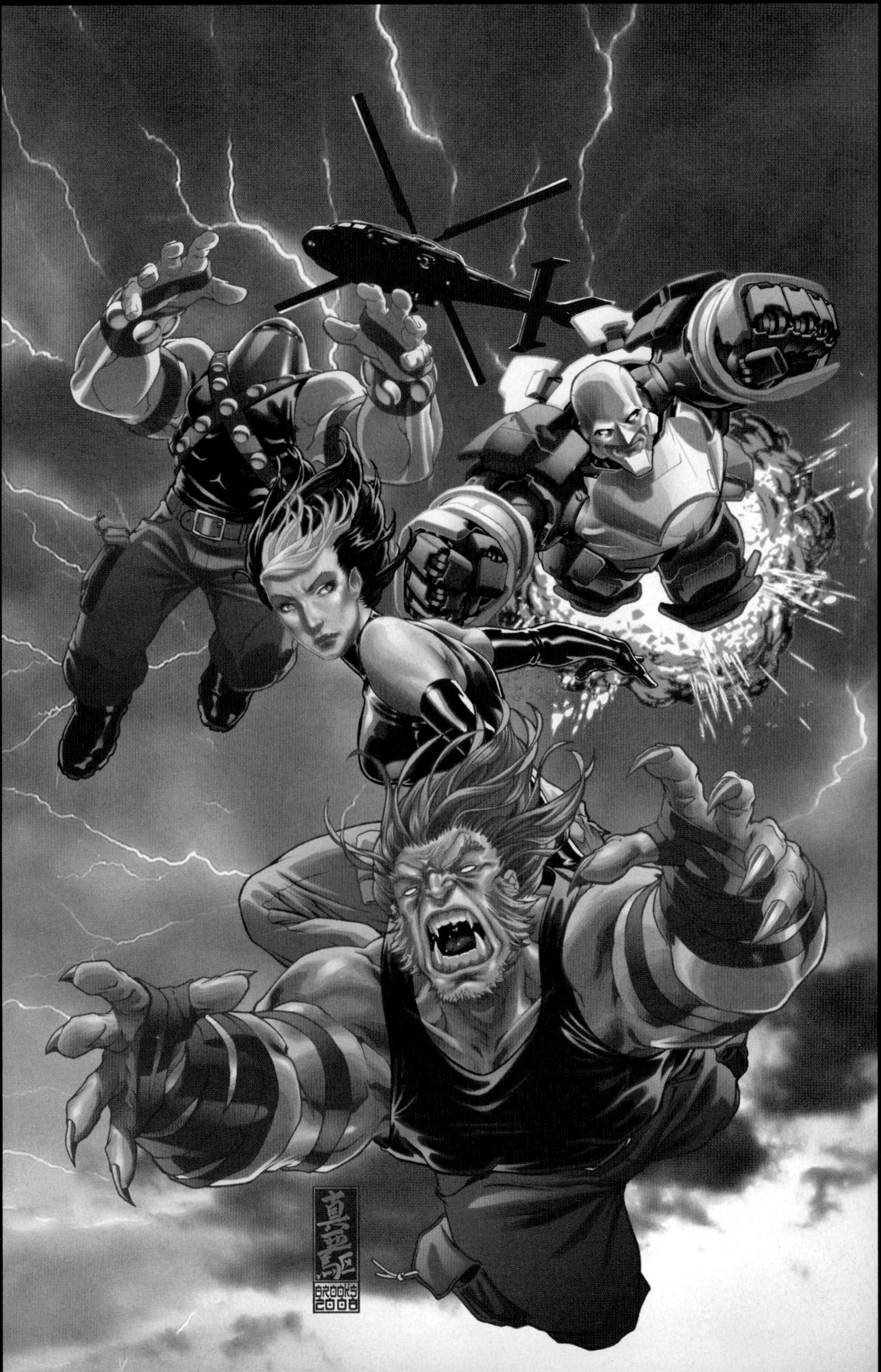
BROOKS
2006

Ultimate X-Men #99

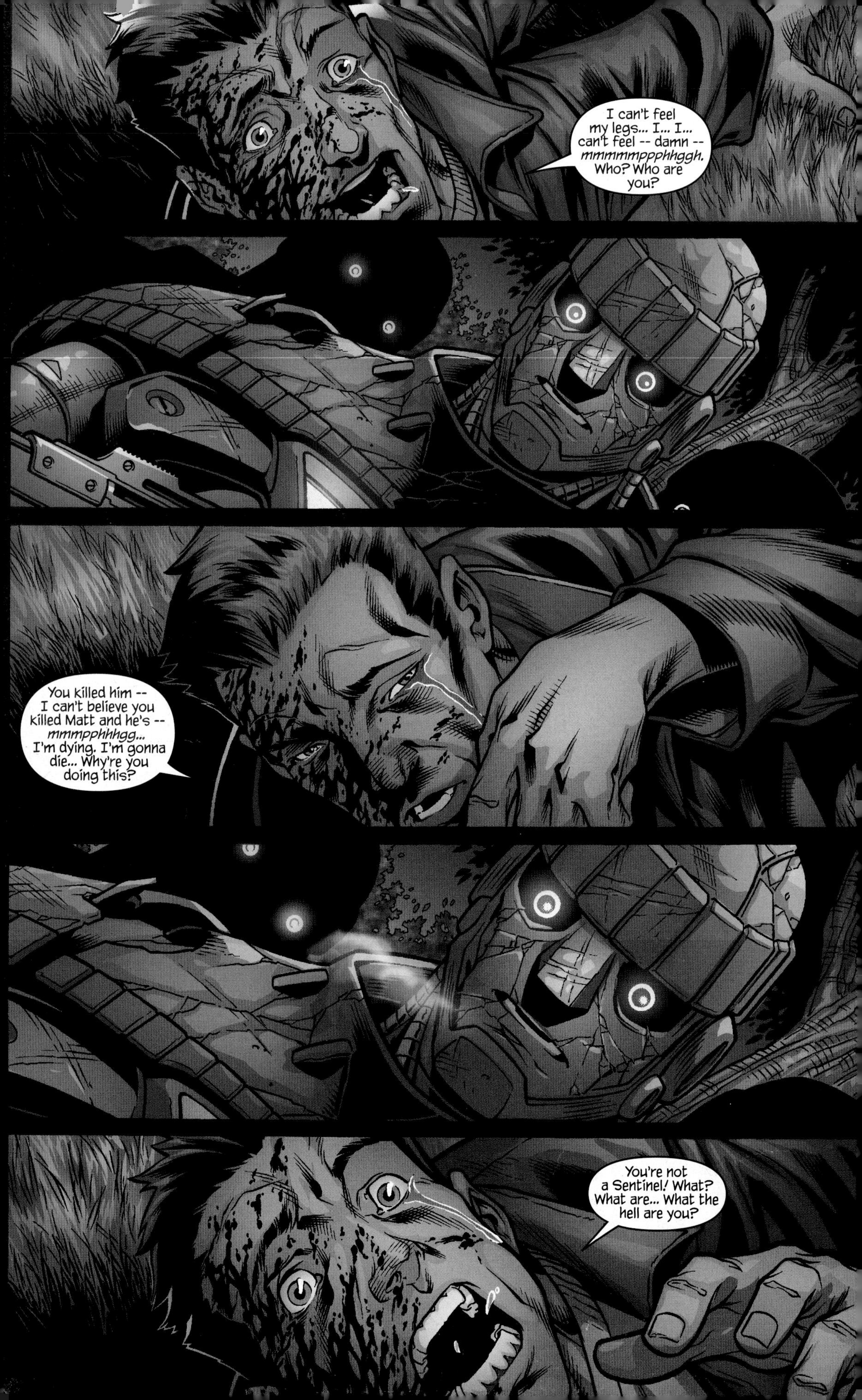
I can't feel my legs... I... I... can't feel -- damn -- *mmmmmppphhggh.* Who? Who are you?
You killed him -- I can't believe you killed Matt and he's -- *mmmpphhhgg...* I'm dying. I'm gonna die... Why're you doing this?
You're not a Sentinel! What? What are... What the hell are you?

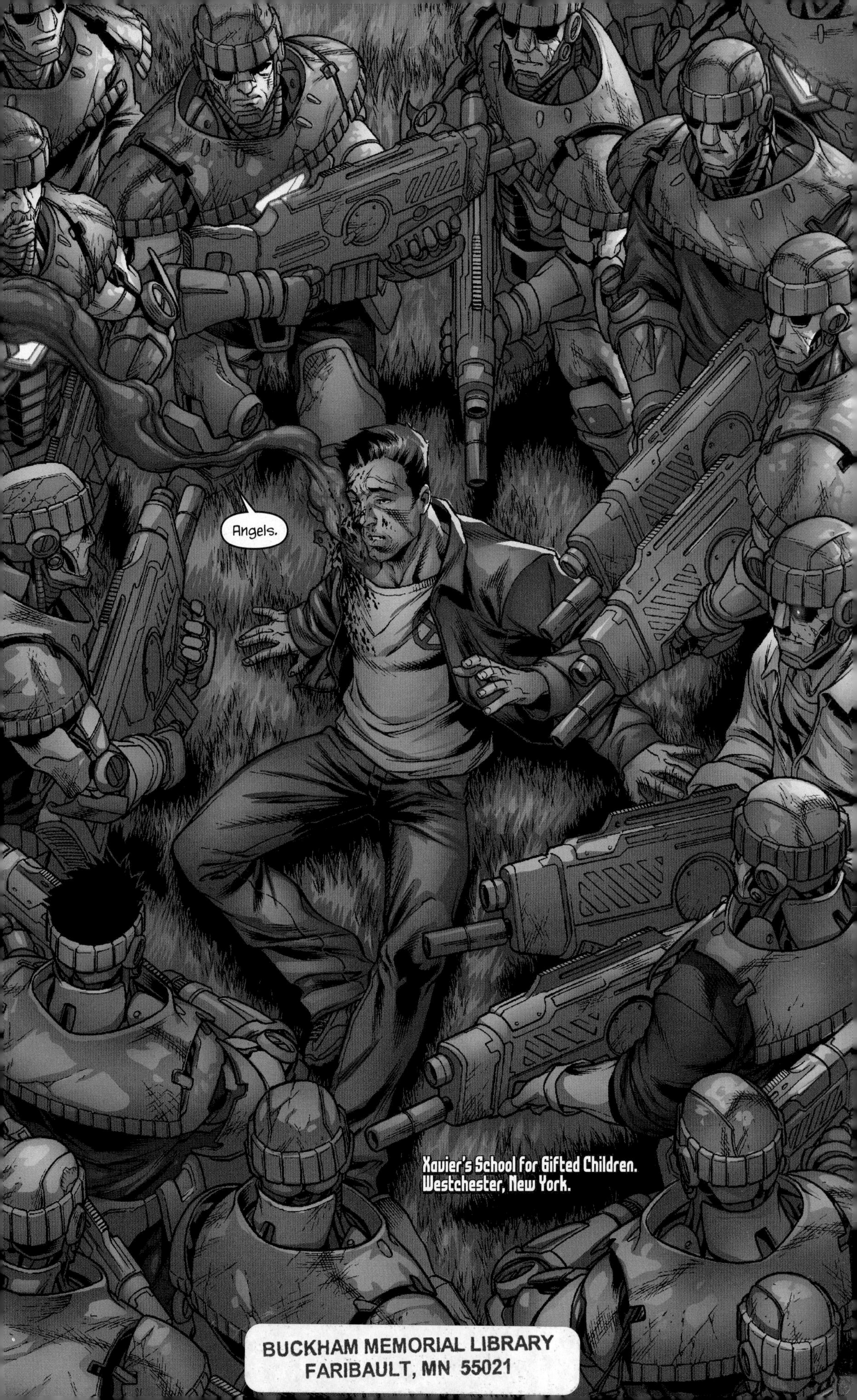
Angels.
Xavier's School for Gifted Children.
Westchester, New York.

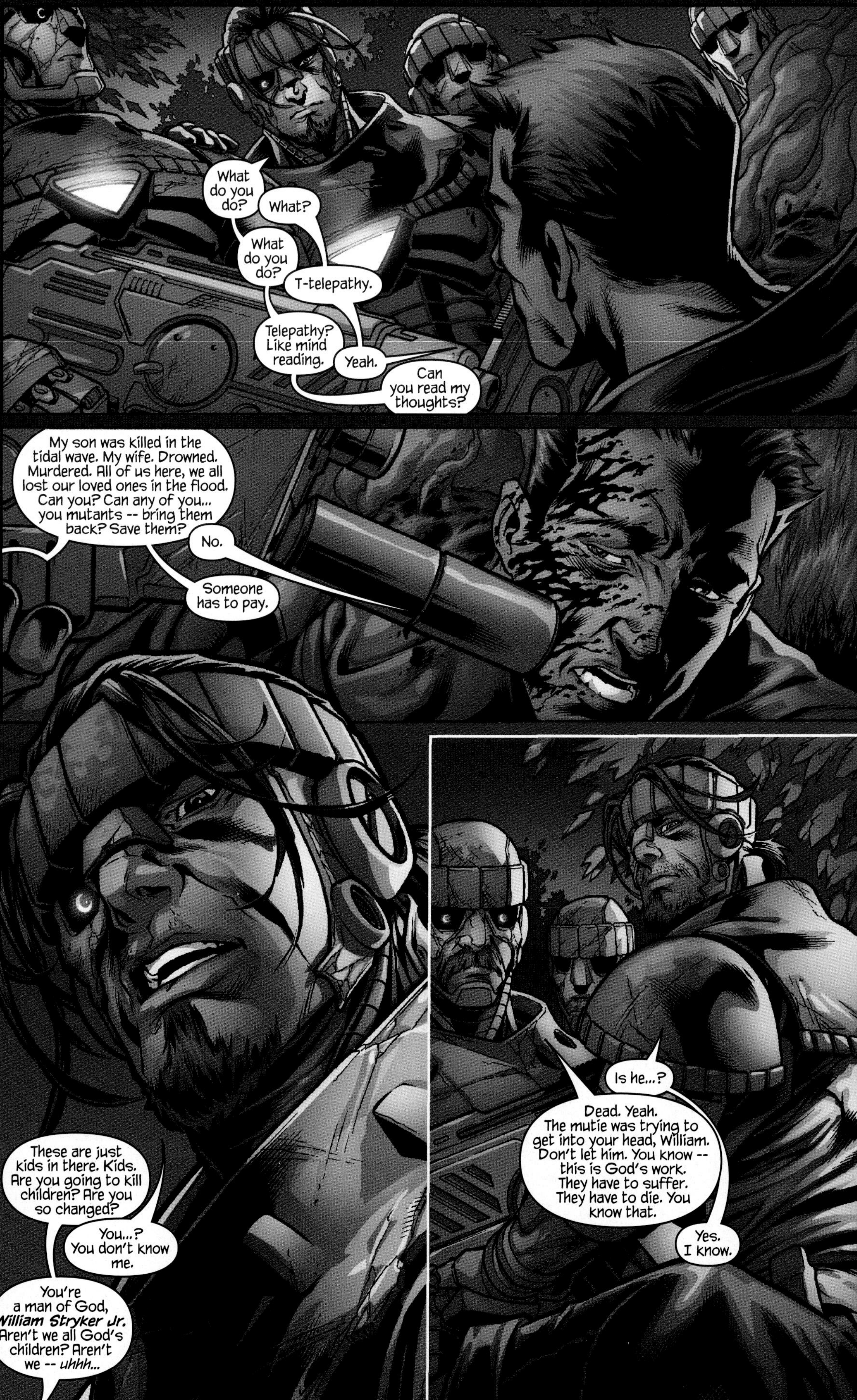

What do you do?
What?
What do you do?
T-telepathy.
Telepathy? Like mind reading.
Yeah.
Can you read my thoughts?
My son was killed in the tidal wave. My wife. Drowned. Murdered. All of us here, we all lost our loved ones in the flood. Can you? Can any of you... you mutants -- bring them back? Save them?
No.
Someone has to pay.
These are just kids in there. Kids. Are you going to kill children? Are you so changed?
You...? You don't know me.
You're a man of God, ***William Stryker Jr.*** Aren't we all God's children? Aren't we -- *uhhh...*
Is he...?
Dead. Yeah. The mutie was trying to get into your head, William. Don't let him. You know -- this is God's work. They have to suffer. They have to die. You know that.
Yes. I know.

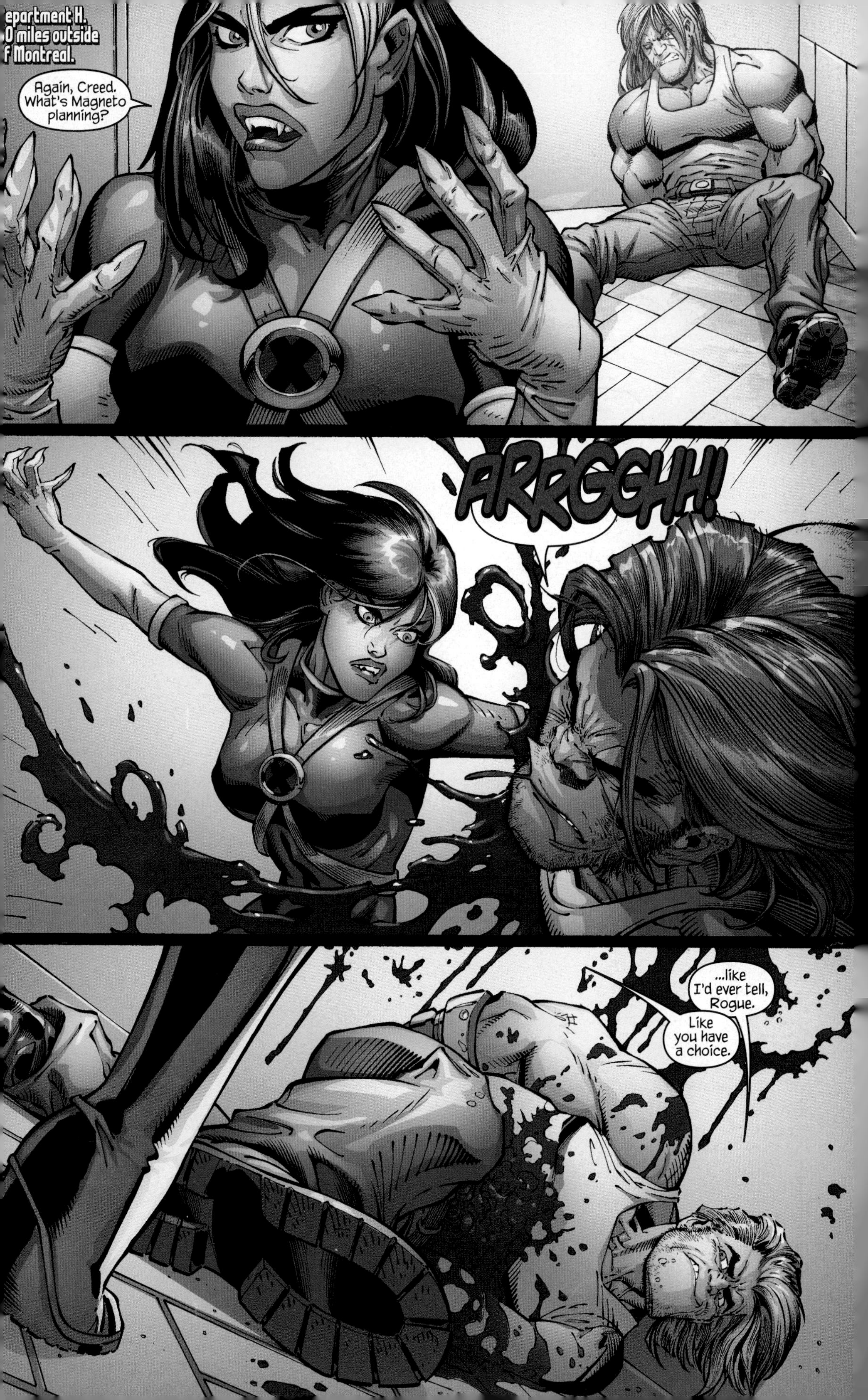
epartment H.
0 miles outside
f Montreal.
Again, Creed. What's Magneto planning?
ARRGGHH!
...like I'd ever tell, Rogue.
Like you have a choice.

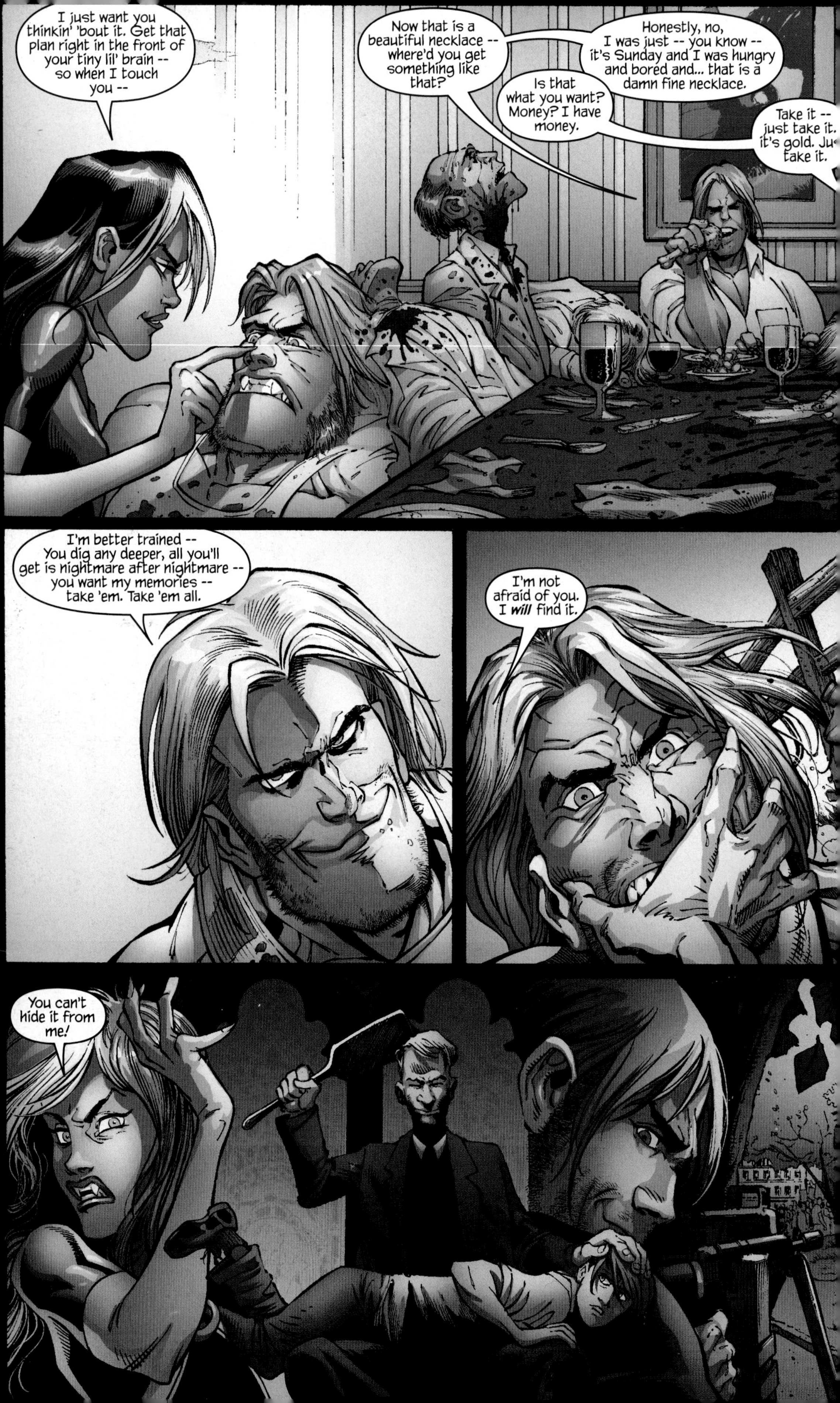
I just want you thinkin' 'bout it. Get that plan right in the front of your tiny lil' brain -- so when I touch you --
Now that is a beautiful necklace -- where'd you get something like that?
Honestly, no, I was just -- you know -- it's Sunday and I was hungry and bored and... that is a damn fine necklace.
Is that what you want? Money? I have money.
Take it -- just take it. it's gold. Ju take it.
I'm better trained -- You dig any deeper, all you'll get is nightmare after nightmare -- you want my memories -- take 'em. Take 'em all.
I'm not afraid of you. I *will* find it.
You can't hide it from me!

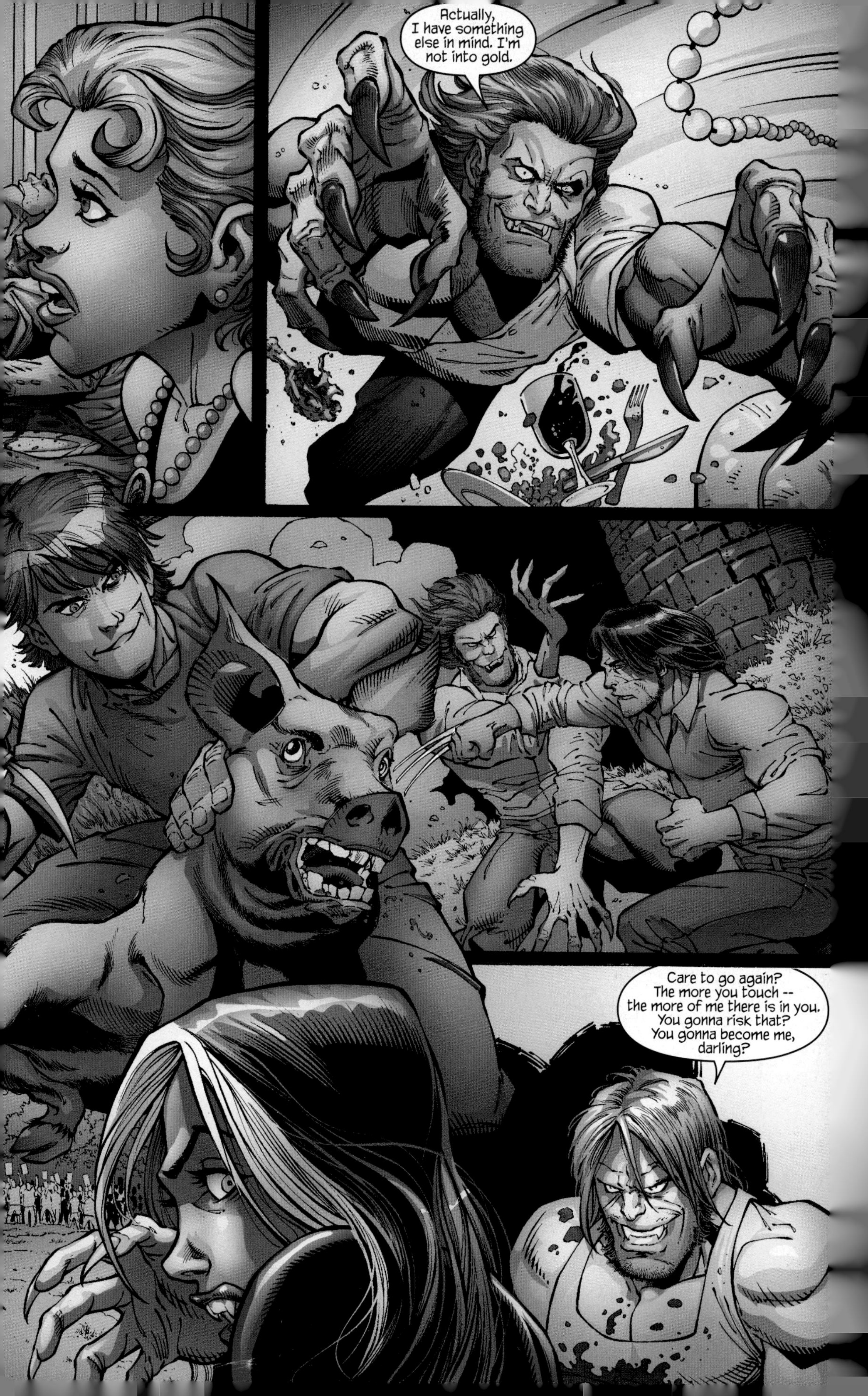
Actually, I have something else in mind. I'm not into gold.
Care to go again? The more you touch -- the more of me there is in you. You gonna risk that? You gonna become me, darling?

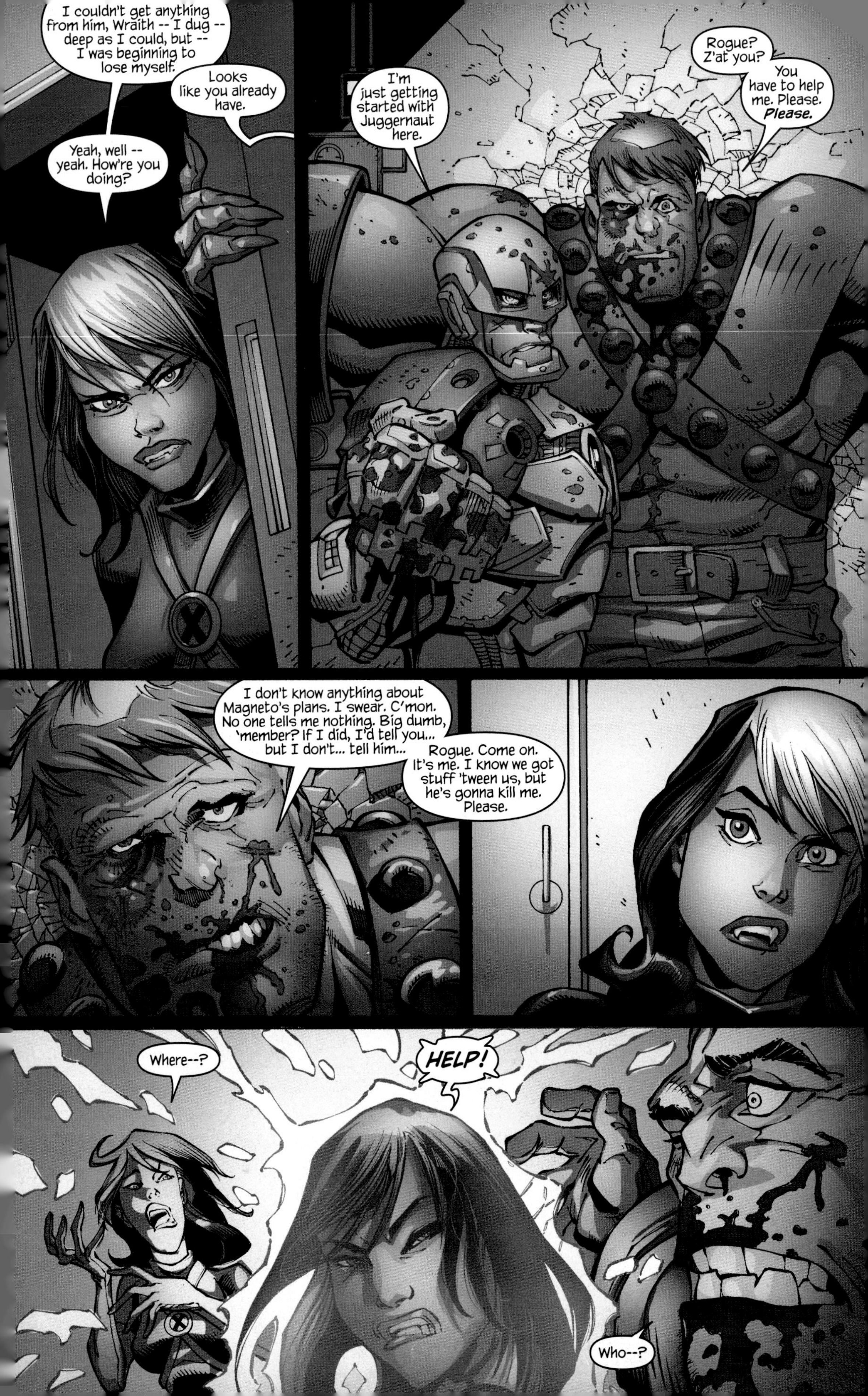
I couldn't get anything from him, Wraith -- I dug -- deep as I could, but -- I was beginning to lose myself.
Looks like you already have.
Yeah, well -- yeah. How're you doing?
I'm just getting started with Juggernaut here.
Rogue? Z'at you?
You have to help me. Please. *Please.*
I don't know anything about Magneto's plans. I swear. C'mon. No one tells me nothing. Big dumb, 'member? If I did, I'd tell you... but I don't... tell him...
Rogue. Come on. It's me. I know we got stuff 'tween us, but he's gonna kill me. Please.
Where--?
HELP!
Who--?

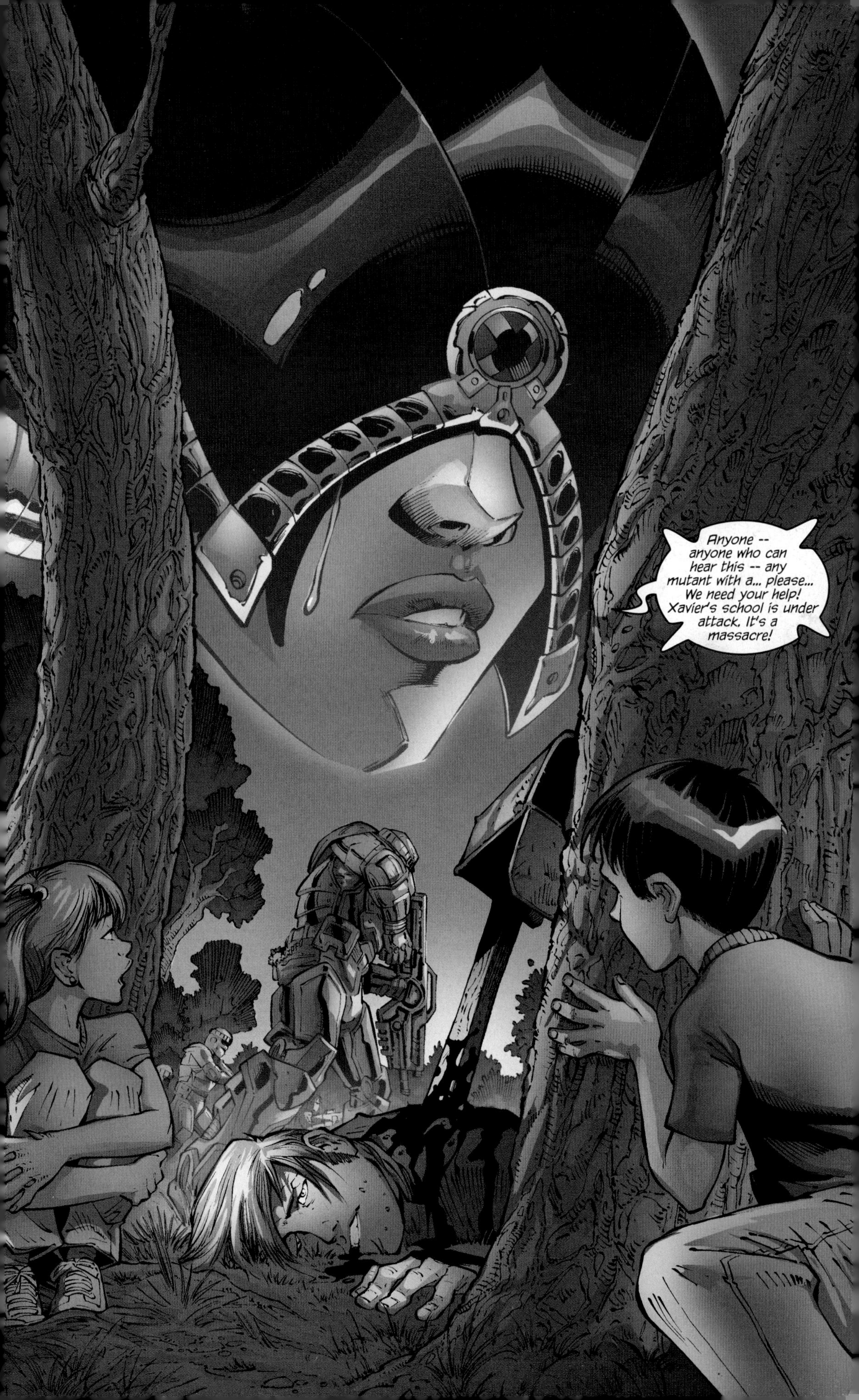
Anyone -- anyone who can hear this -- any mutant with a... please... We need your help! Xavier's school is under attack. It's a massacre!

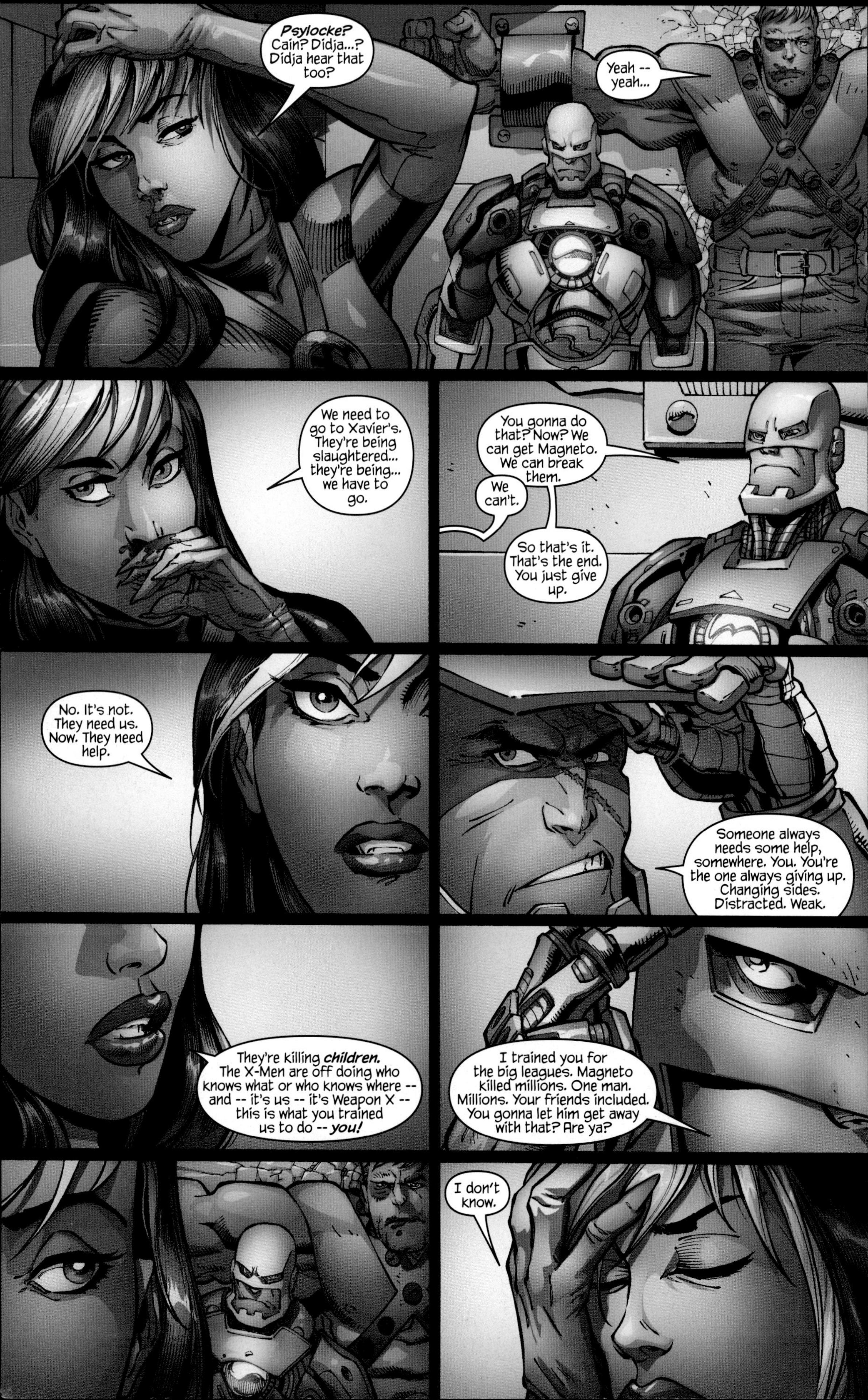

Psylocke? Cain? Didja...? Didja hear that too?
Yeah -- yeah...
We need to go to Xavier's. They're being slaughtered... they're being... we have to go.
You gonna do that? Now? We can get Magneto. We can break them.
We can't.
So that's it. That's the end. You just give up.
No. It's not. They need us. Now. They need help.
Someone always needs some help, somewhere. You. You're the one always giving up. Changing sides. Distracted. Weak.
They're killing ***children.*** The X-Men are off doing who knows what or who knows where -- and -- it's us -- it's Weapon X -- this is what you trained us to do -- ***you!***
I trained you for the big leagues. Magneto killed millions. One man. Millions. Your friends included. You gonna let him get away with that? Are ya?
I don't know.

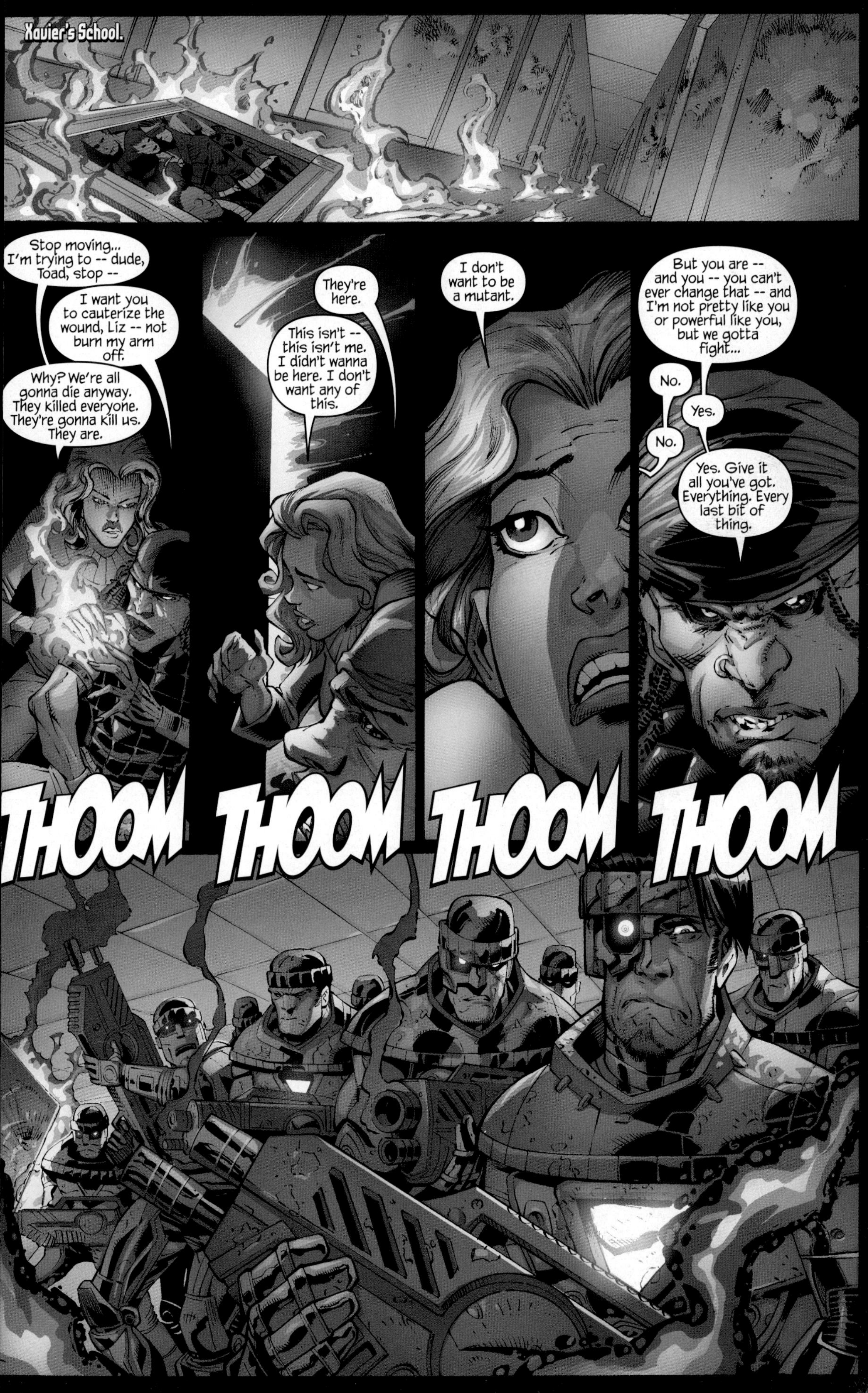
Xavier's School.
Stop moving... I'm trying to -- dude, Toad, stop --
I want you to cauterize the wound, Liz -- not burn my arm off.
Why? We're all gonna die anyway. They killed everyone. They're gonna kill us. They are.
They're here.
This isn't -- this isn't me. I didn't wanna be here. I don't want any of this.
I don't want to be a mutant.
But you are -- and you -- you can't ever change that -- and I'm not pretty like you or powerful like you, but we gotta fight...
No.
Yes.
No.
Yes. Give it all you've got. Everything. Every last bit of thing.
THOOM
THOOM
THOOM
THOOM

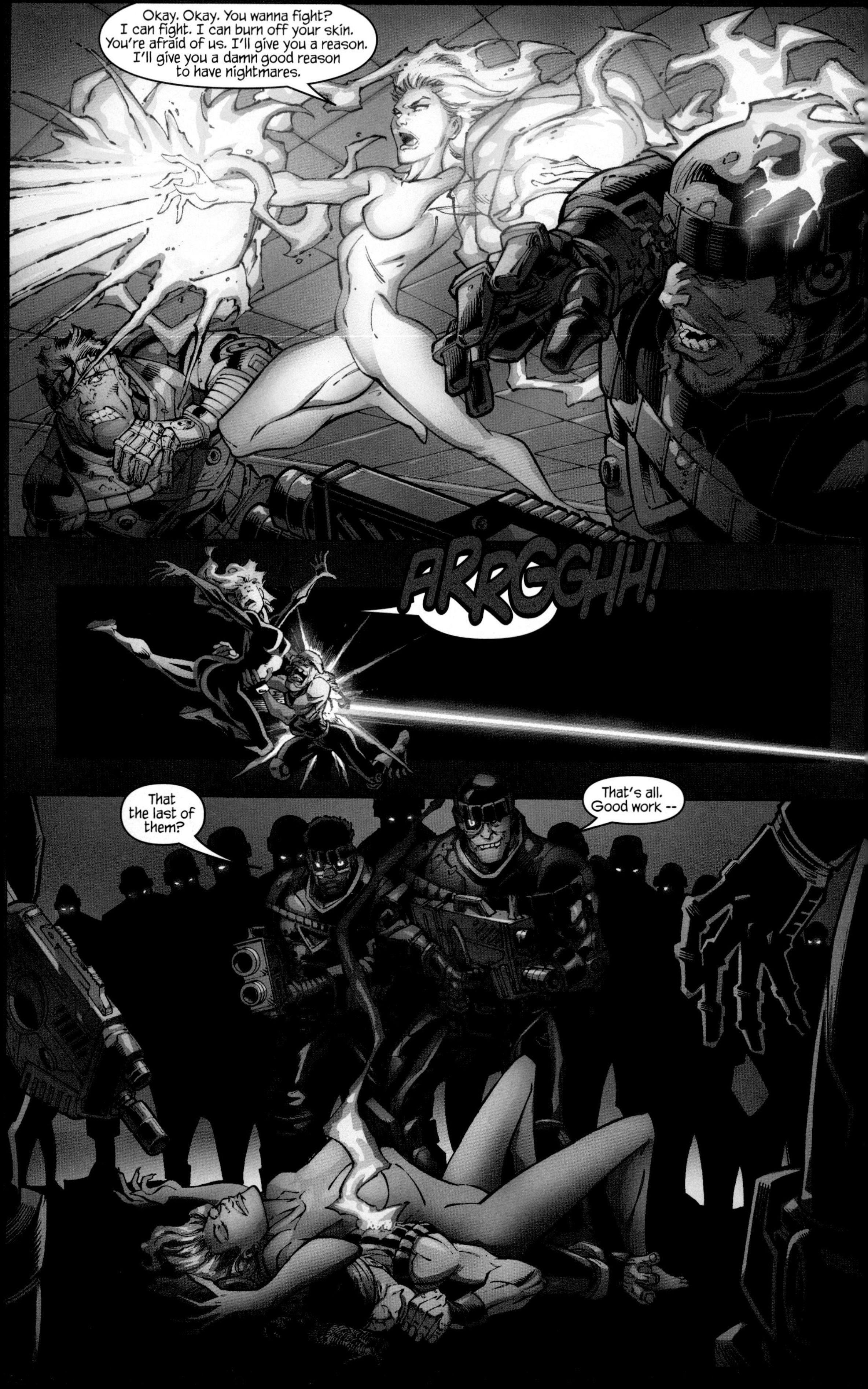
Okay. Okay. You wanna fight? I can fight. I can burn off your skin. You're afraid of us. I'll give you a reason. I'll give you a damn good reason to have nightmares.
ARRGGHH!
That the last of them?
That's all. Good work --

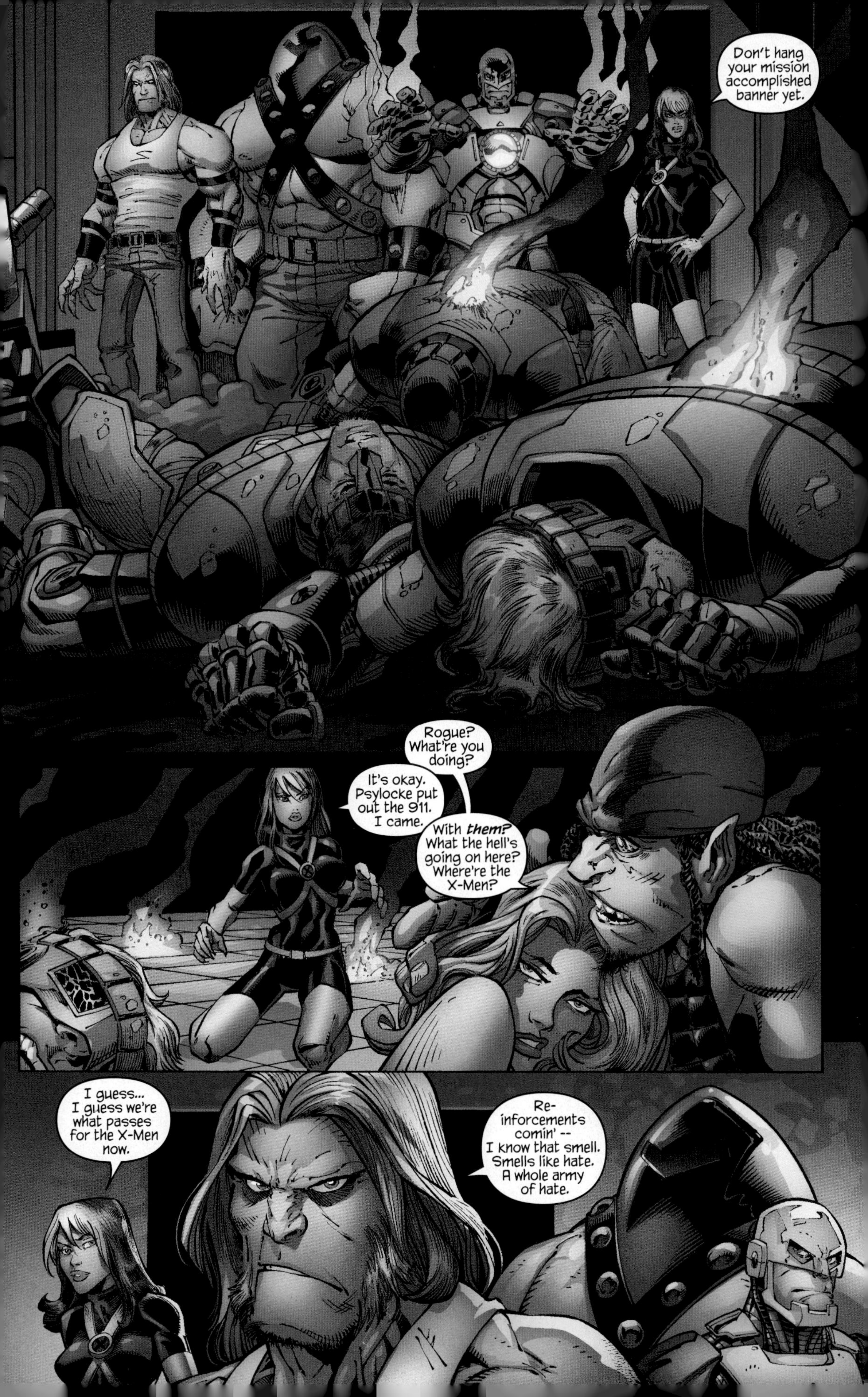
Don't hang your mission accomplished banner yet.
Rogue? What're you doing?
It's okay. Psylocke put out the 911. I came.
With *them?* What the hell's going on here? Where're the X-Men?
I guess... I guess we're what passes for the X-Men now.
Re-inforcements comin' -- I know that smell. Smells like hate. A whole army of hate.

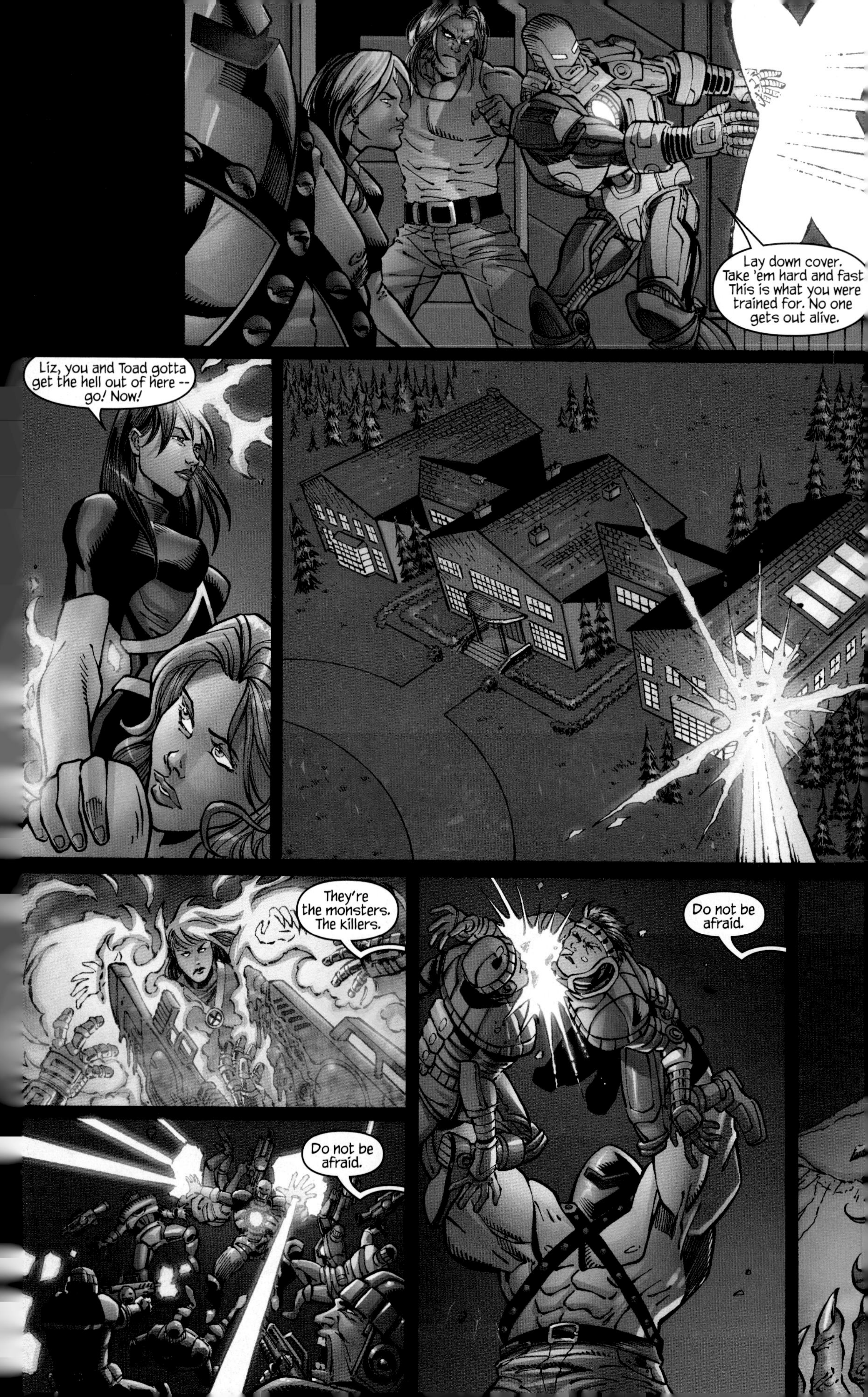
Lay down cover. Take 'em hard and fast This is what you were trained for. No one gets out alive.
Liz, you and Toad gotta get the hell out of here -- go! Now!
They're the monsters. The killers.
Do not be afraid.
Do not be afraid.

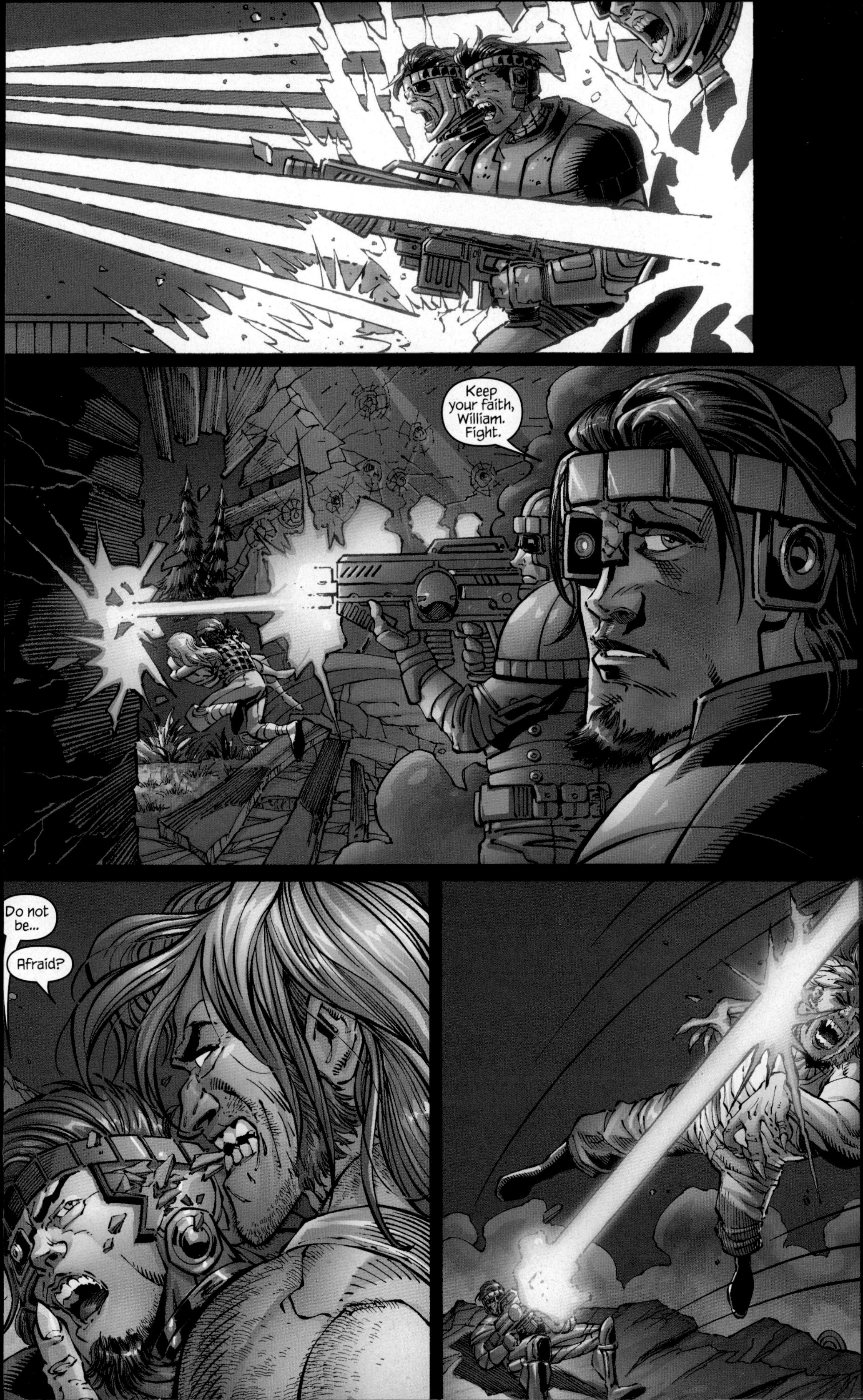
Keep your faith, William. Fight.
Do not be...
Afraid?

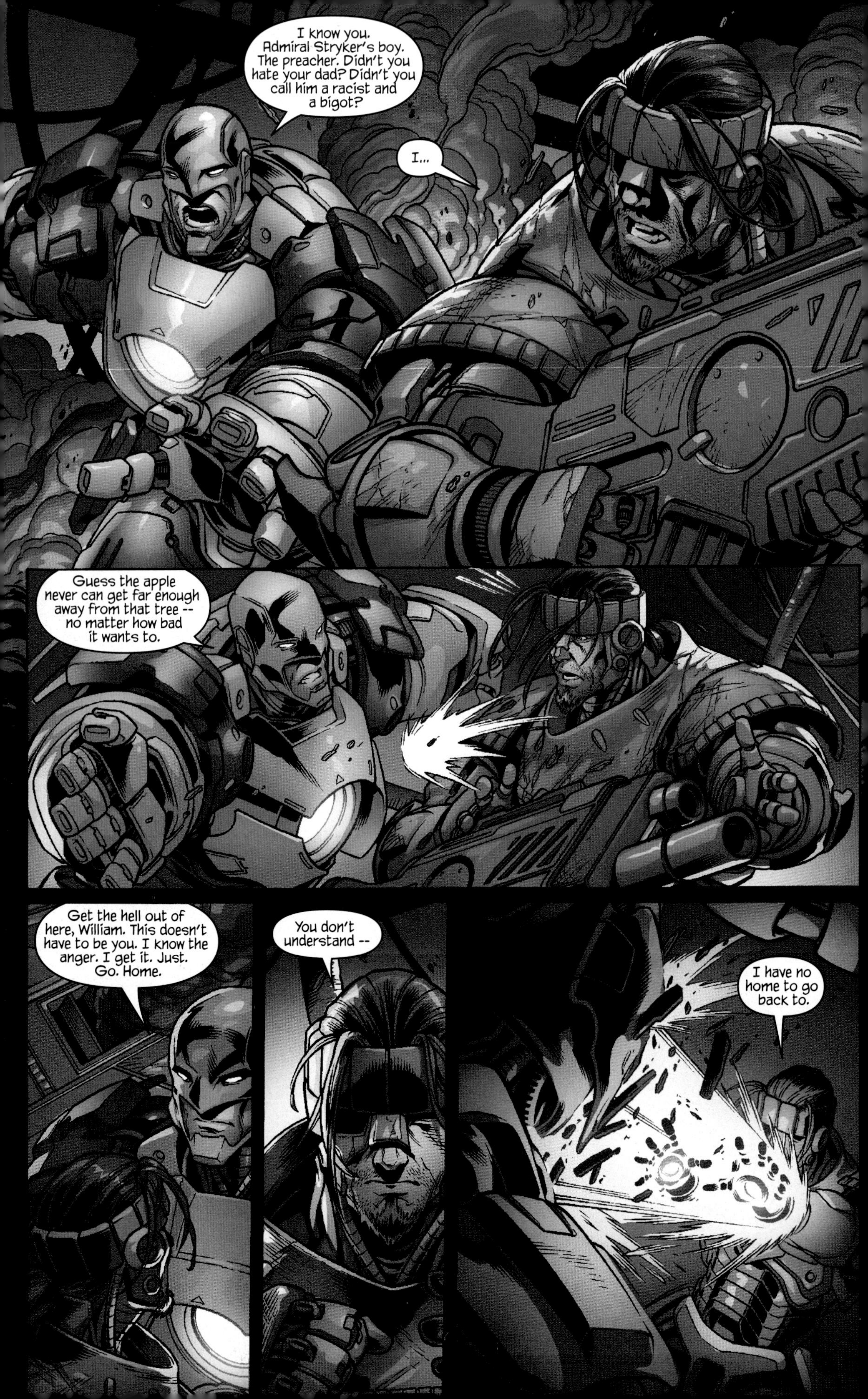
I know you. Admiral Stryker's boy. The preacher. Didn't you hate your dad? Didn't you call him a racist and a bigot?
I...
Guess the apple never can get far enough away from that tree -- no matter how bad it wants to.
Get the hell out of here, William. This doesn't have to be you. I know the anger. I get it. Just. Go. Home.
You don't understand --
I have no home to go back to.

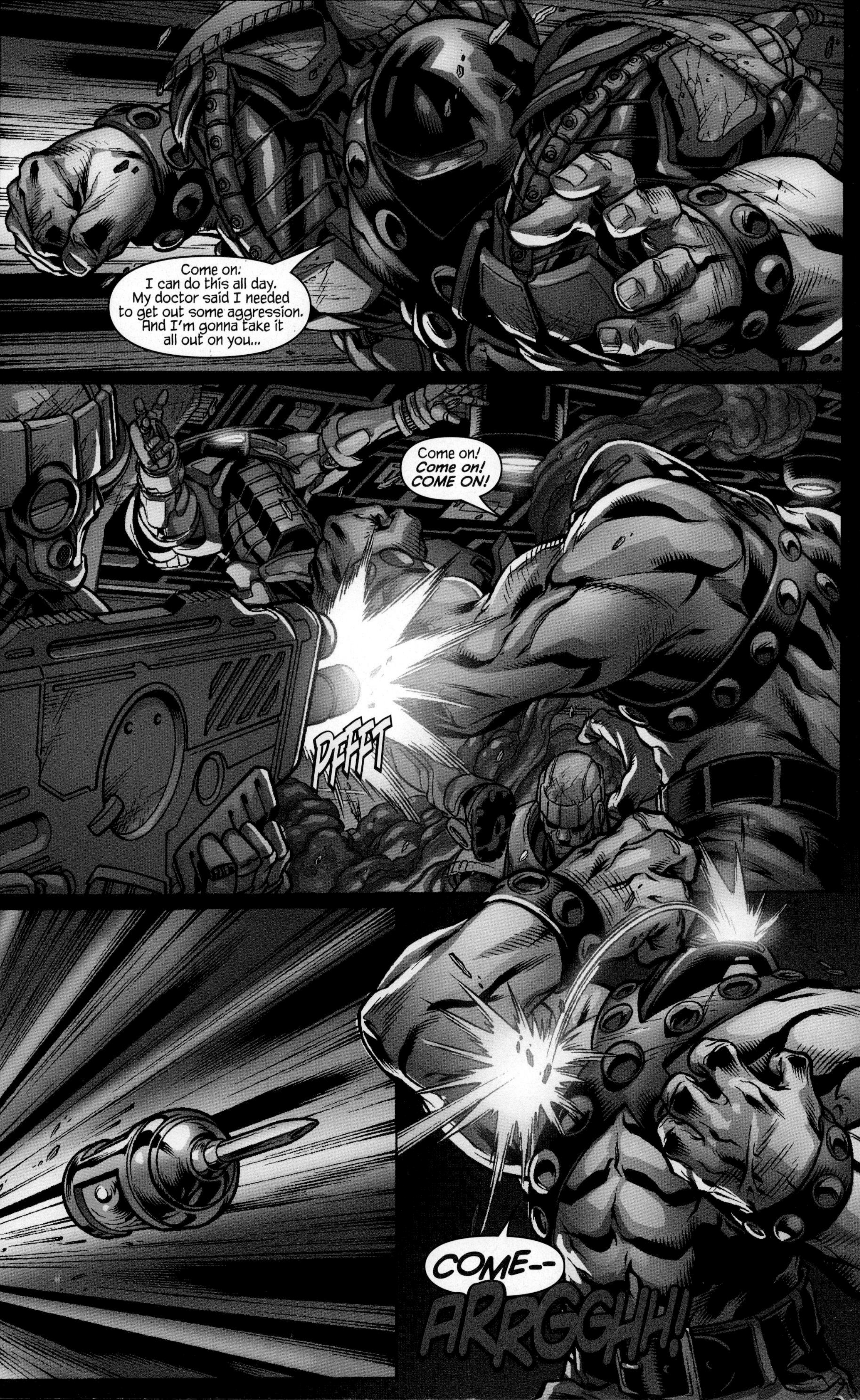
Come on. I can do this all day. My doctor said I needed to get out some aggression. And I'm gonna take it all out on you...
Come on! *Come on!* COME ON!
DFFFT
COME--
ARRGGHH!

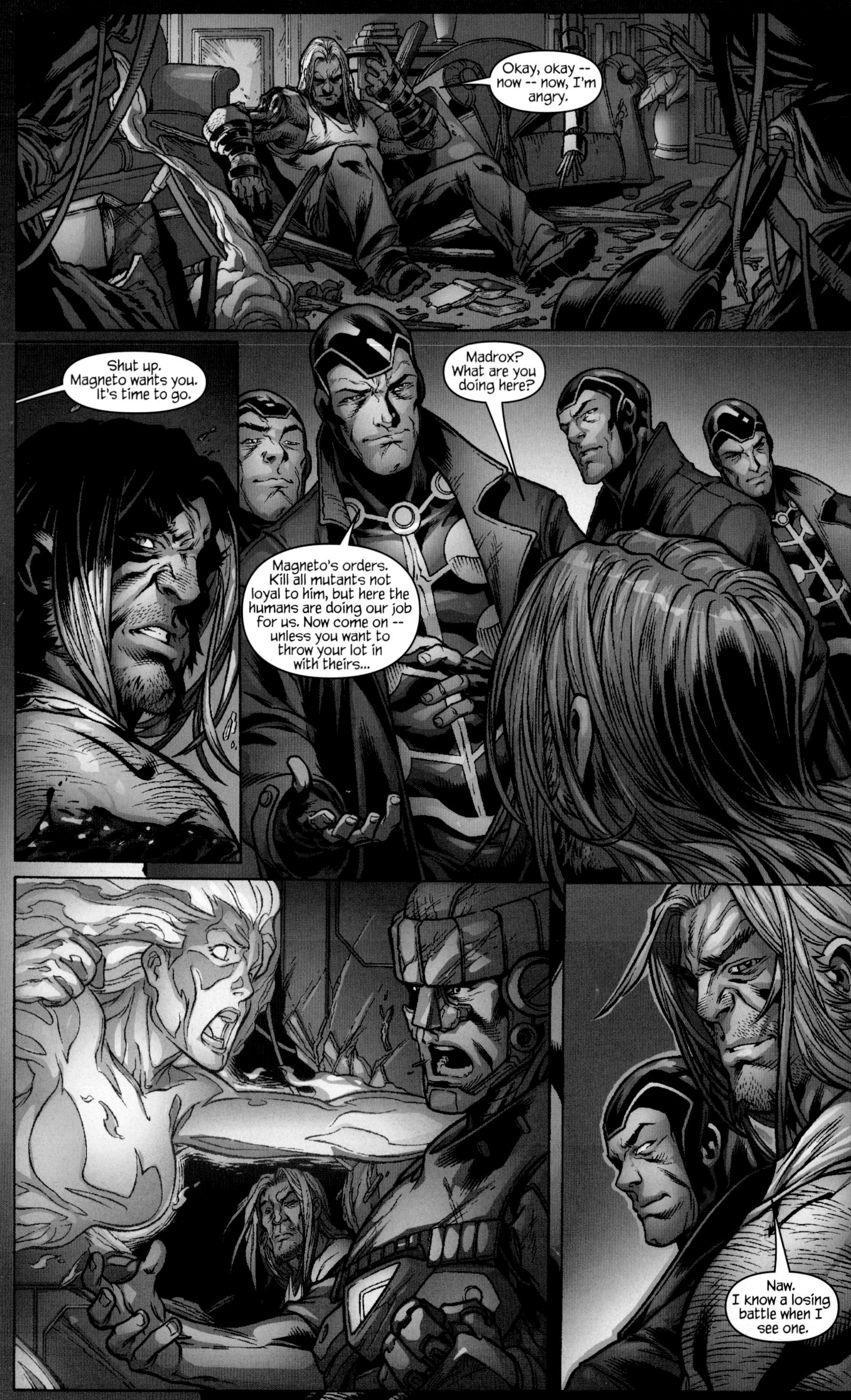
Okay, okay -- now -- now, I'm angry.
Shut up. Magneto wants you. It's time to go.
Madrox? What are you doing here?
Magneto's orders. Kill all mutants not loyal to him, but here the humans are doing our job for us. Now come on -- unless you want to throw your lot in with theirs...
Naw. I know a losing battle when I see one.

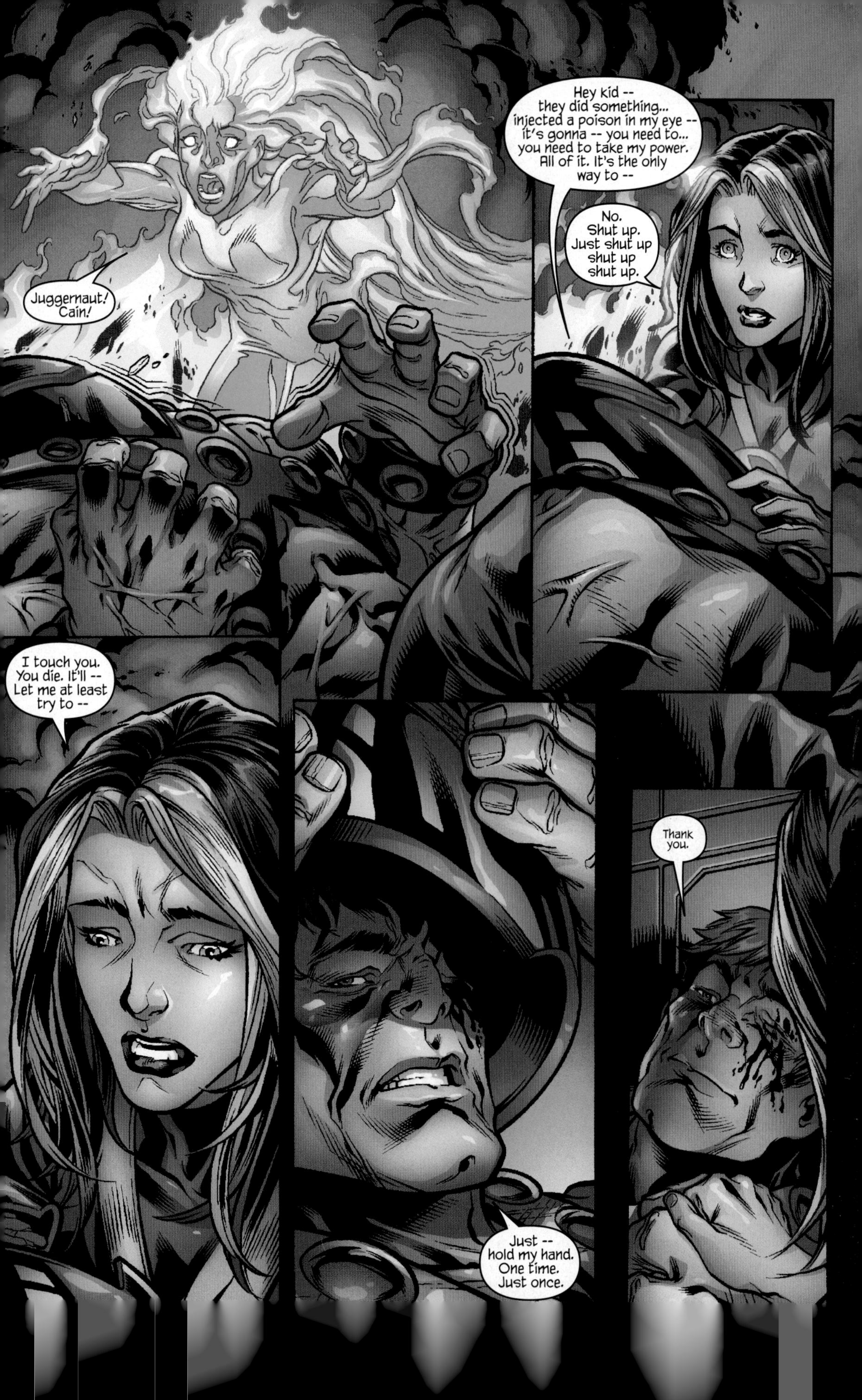
Juggernaut! Cain!
Hey kid -- they did something... injected a poison in my eye -- it's gonna -- you need to... you need to take my power. All of it. It's the only way to --
No. Shut up. Just shut up shut up shut up.
I touch you. You die. It'll -- Let me at least try to --
Just -- hold my hand. One time. Just once.
Thank you.

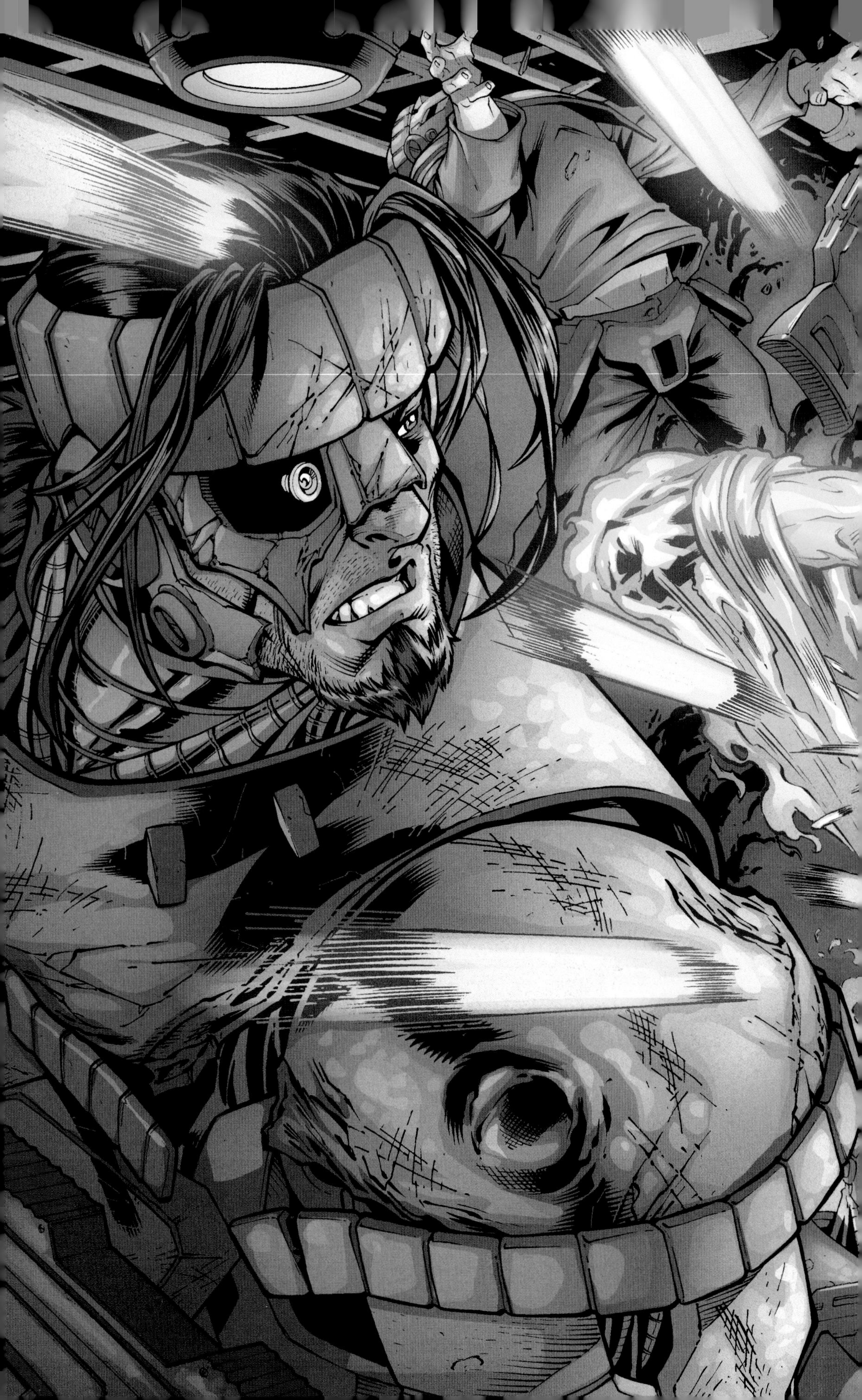

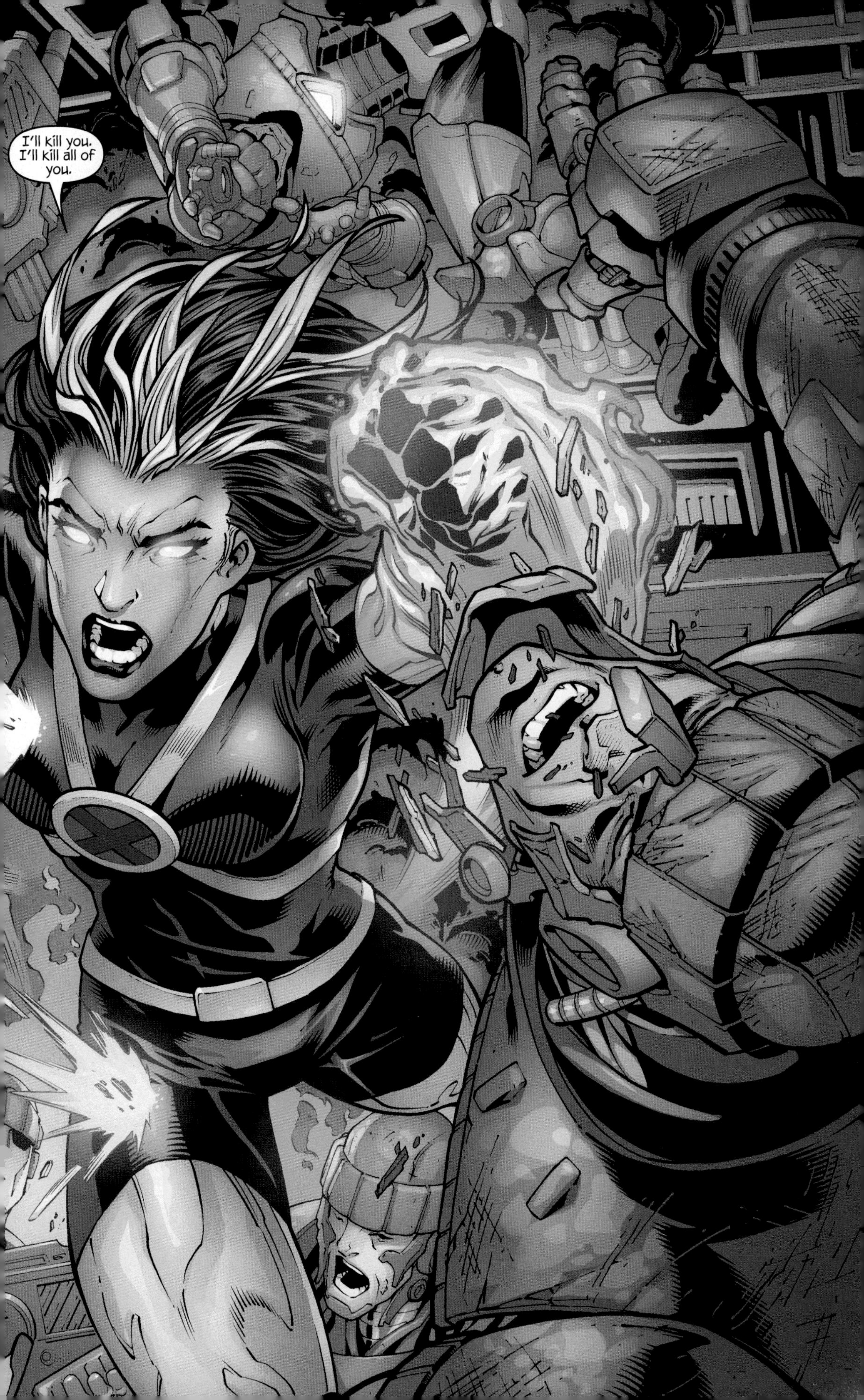
I'll kill you. I'll kill all of you.

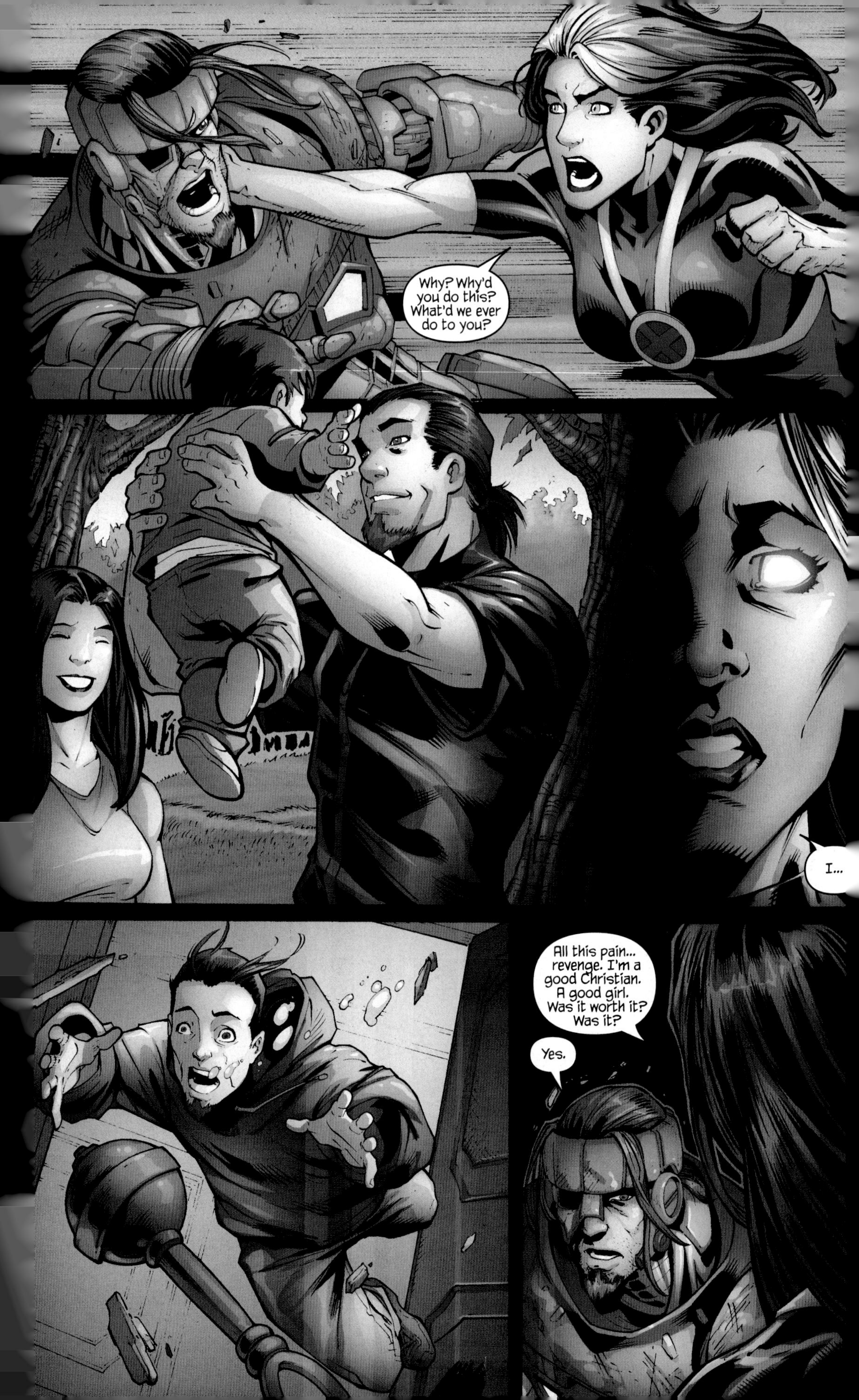
Why? Why'd you do this? What'd we ever do to you?
I...
All this pain... revenge. I'm a good Christian. A good girl. Was it worth it? Was it?
Yes.

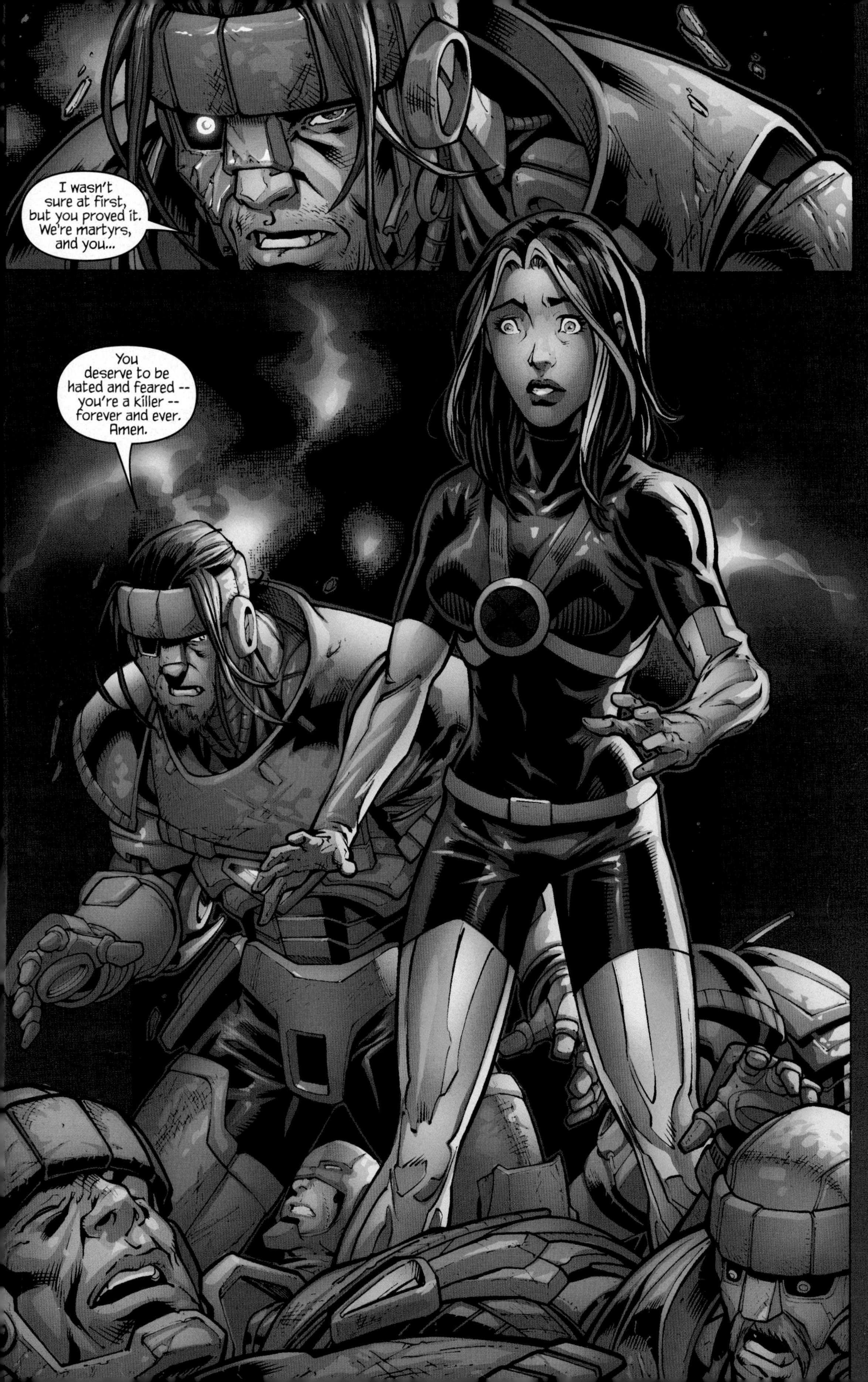
I wasn't sure at first, but you proved it. We're martyrs, and you...
You deserve to be hated and feared -- you're a killer -- forever and ever. Amen.

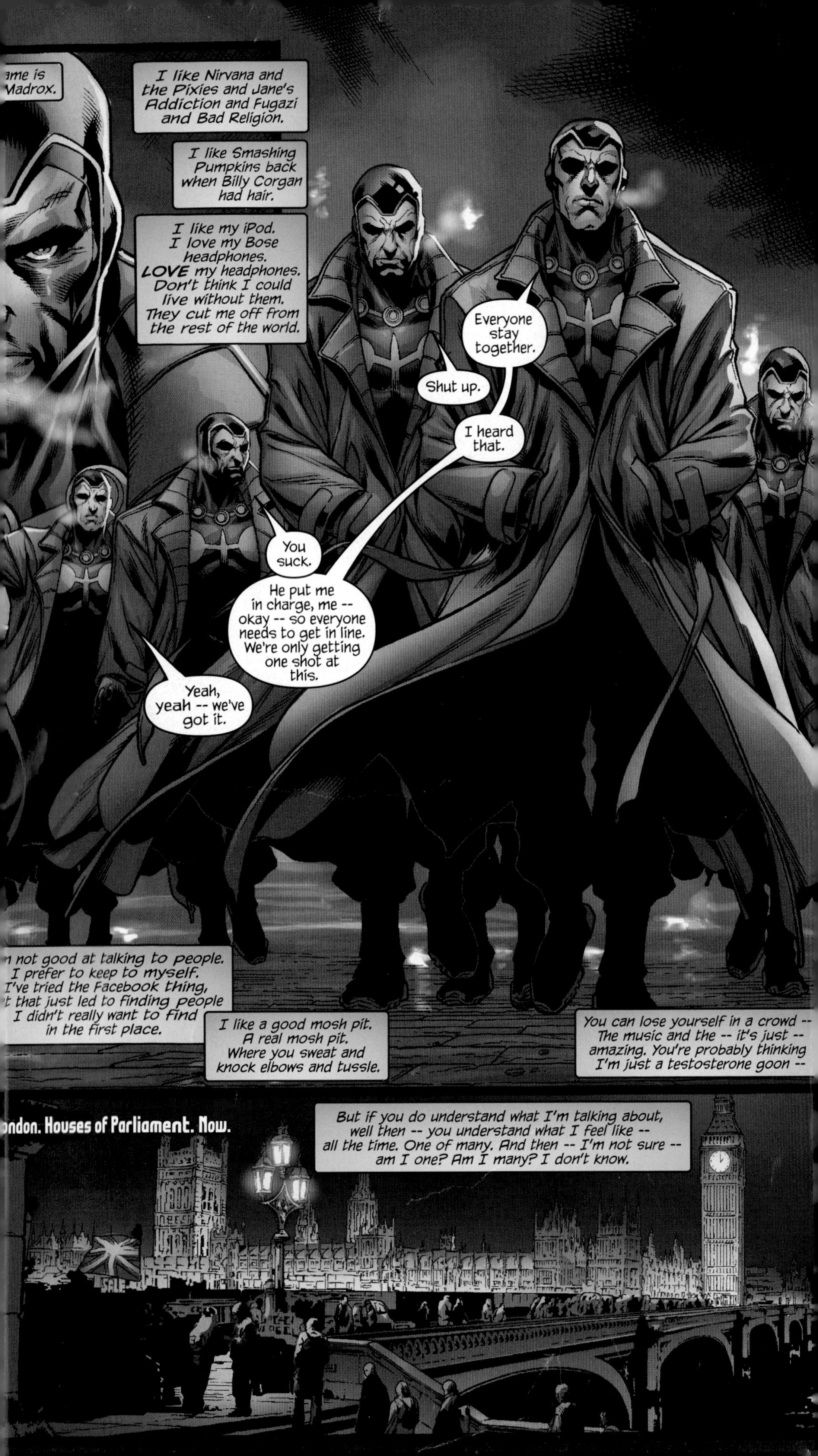
ame is
Madrox.
I like Nirvana and the Pixies and Jane's Addiction and Fugazi and Bad Religion.
I like Smashing Pumpkins back when Billy Corgan had hair.
I like my iPod. I love my Bose headphones. LOVE my headphones. Don't think I could live without them. They cut me off from the rest of the world.
Everyone stay together.
Shut up.
I heard that.
You suck.
He put me in charge, me -- okay -- so everyone needs to get in line. We're only getting one shot at this.
Yeah, yeah -- we've got it.
n not good at talking to people. I prefer to keep to myself. I've tried the Facebook thing, t that just led to finding people I didn't really want to find in the first place.
I like a good mosh pit. A real mosh pit. Where you sweat and knock elbows and tussle.
You can lose yourself in a crowd -- The music and the -- it's just -- amazing. You're probably thinking I'm just a testosterone goon --
ondon. Houses of Parliament. Now.
But if you do understand what I'm talking about, well then -- you understand what I feel like -- all the time. One of many. And then -- I'm not sure -- am I one? Am I many? I don't know.

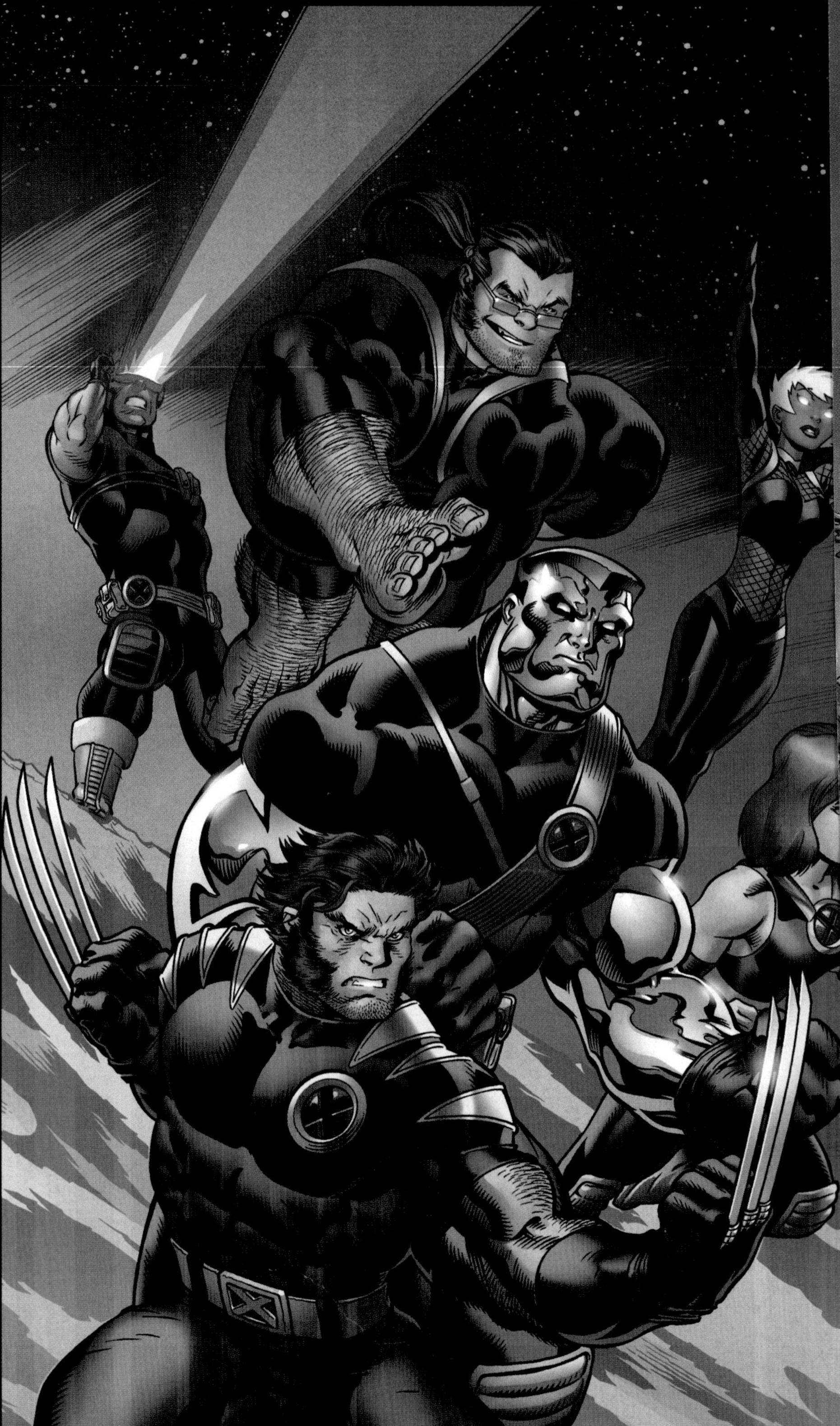

ULTIMATE X-MEN #100

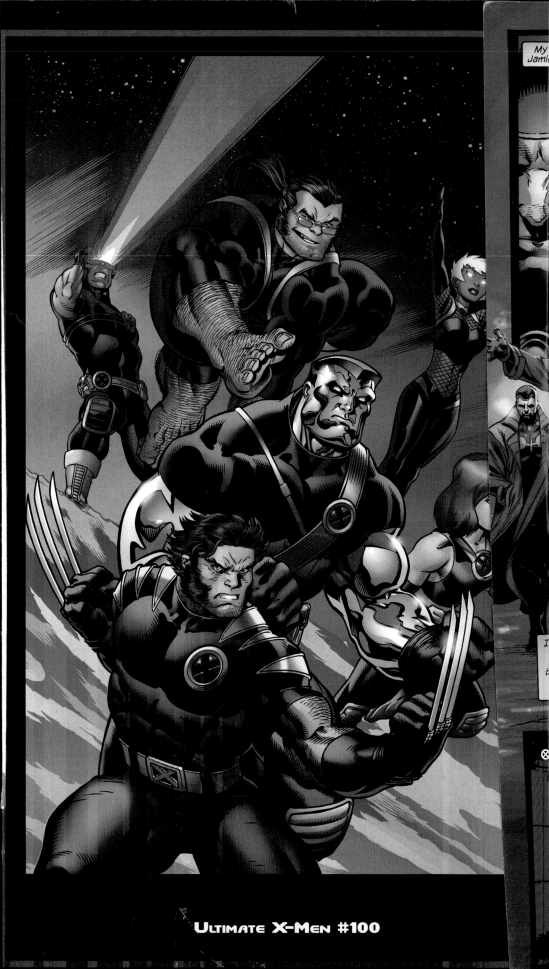

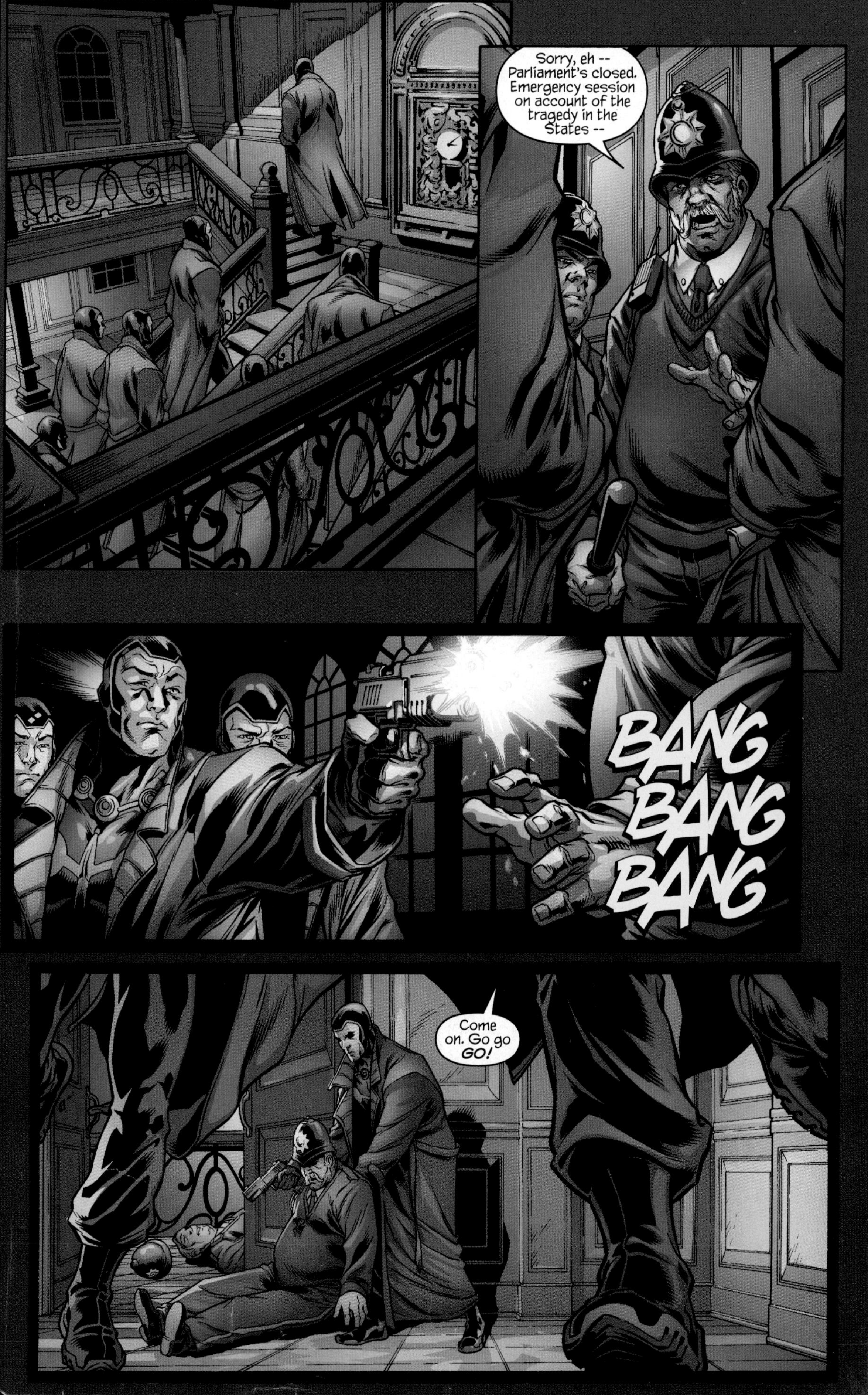

Sorry, eh -- Parliament's closed. Emergency session on account of the tragedy in the States --
BANG BANG BANG
Come on. Go go *GO!*

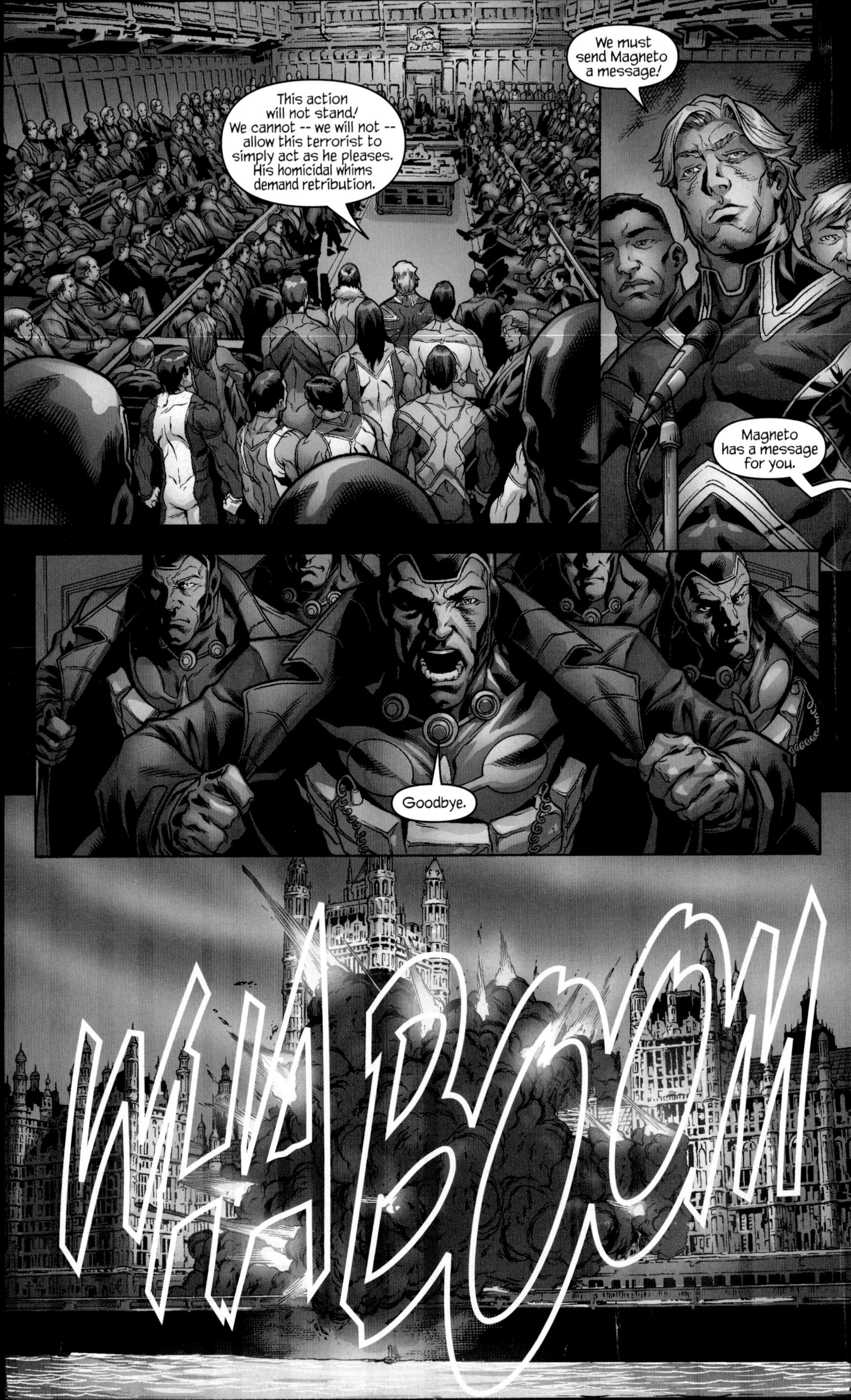
This action will not stand! We cannot -- we will not -- allow this terrorist to simply act as he pleases. His homicidal whims demand retribution.
We must send Magneto a message!
Magneto has a message for you.
Goodbye.
WHABOOM

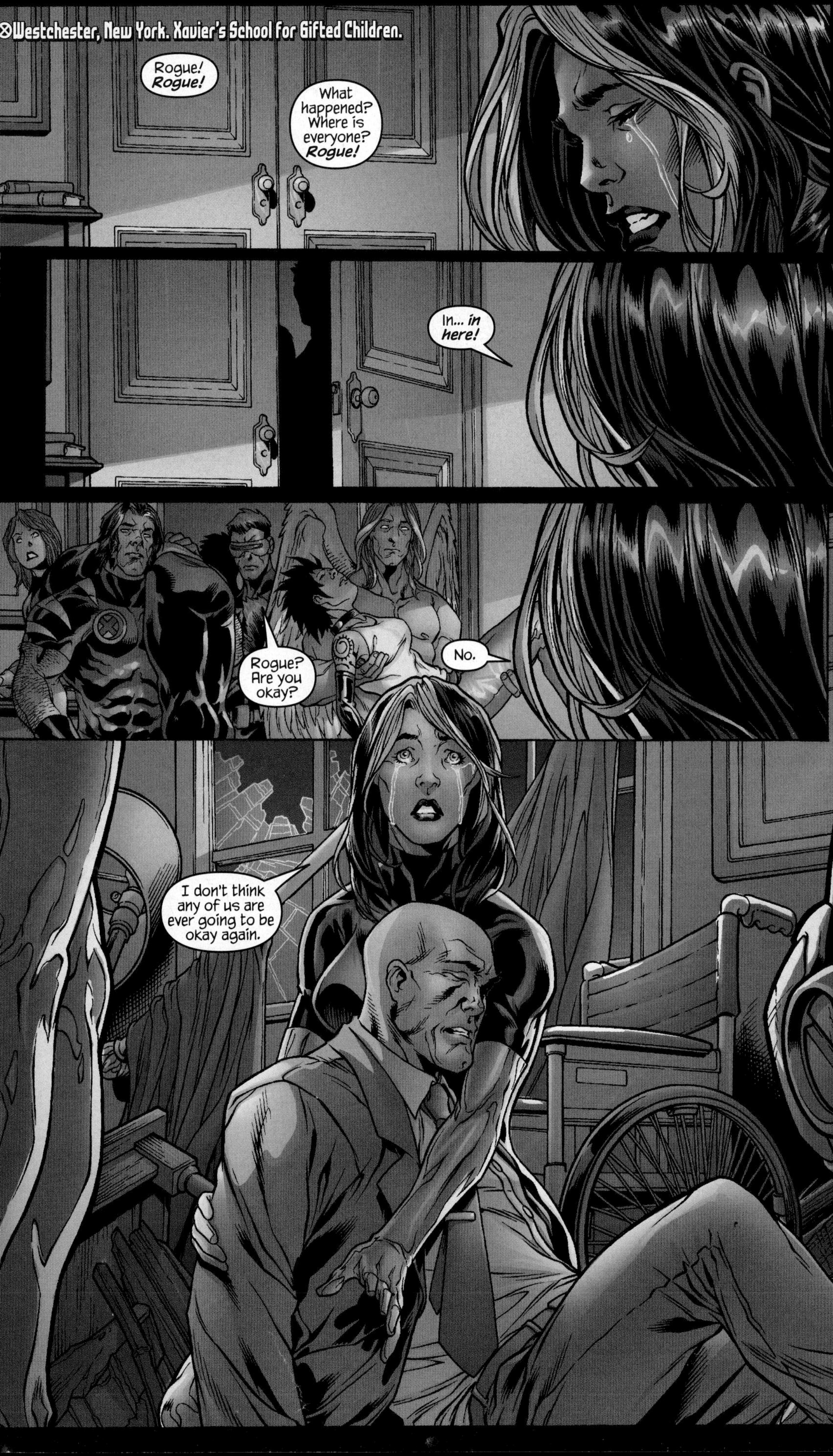
Westchester, New York. Xavier's School for Gifted Children.
Rogue! Rogue!
What happened? Where is everyone? Rogue!
In... in here!
Rogue? Are you okay?
No.
I don't think any of us are ever going to be okay again.

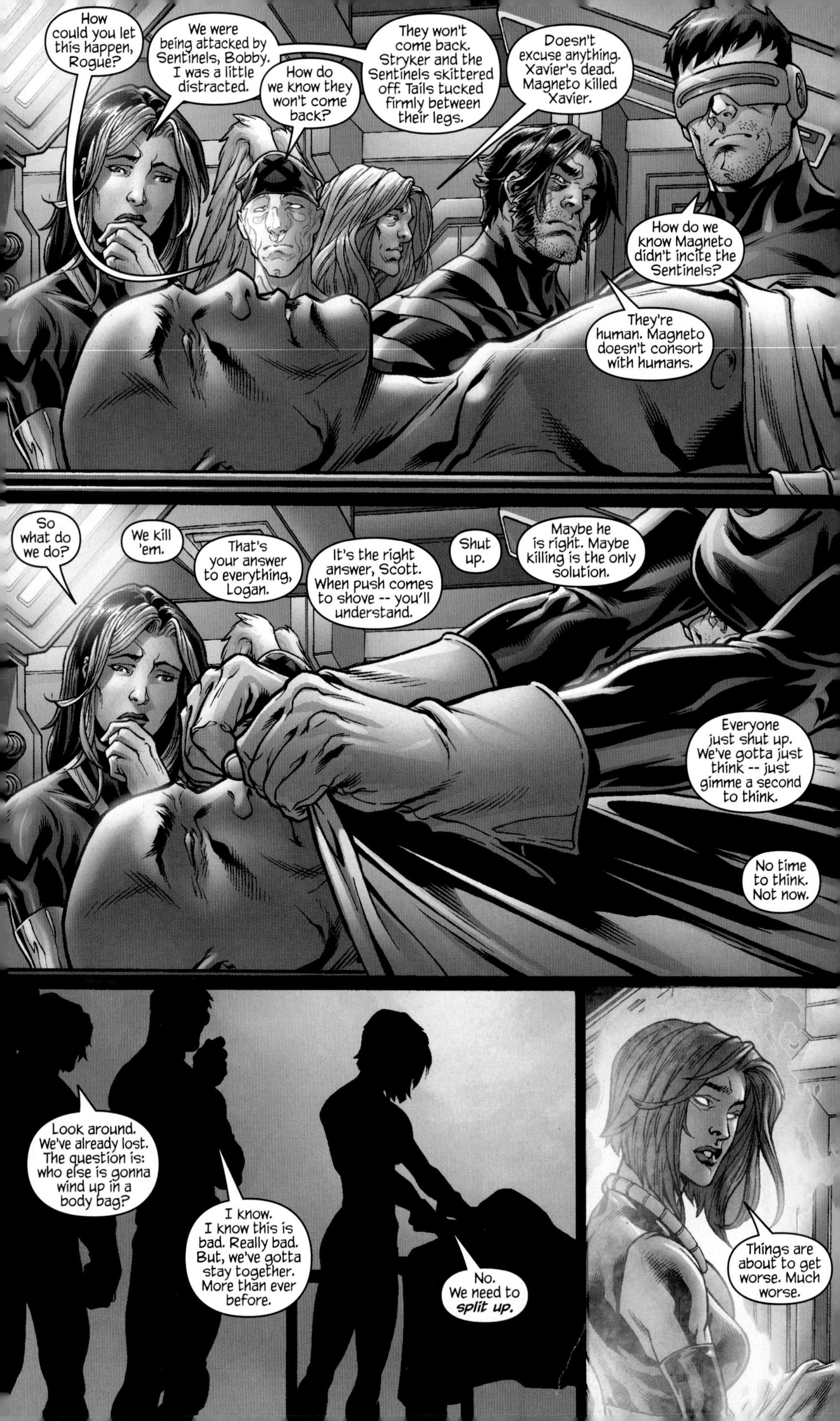
How could you let this happen, Rogue?
We were being attacked by Sentinels, Bobby. I was a little distracted.
How do we know they won't come back?
They won't come back. Stryker and the Sentinels skittered off. Tails tucked firmly between their legs.
Doesn't excuse anything. Xavier's dead. Magneto killed Xavier.
How do we know Magneto didn't incite the Sentinels?
They're human. Magneto doesn't consort with humans.
So what do we do?
We kill 'em.
That's your answer to everything, Logan.
It's the right answer, Scott. When push comes to shove -- you'll understand.
Shut up.
Maybe he is right. Maybe killing is the only solution.
Everyone just shut up. We've gotta just think -- just gimme a second to think.
No time to think. Not now.
Look around. We've already lost. The question is: who else is gonna wind up in a body bag?
I know. I know this is bad. Really bad. But, we've gotta stay together. More than ever before.
No. We need to *split up.*
Things are about to get worse. Much worse.

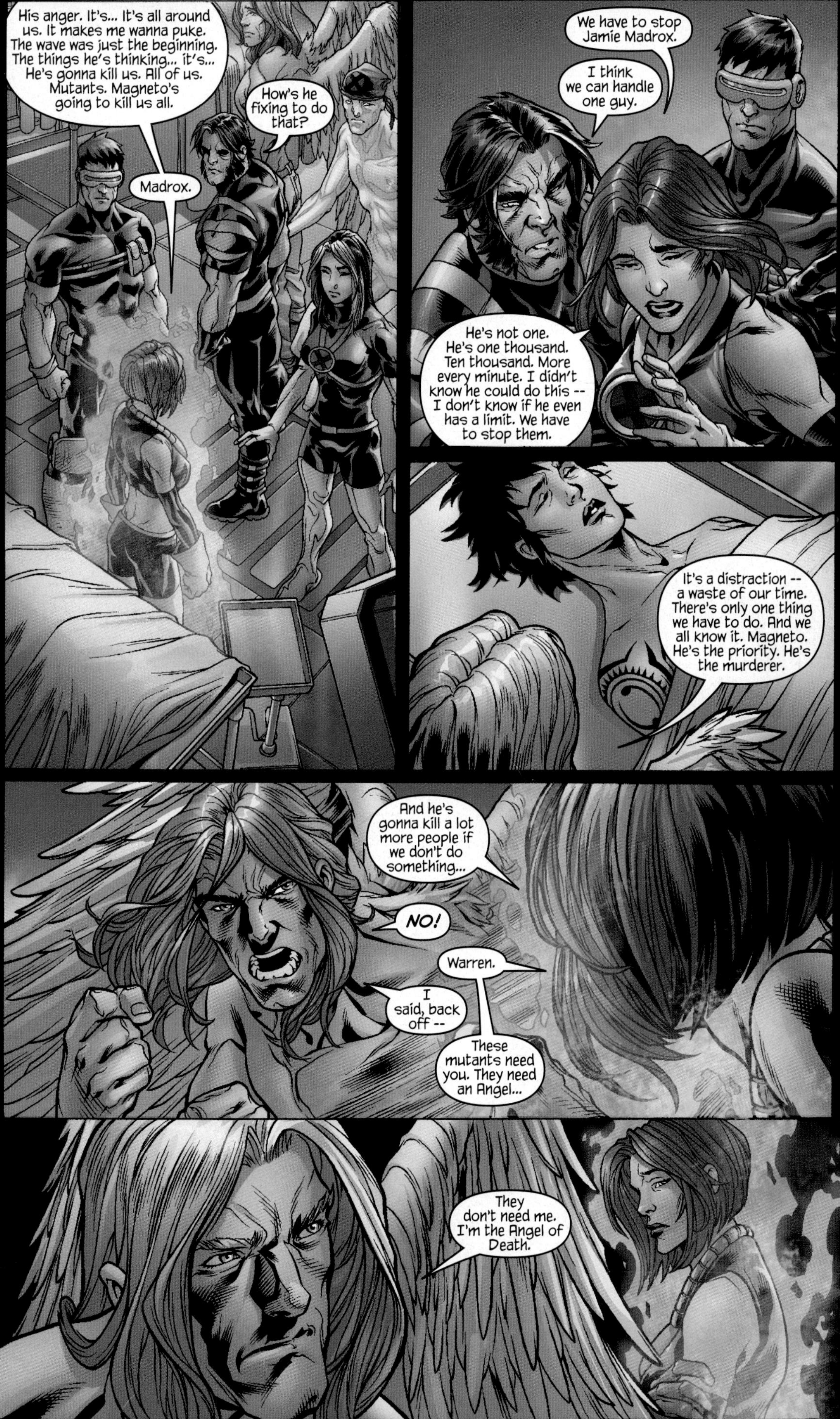

His anger. It's... It's all around us. It makes me wanna puke. The wave was just the beginning. The things he's thinking... it's... He's gonna kill us. All of us. Mutants. Magneto's going to kill us all.
How's he fixing to do that?
Madrox.
We have to stop Jamie Madrox.
I think we can handle one guy.
He's not one. He's one thousand. Ten thousand. More every minute. I didn't know he could do this -- I don't know if he even has a limit. We have to stop them.
It's a distraction -- a waste of our time. There's only one thing we have to do. And we all know it. Magneto. He's the priority. He's the murderer.
And he's gonna kill a lot more people if we don't do something...
NO!
Warren.
I said, back off --
These mutants need you. They need an Angel...
They don't need me. I'm the Angel of Death.

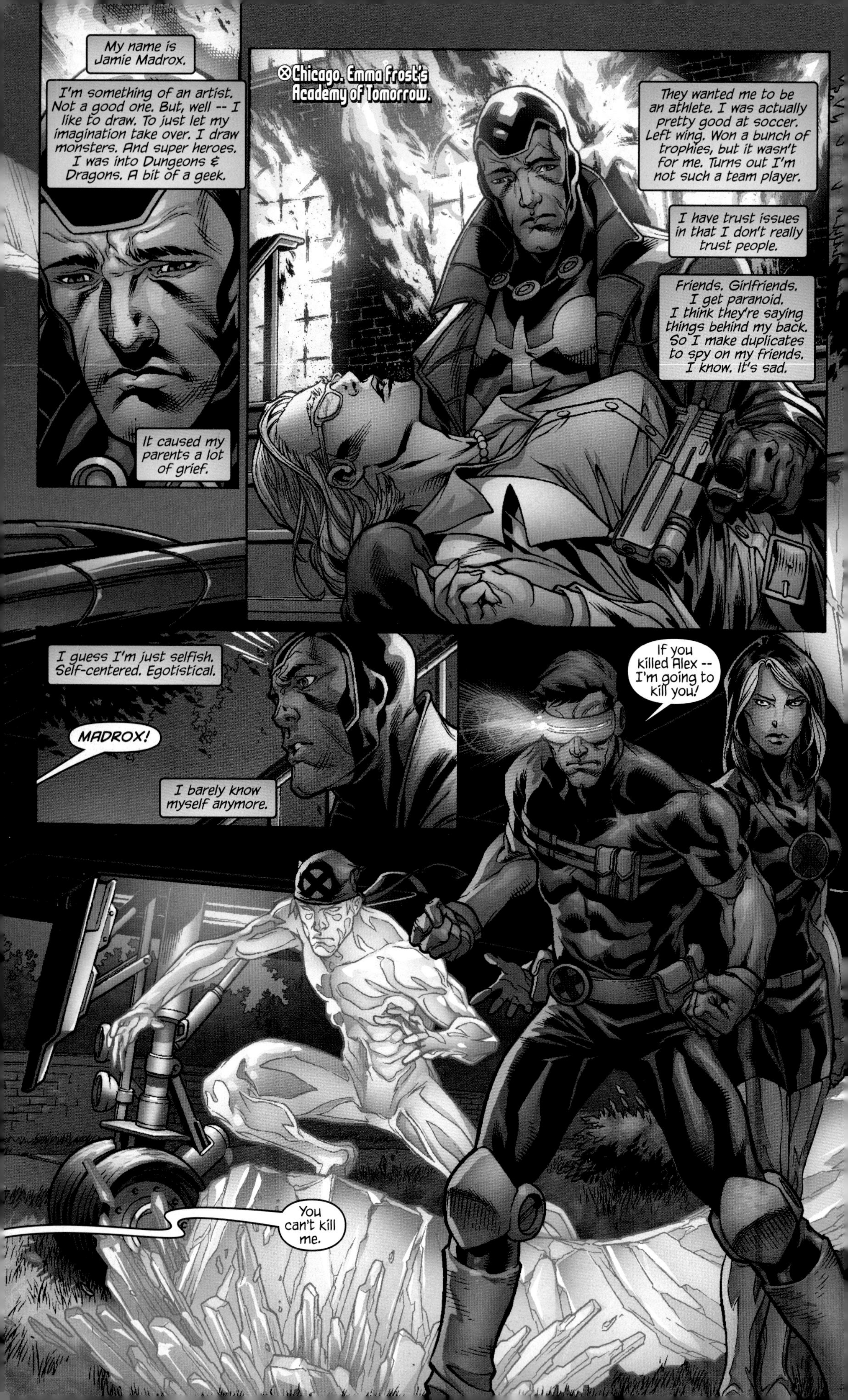
My name is Jamie Madrox.
I'm something of an artist. Not a good one. But, well -- I like to draw. To just let my imagination take over. I draw monsters. And super heroes. I was into Dungeons & Dragons. A bit of a geek.
It caused my parents a lot of grief.
Chicago. Emma Frost's Academy of Tomorrow.
They wanted me to be an athlete. I was actually pretty good at soccer. Left wing. Won a bunch of trophies, but it wasn't for me. Turns out I'm not such a team player.
I have trust issues in that I don't really trust people.
Friends. Girlfriends. I get paranoid. I think they're saying things behind my back. So I make duplicates to spy on my friends. I know. It's sad.
I guess I'm just selfish. Self-centered. Egotistical.
MADROX!
I barely know myself anymore.
If you killed Alex -- I'm going to kill you!
You can't kill me.

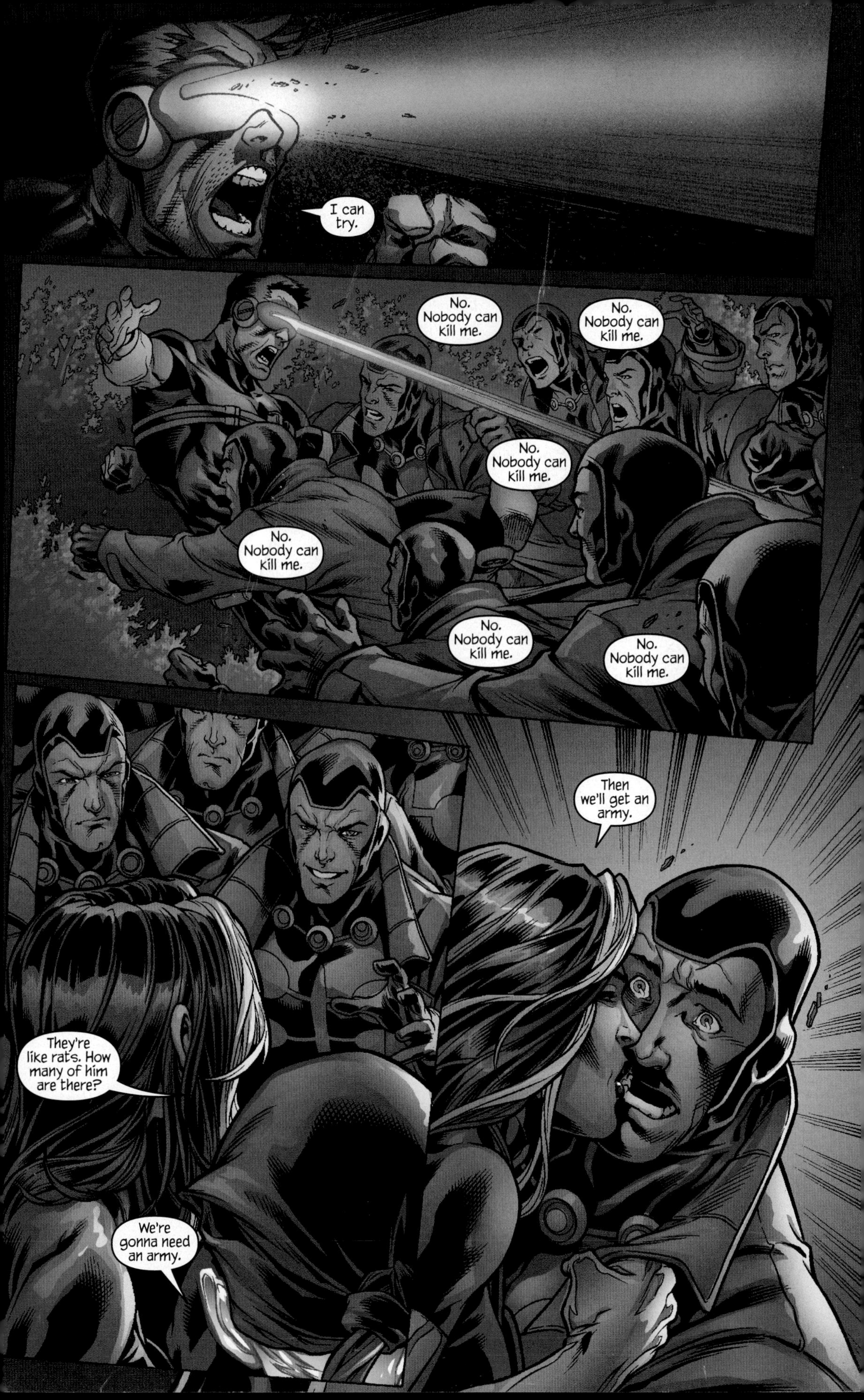

I can try.
No. Nobody can kill me.
No. Nobody can kill me.
No. Nobody can kill me.
No. Nobody can kill me.
No. Nobody can kill me.
No. Nobody can kill me.
They're like rats. How many of him are there?
We're gonna need an army.
Then we'll get an army.

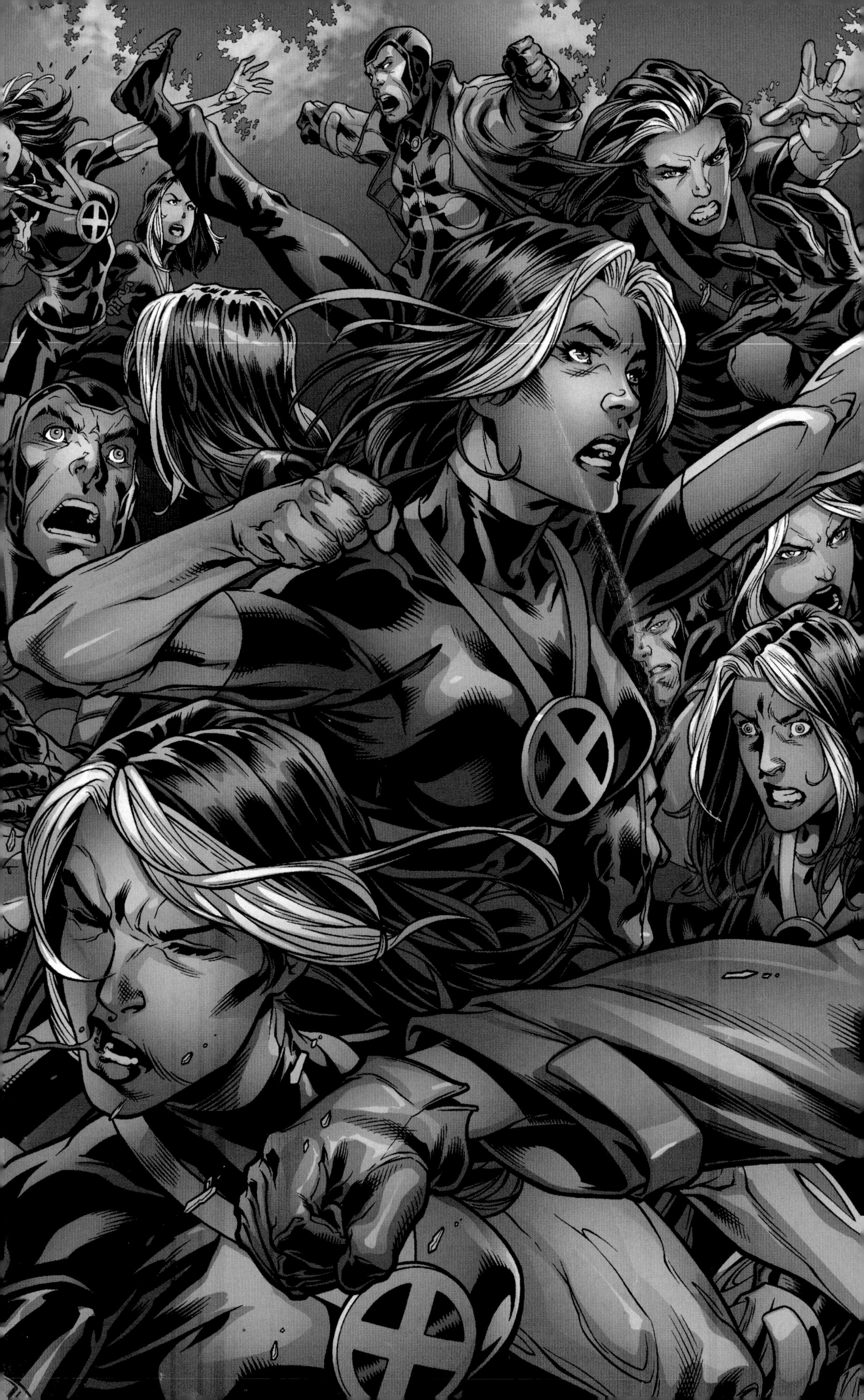

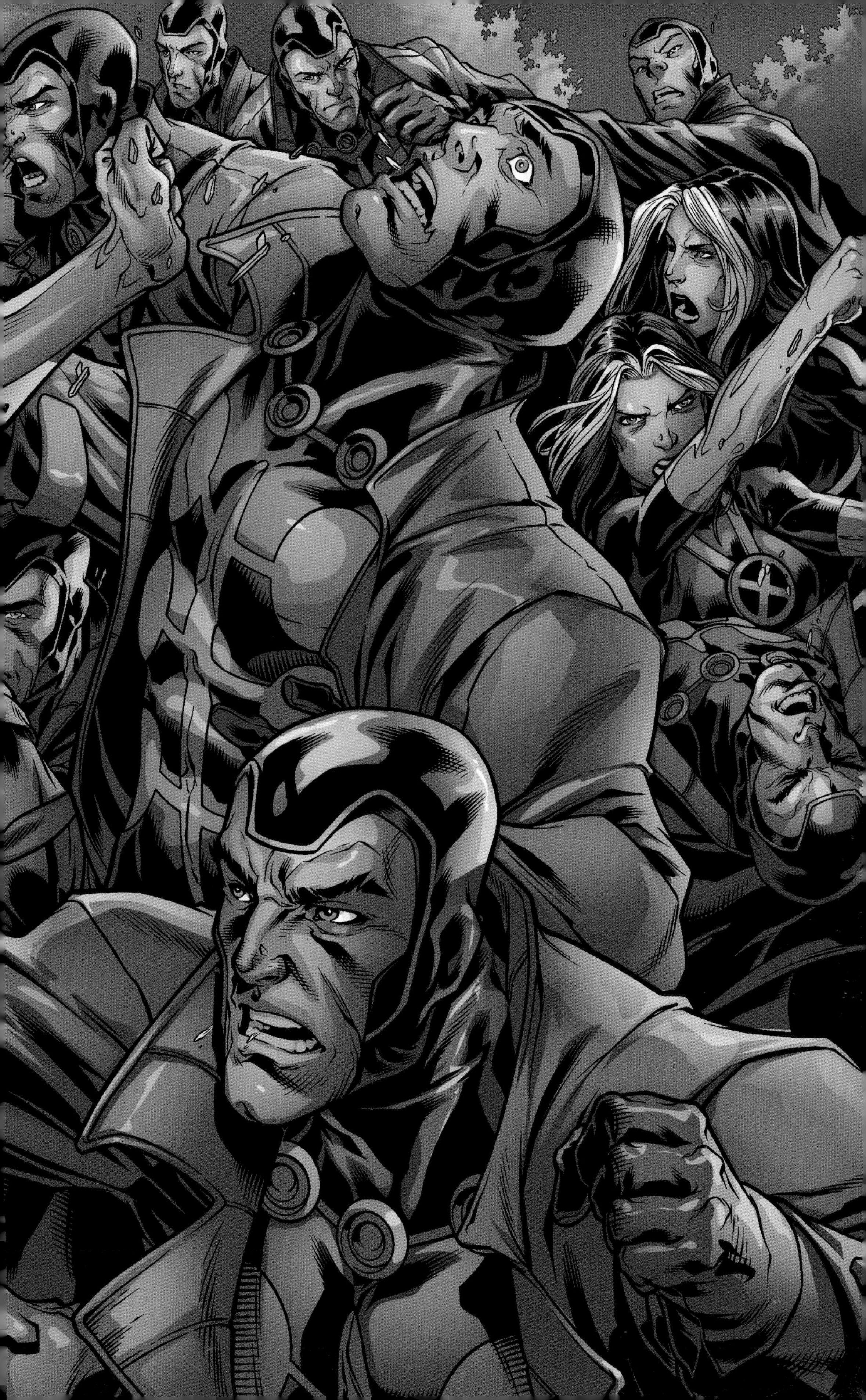

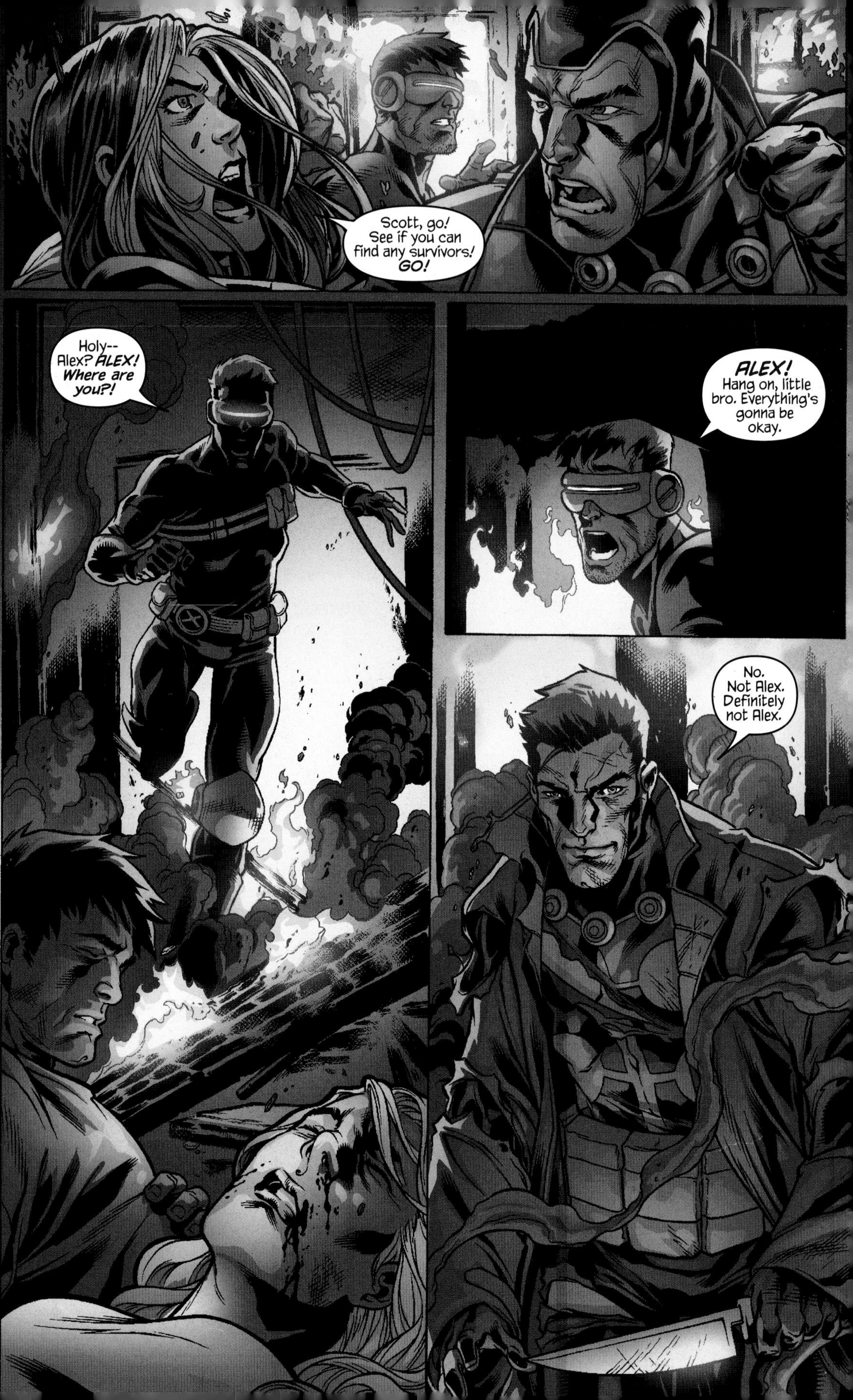

Scott, go! See if you can find any survivors! GO!
Holy-- Alex? ALEX! Where are you?!
ALEX! Hang on, little bro. Everything's gonna be okay.
No. Not Alex. Definitely not Alex.

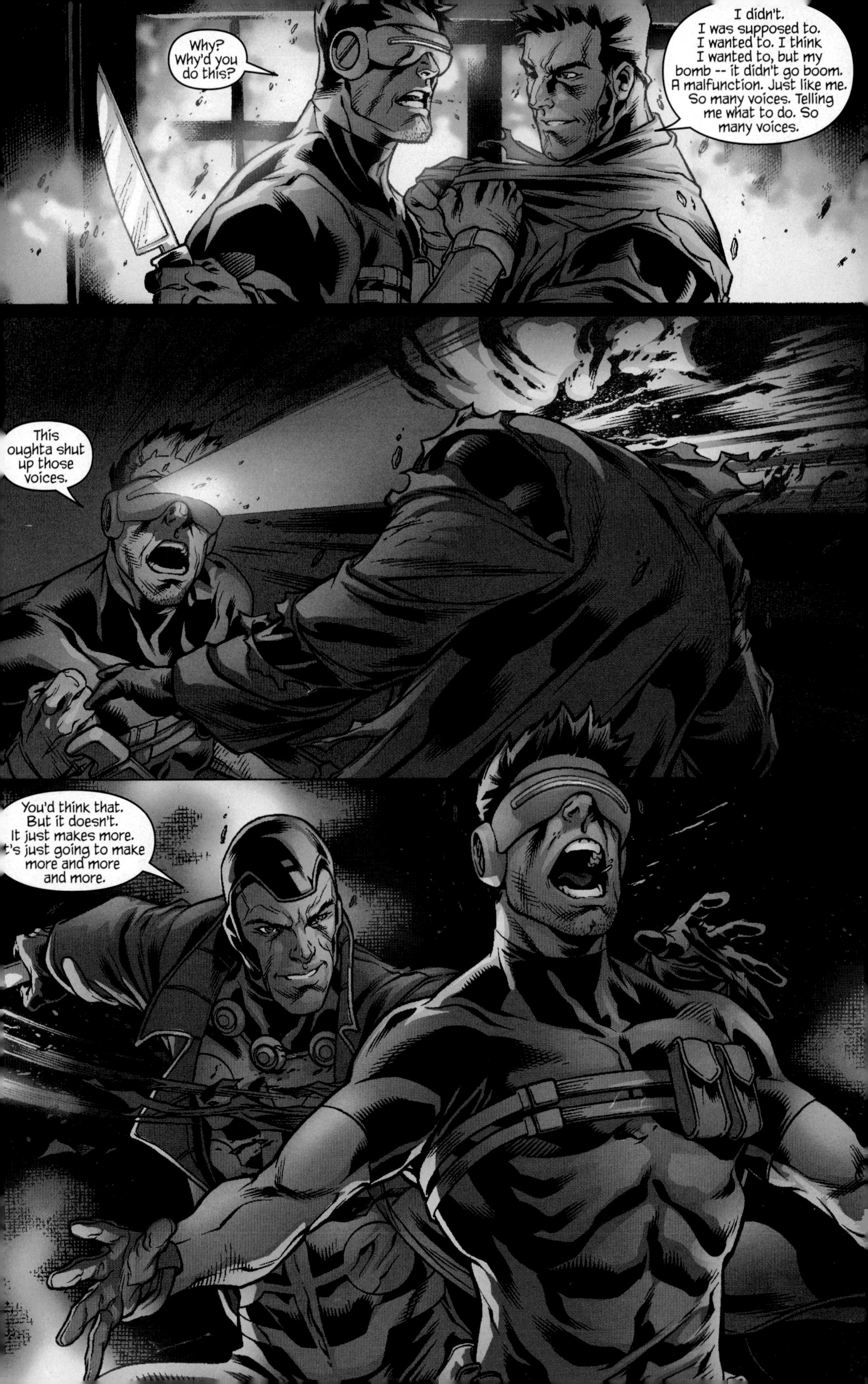
Why? Why'd you do this?
I didn't. I was supposed to. I wanted to. I think I wanted to, but my bomb -- it didn't go boom. A malfunction. Just like me. So many voices. Telling me what to do. So many voices.
This oughta shut up those voices.
You'd think that. But it doesn't. It just makes more. t's just going to make more and more and more.

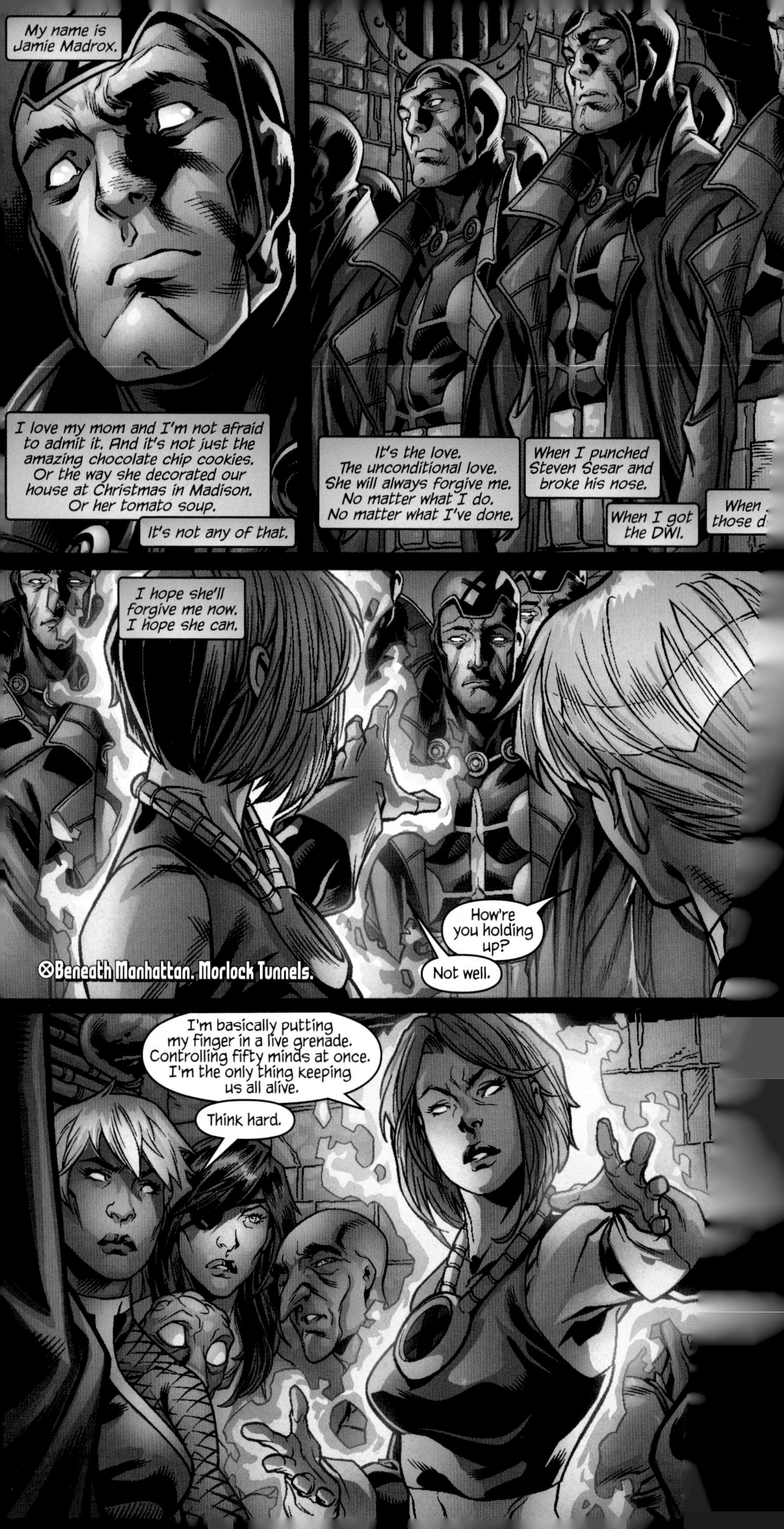

My name is Jamie Madrox.
I love my mom and I'm not afraid to admit it. And it's not just the amazing chocolate chip cookies. Or the way she decorated our house at Christmas in Madison. Or her tomato soup.
It's not any of that.
It's the love. The unconditional love. She will always forgive me. No matter what I do. No matter what I've done.
When I punched Steven Sesar and broke his nose.
When I got the DWI.
When
those
I hope she'll forgive me now. I hope she can.
Beneath Manhattan. Morlock Tunnels.
How're you holding up?
Not well.
I'm basically putting my finger in a live grenade. Controlling fifty minds at once. I'm the only thing keeping us all alive.
Think hard.

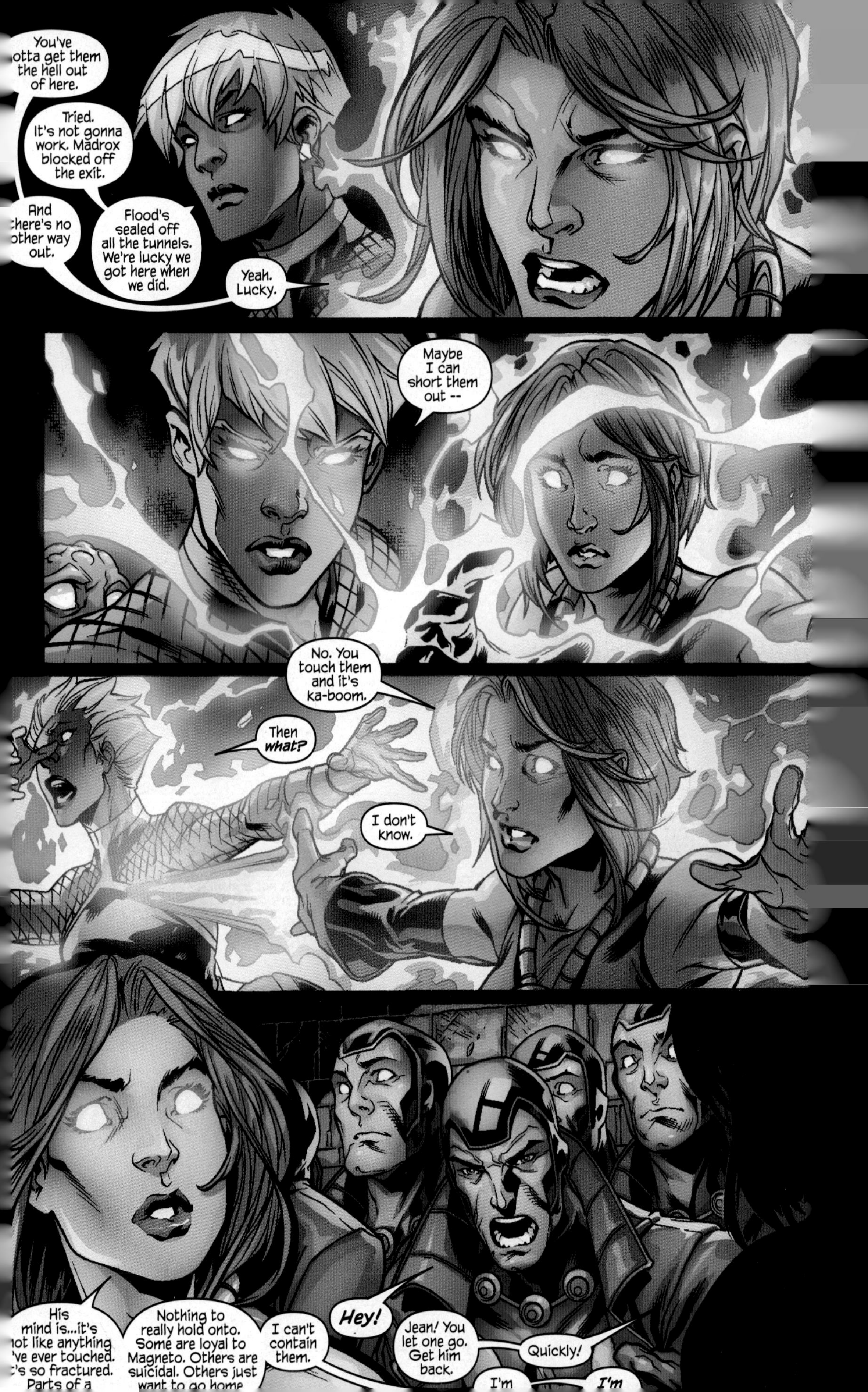

You've otta get them the hell out of here.
Tried. It's not gonna work. Madrox blocked off the exit.
And here's no other way out.
Flood's sealed off all the tunnels. We're lucky we got here when we did.
Yeah. Lucky.
Maybe I can short them out --
No. You touch them and it's ka-boom.
Then *what?*
I don't know.
His mind is...it's ot like anything 've ever touched. 's so fractured. Parts of a
Nothing to really hold onto. Some are loyal to Magneto. Others are suicidal. Others just want to go home
I can't contain them.
Hey!
Jean! You let one go. Get him back.
Quickly!
I'm
I'm

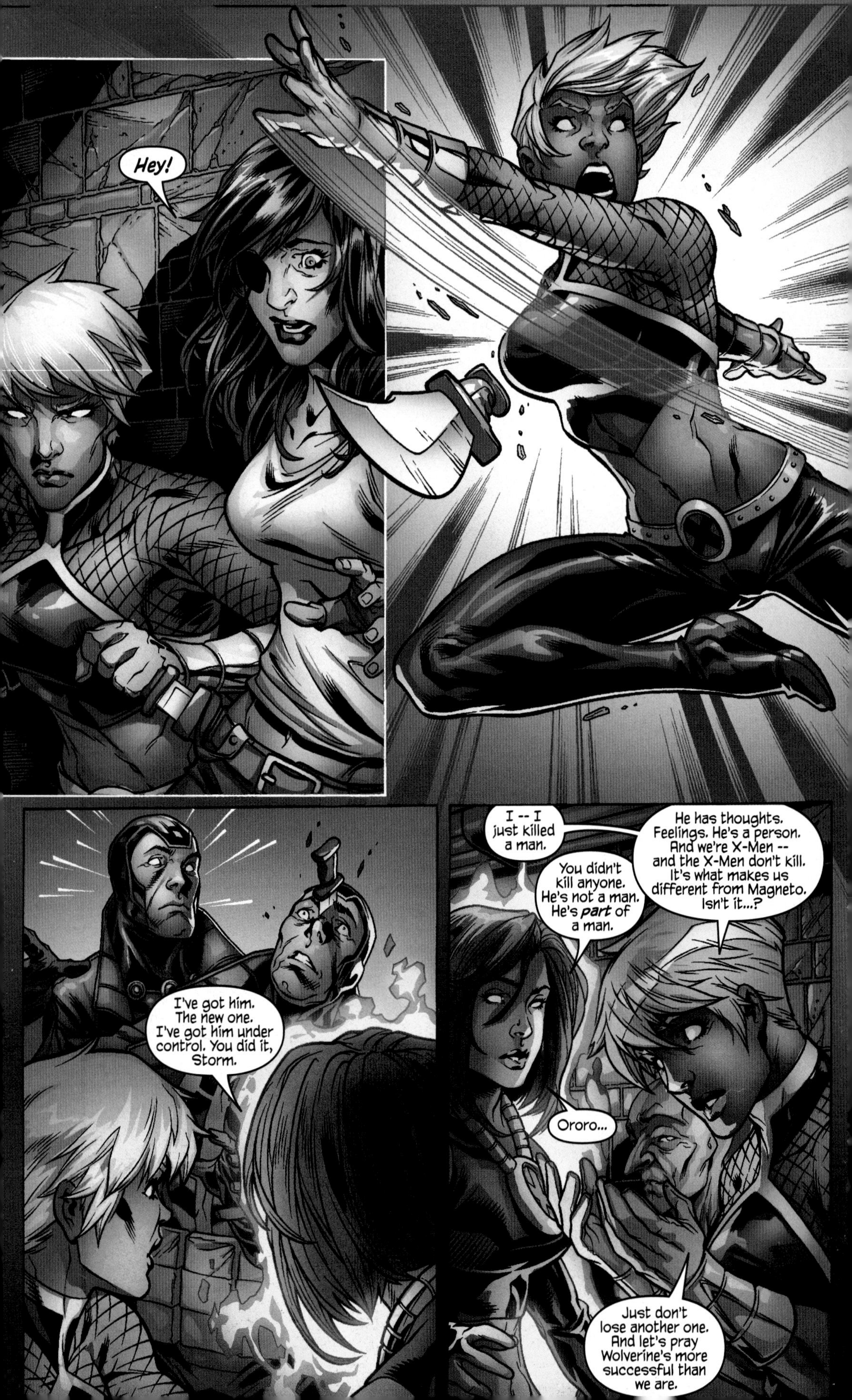
Hey!
I've got him. The new one. I've got him under control. You did it, Storm.
I -- I just killed a man.
You didn't kill anyone. He's not a man. He's *part* of a man.
He has thoughts. Feelings. He's a person. And we're X-Men -- and the X-Men don't kill. It's what makes us different from Magneto. Isn't it...?
Ororo...
Just don't lose another one. And let's pray Wolverine's more successful than we are.

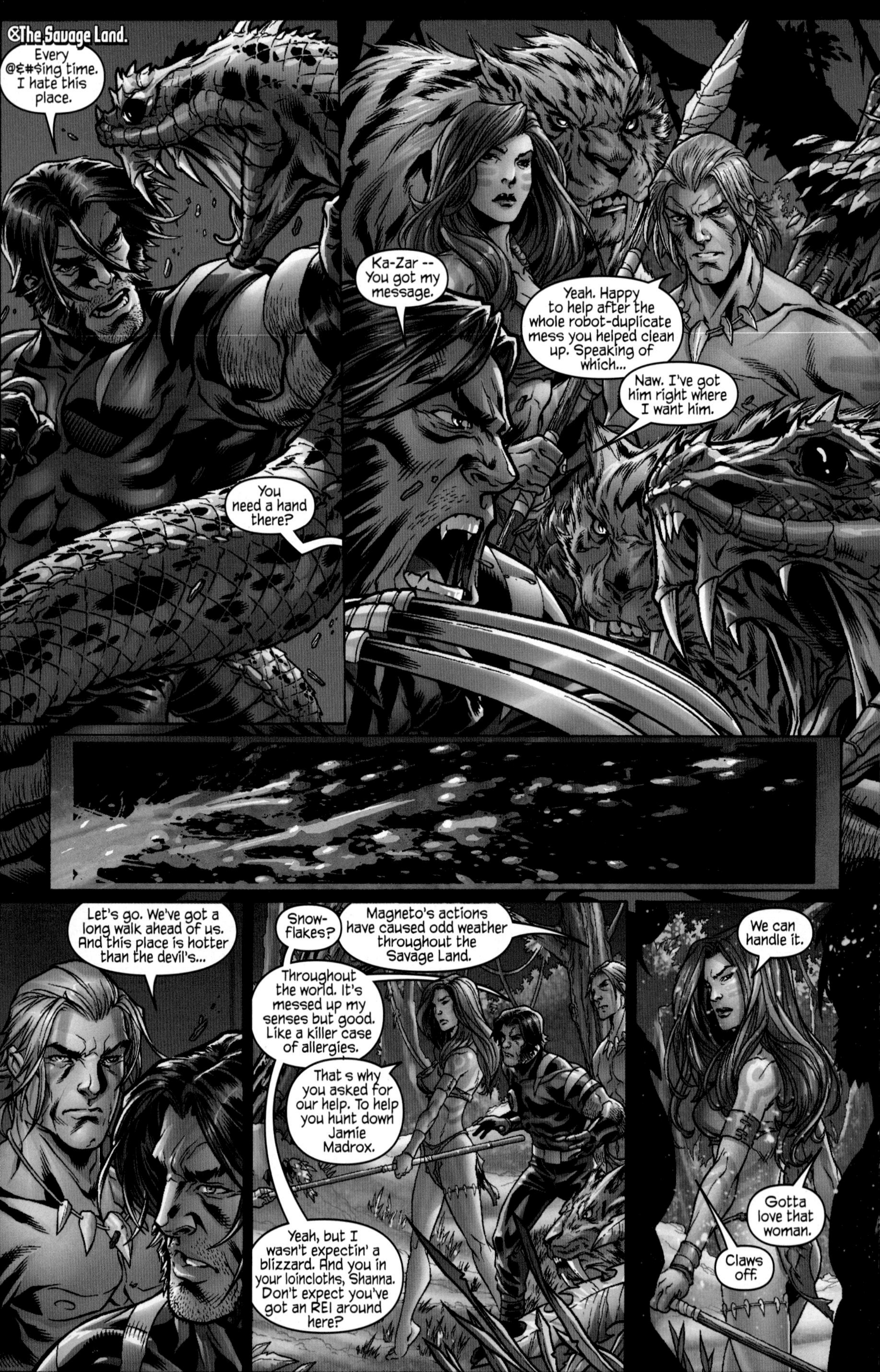

The Savage Land.
Every @¢#$ing time. I hate this place.
You need a hand there?
Ka-Zar -- You got my message.
Yeah. Happy to help after the whole robot-duplicate mess you helped clean up. Speaking of which...
Naw. I've got him right where I want him.
Let's go. We've got a long walk ahead of us. And this place is hotter than the devil's...
Snow-flakes?
Magneto's actions have caused odd weather throughout the Savage Land.
Throughout the world. It's messed up my senses but good. Like a killer case of allergies.
That s why you asked for our help. To help you hunt down Jamie Madrox.
Yeah, but I wasn't expectin' a blizzard. And you in your loincloths, Shanna. Don't expect you've got an REI around here?
We can handle it.
Gotta love that woman.
Claws off.

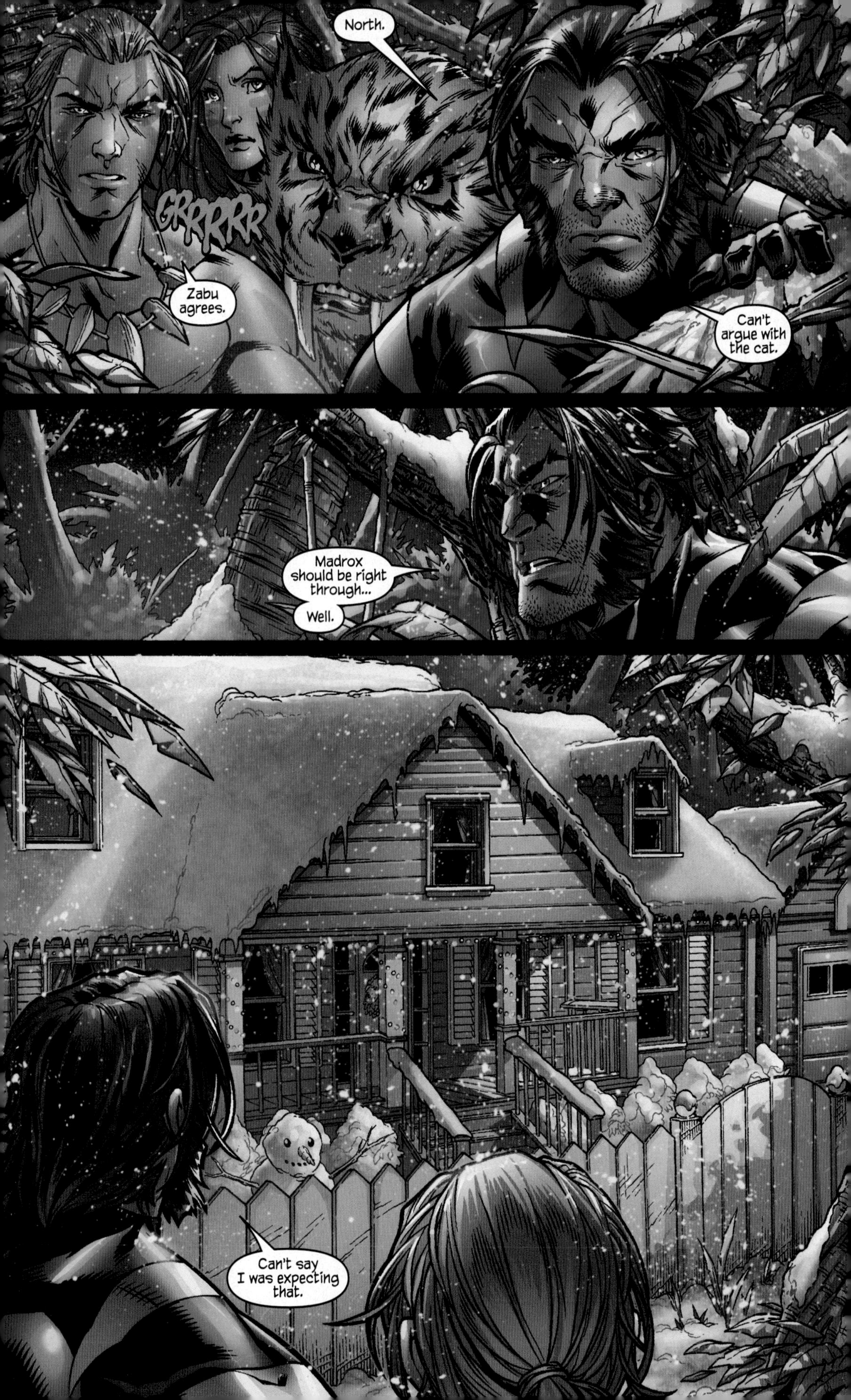
North.
GRRRRR
Zabu agrees.
Can't argue with the cat.
Madrox should be right through...
Well.
Can't say I was expecting that.

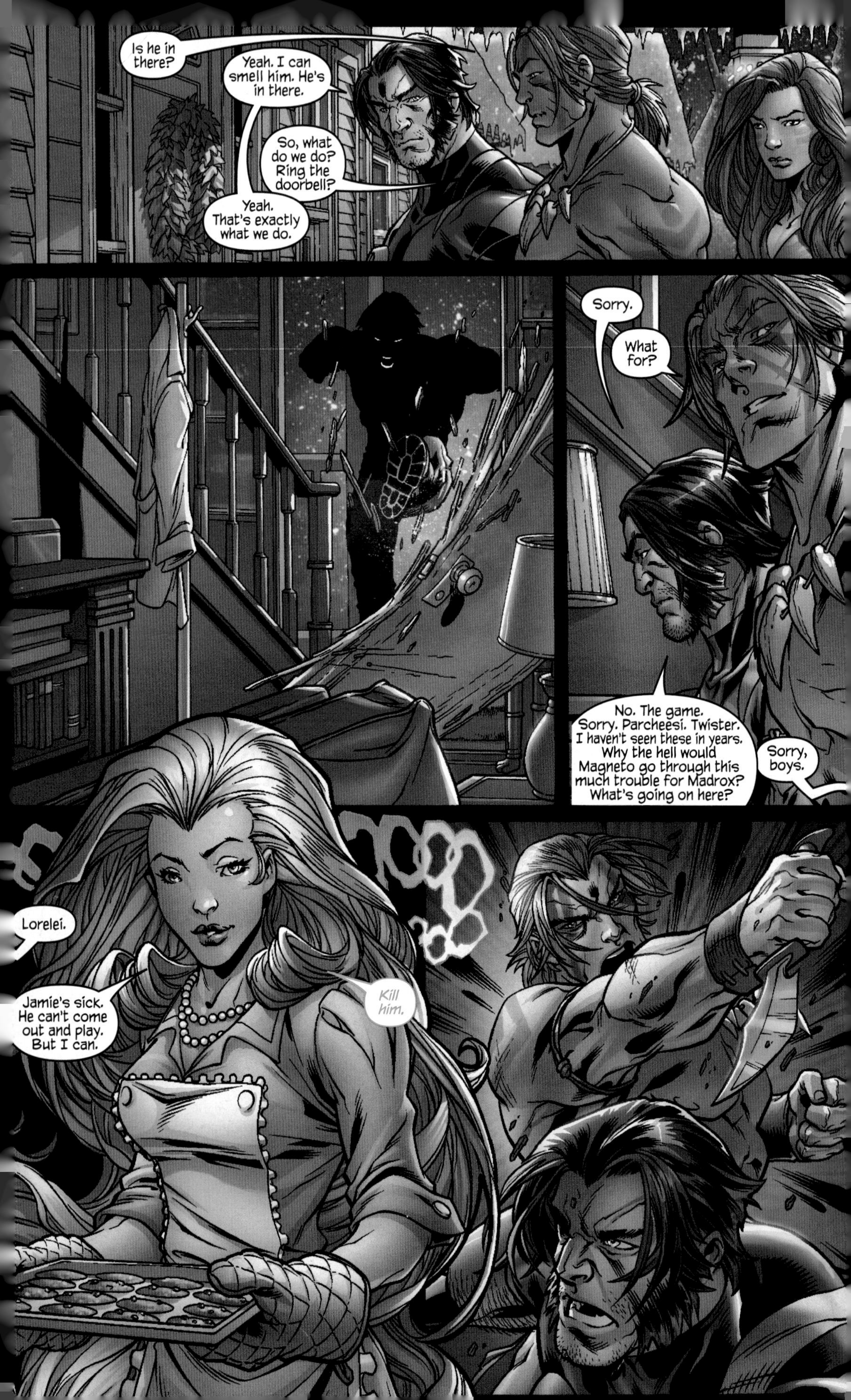
Is he in there?
Yeah. I can smell him. He's in there.
So, what do we do? Ring the doorbell?
Yeah. That's exactly what we do.
Sorry.
What for?
No. The game. Sorry. Parcheesi. Twister. I haven't seen these in years. Why the hell would Magneto go through this much trouble for Madrox? What's going on here?
Sorry, boys.
Lorelei.
Jamie's sick. He can't come out and play. But I can.
Kill him.

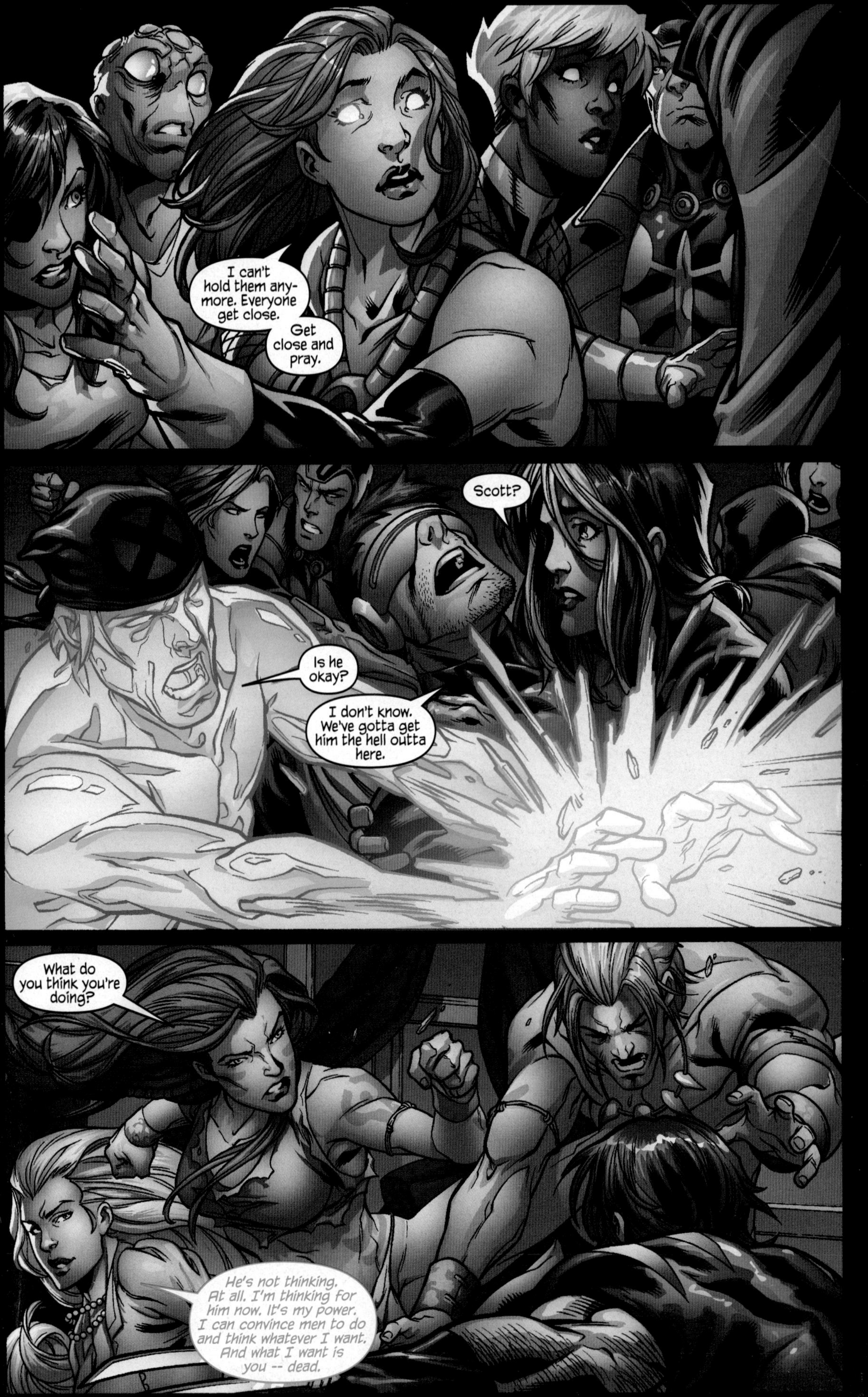
I can't hold them any-more. Everyone get close.
Get close and pray.
Scott?
Is he okay?
I don't know. We've gotta get him the hell outta here.
What do you think you're doing?
He's not thinking. At all. I'm thinking for him now. It's my power. I can convince men to do and think whatever I want. And what I want is you -- dead.

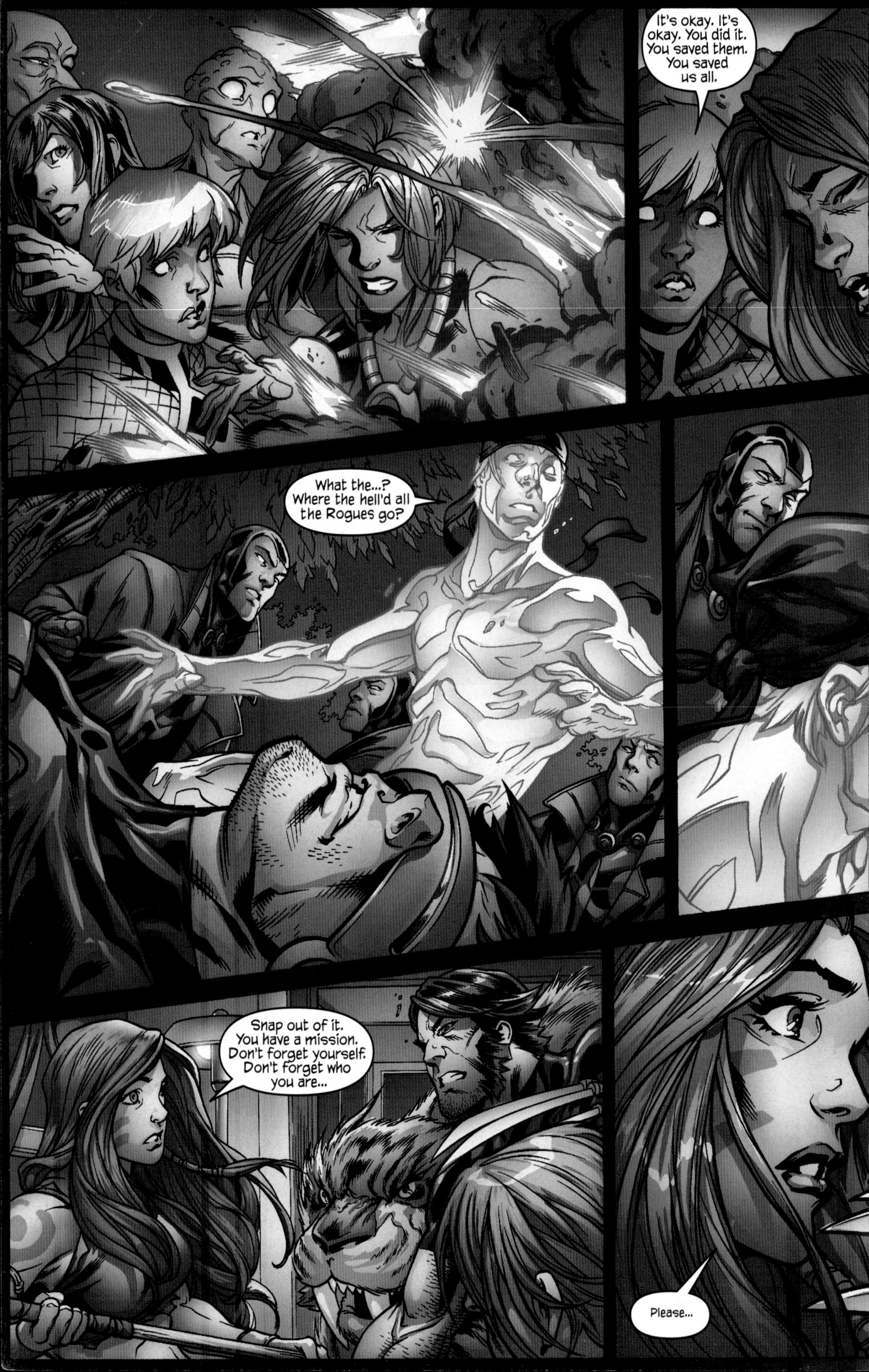
It's okay. It's okay. You did it. You saved them. You saved us all.
What the...? Where the hell'd all the Rogues go?
Snap out of it. You have a mission. Don't forget yourself. Don't forget who you are...
Please...

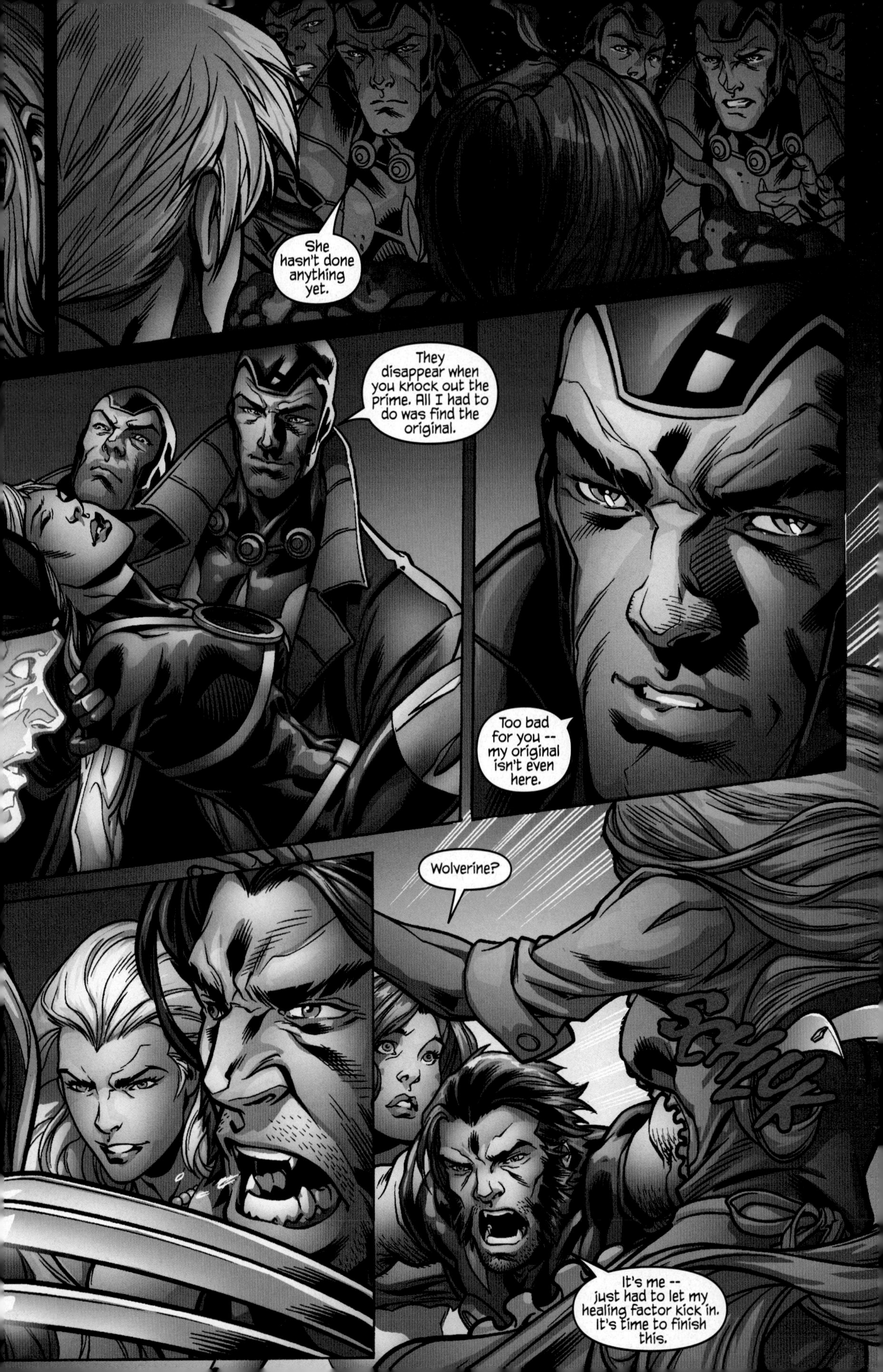
She hasn't done anything yet.
They disappear when you knock out the prime. All I had to do was find the original.
Too bad for you -- my original isn't even here.
Wolverine?
SCHLIK
It's me -- just had to let my healing factor kick in. It's time to finish this.

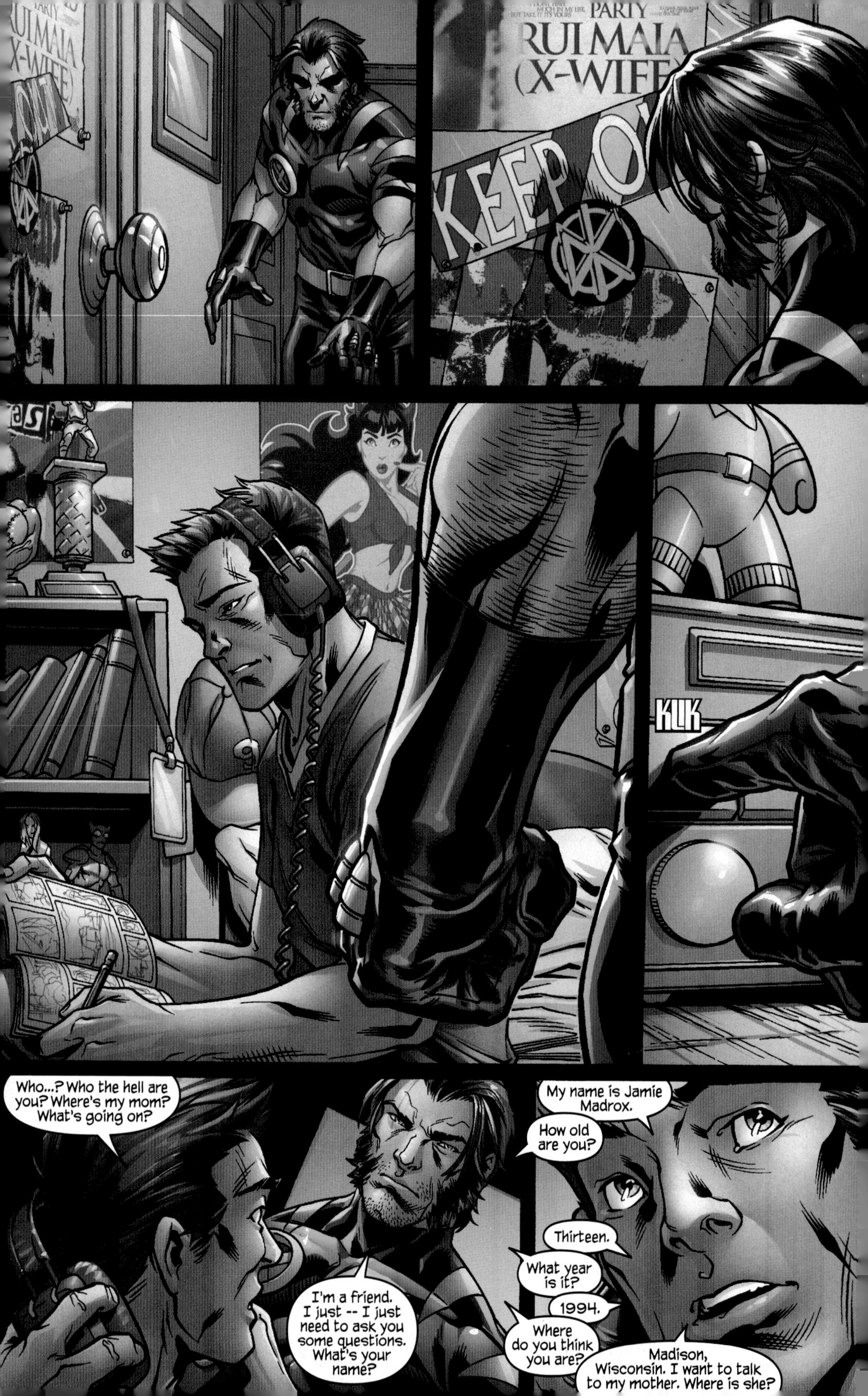

KLIK
Who...? Who the hell are you? Where's my mom? What's going on?
I'm a friend. I just -- I just need to ask you some questions. What's your name?
My name is Jamie Madrox.
How old are you?
Thirteen.
What year is it?
1994.
Where do you think you are?
Madison, Wisconsin. I want to talk to my mother. Where is she?

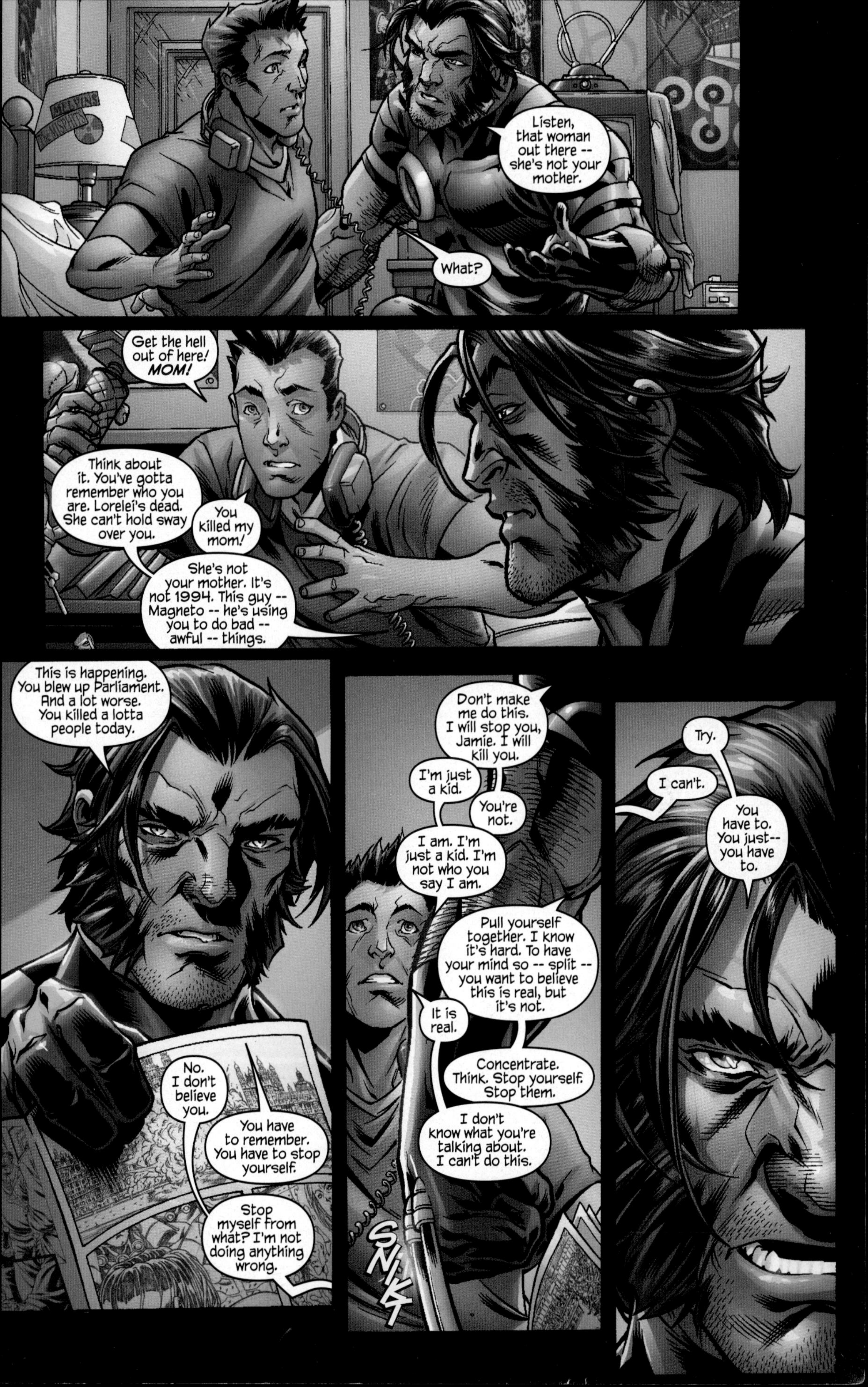
Listen, that woman out there -- she's not your mother.
What?
Get the hell out of here! MOM!
Think about it. You've gotta remember who you are. Lorelei's dead. She can't hold sway over you.
You killed my mom!
She's not your mother. It's not 1994. This guy -- Magneto -- he's using you to do bad -- awful -- things.
This is happening. You blew up Parliament. And a lot worse. You killed a lotta people today.
No. I don't believe you.
You have to remember. You have to stop yourself.
Stop myself from what? I'm not doing anything wrong.
Don't make me do this. I will stop you, Jamie. I will kill you.
I'm just a kid.
You're not.
I am. I'm just a kid. I'm not who you say I am.
Pull yourself together. I know it's hard. To have your mind so -- split -- you want to believe this is real, but it's not.
It is real.
Concentrate. Think. Stop yourself. Stop them.
I don't know what you're talking about. I can't do this.
SNIKT
Try.
I can't.
You have to. You just-- you have to.

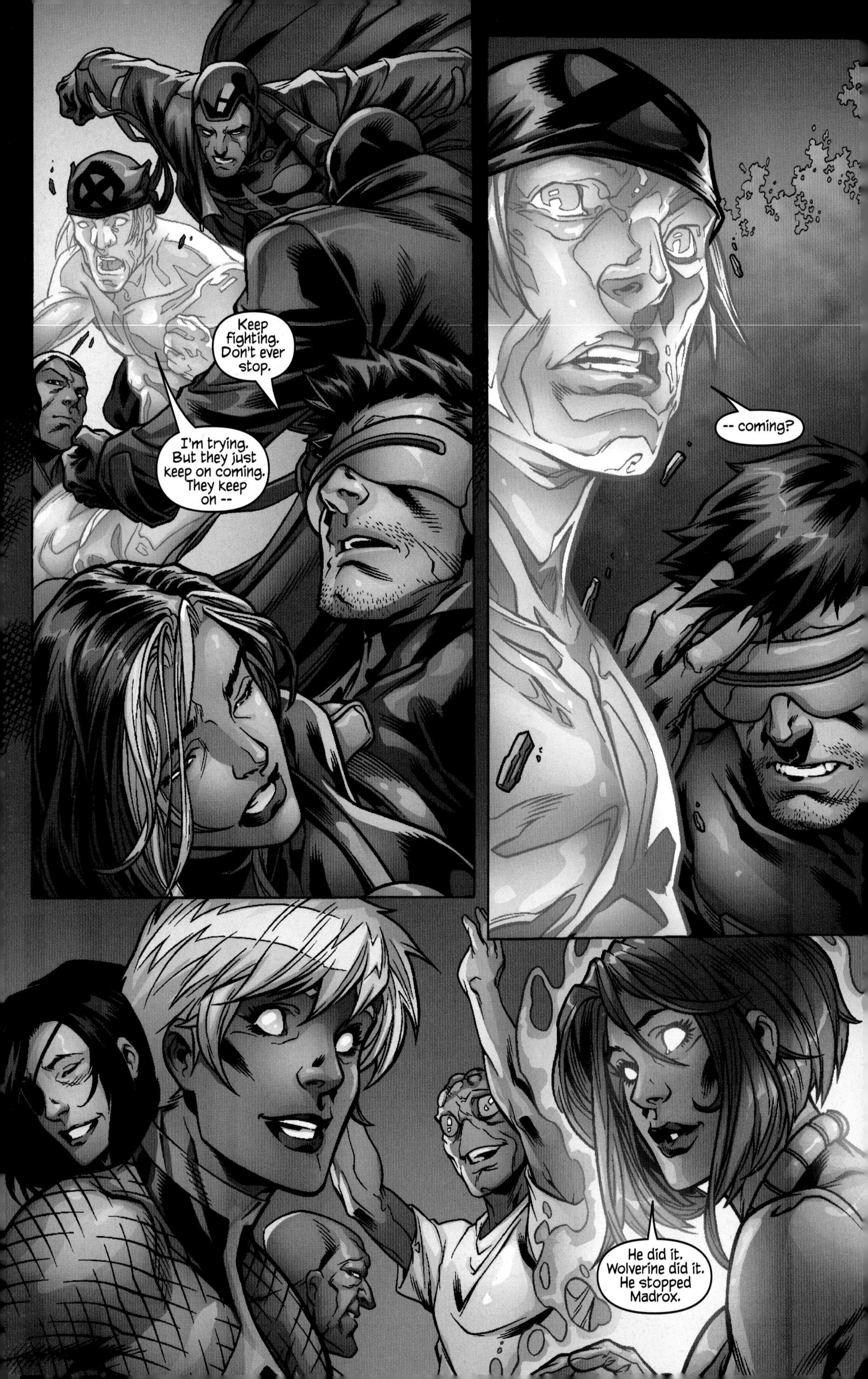
Keep fighting. Don't ever stop.
I'm trying. But they just keep on coming. They keep on --
-- coming?
He did it. Wolverine did it. He stopped Madrox.

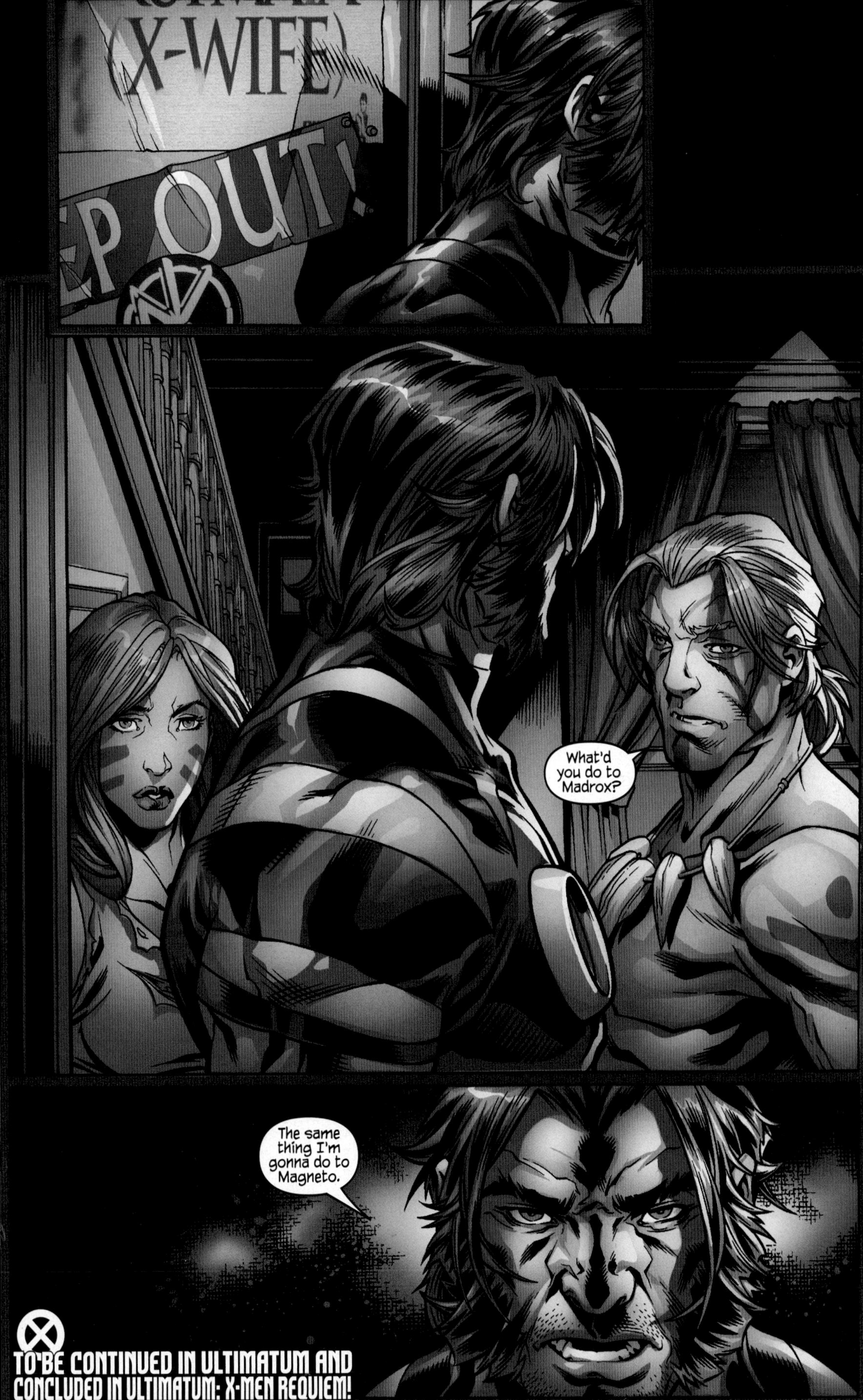
(X-WIFE)
EP OUT
What'd you do to Madrox?
The same thing I'm gonna do to Magneto.
TO BE CONTINUED IN ULTIMATUM AND CONCLUDED IN ULTIMATUM: X-MEN REQUIEM!

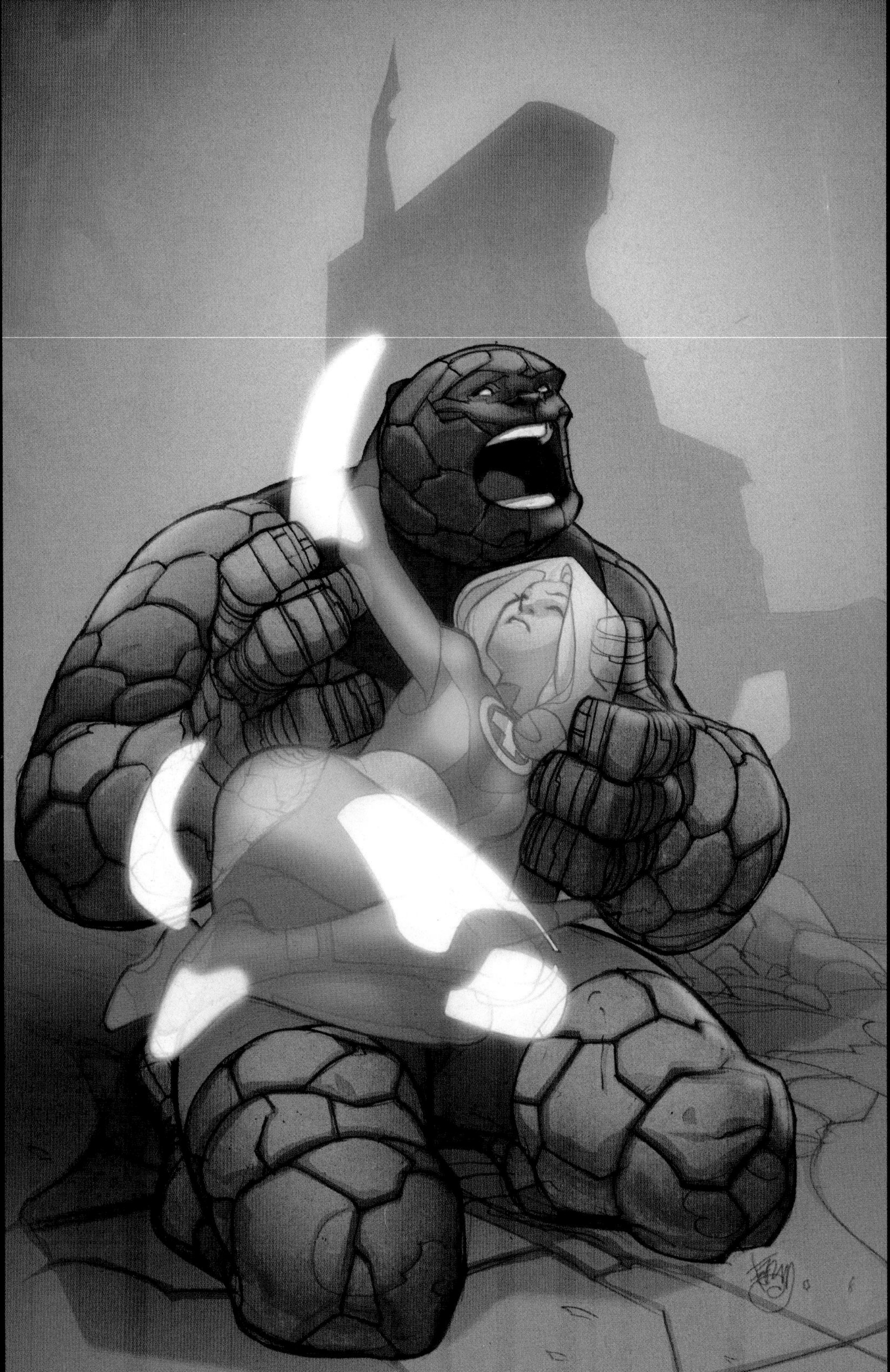

ULTIMATE FANTASTIC FOUR #58

After an inter-dimensional accident, young **Reed Richards**, **Sue Storm**, her brother **Johnny**, and Reed's friend **Ben Grimm** are changed forever. The quartet's genetic structures are scrambled and recombined in a fantastically strange way. Reed's body stretches and flows like water. Ben looks like a thing carved from desert rock. Sue can become invisible. Johnny generates flame. Together, they are the...

PREVIOUSLY IN ULTIMATE FANTASTIC FOUR:

Doom. Nihil. Namor. Psycho Man. Thanos. The Seven.

Reed thought the Fantastic Four had faced the worst the universe could offer — and after surviving some rocky times with Sue, he had finally worked up the nerve to take their relationship to the next level and propose to her. But when the Ultimatum event hit New York — drowning the city in a tidal wave of destruction and leaving Johnny missing and Sue lying near death — Reed had no choice but to track down the man he believed responsible for the devastation...

...which left Benjamin Grimm alone to pick up the pieces. Truly alone for the first time since Reed's science experiment-gone-wrong turned him into the rocky Thing, who will Ben turn to in his darkest hour...?

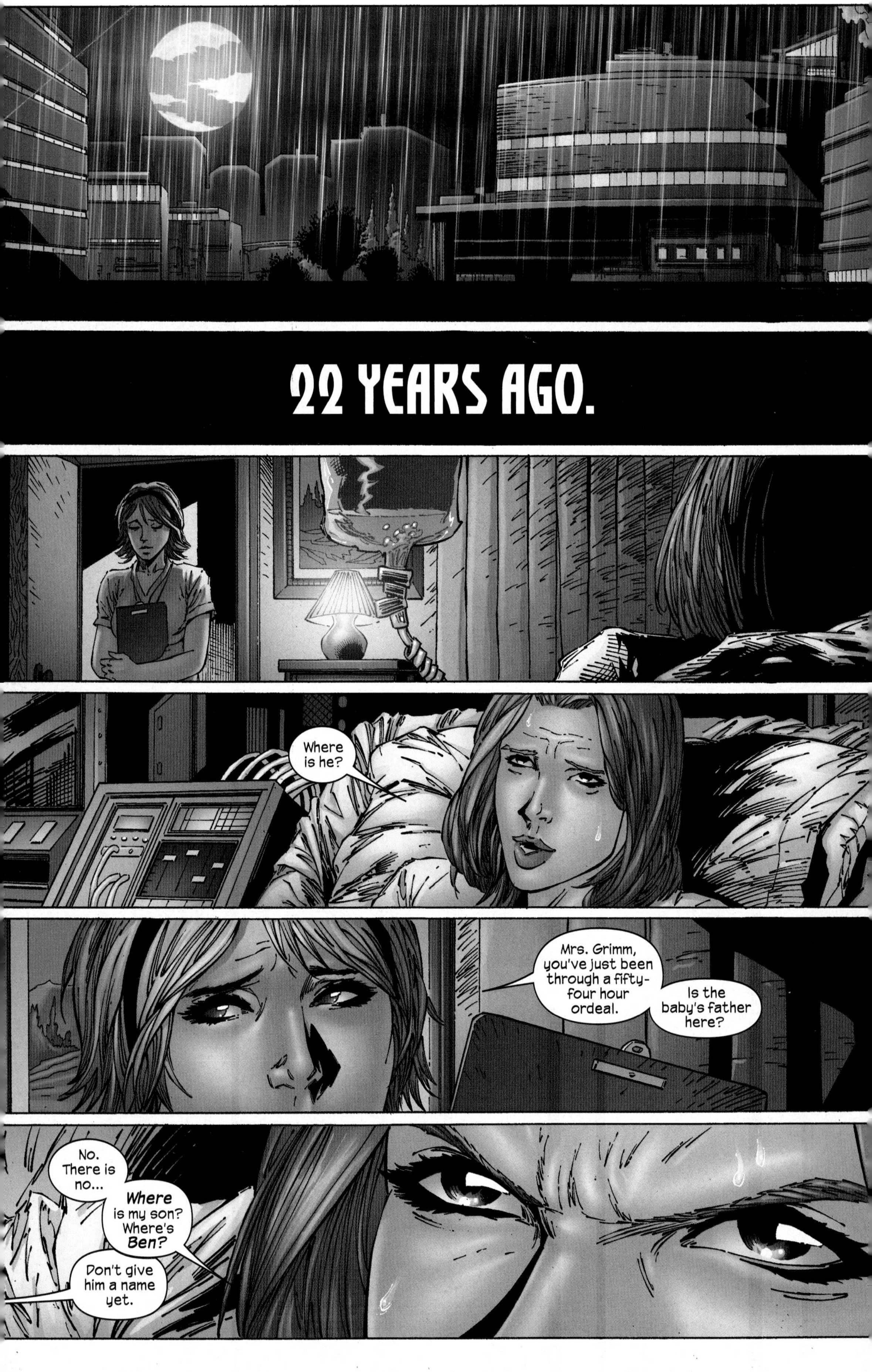
22 YEARS AGO.
Where is he?
Mrs. Grimm, you've just been through a fifty-four hour ordeal.
Is the baby's father here?
No. There is no...
Where is my son? Where's Ben?
Don't give him a name yet.

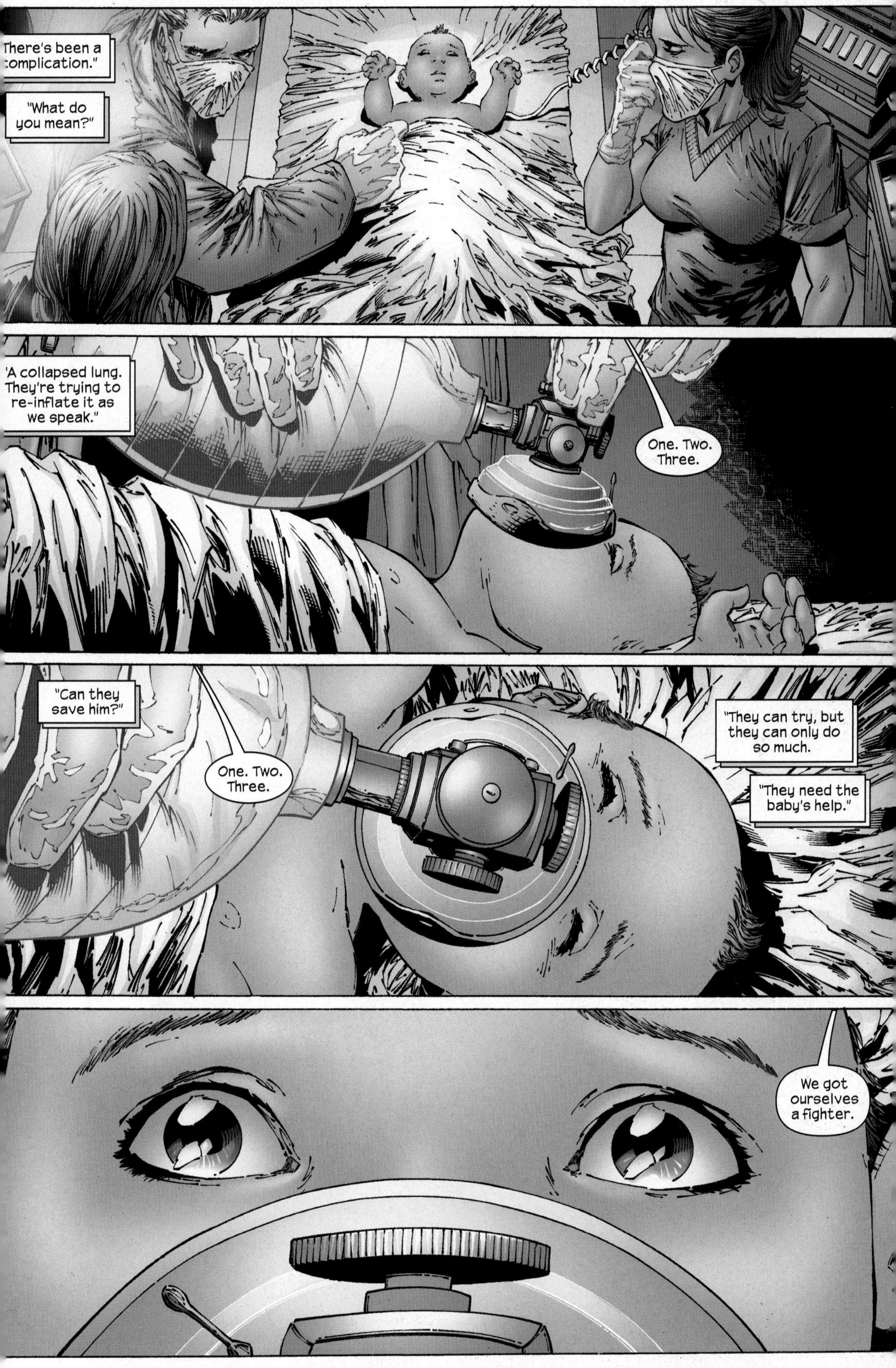
There's been a complication."
"What do you mean?"
'A collapsed lung. They're trying to re-inflate it as we speak."
One. Two. Three.
"Can they save him?"
One. Two. Three.
"They can try, but they can only do so much.
"They need the baby's help."
We got ourselves a fighter.

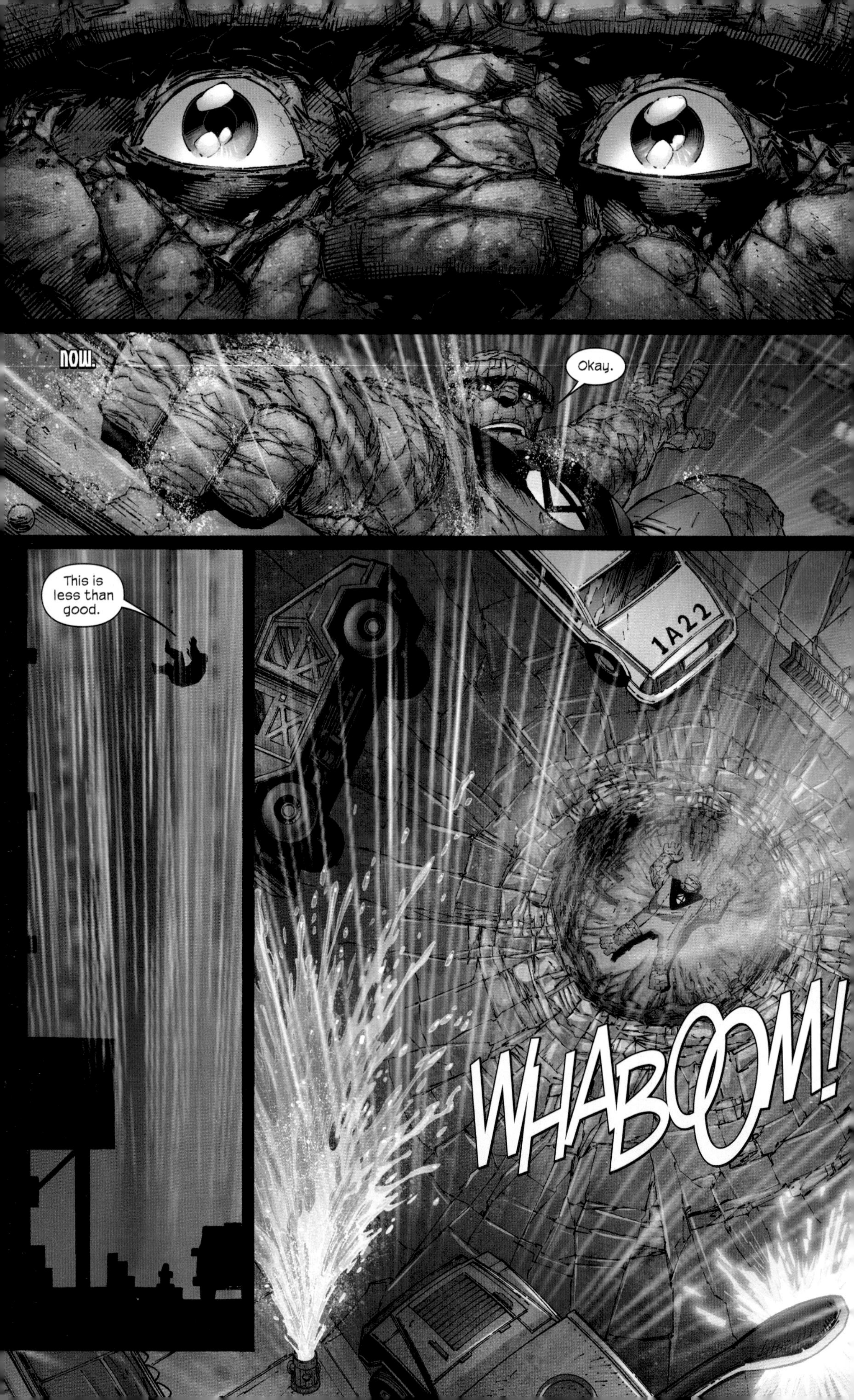
NOW.
Okay.
This is less than good.
1A22
WHABOOM!

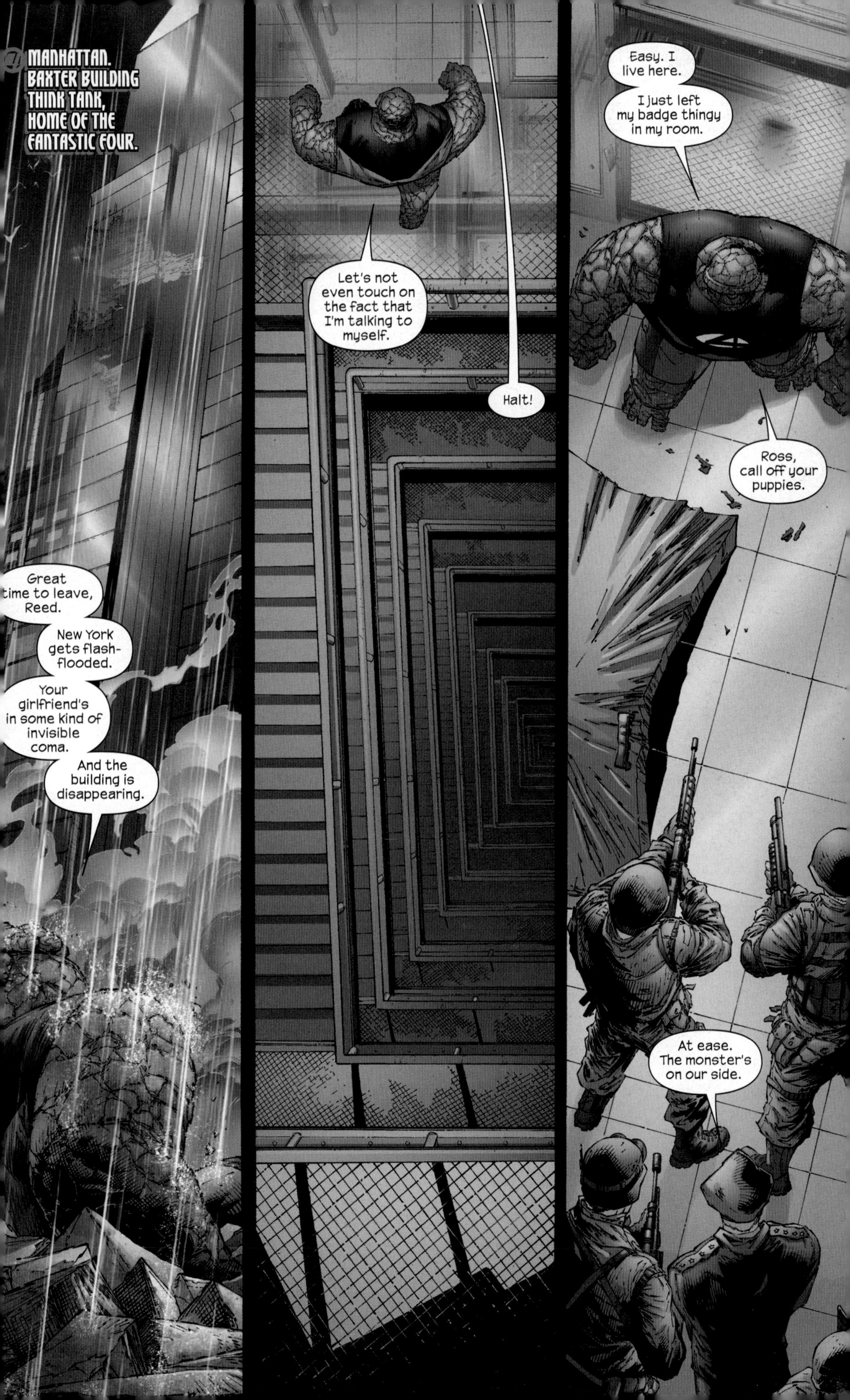
MANHATTAN. BAXTER BUILDING THINK TANK, HOME OF THE FANTASTIC FOUR.
Great time to leave, Reed.
New York gets flash-flooded.
Your girlfriend's in some kind of invisible coma.
And the building is disappearing.
Let's not even touch on the fact that I'm talking to myself.
Halt!
Easy. I live here.
I just left my badge thingy in my room.
Ross, call off your puppies.
At ease. The monster's on our side.

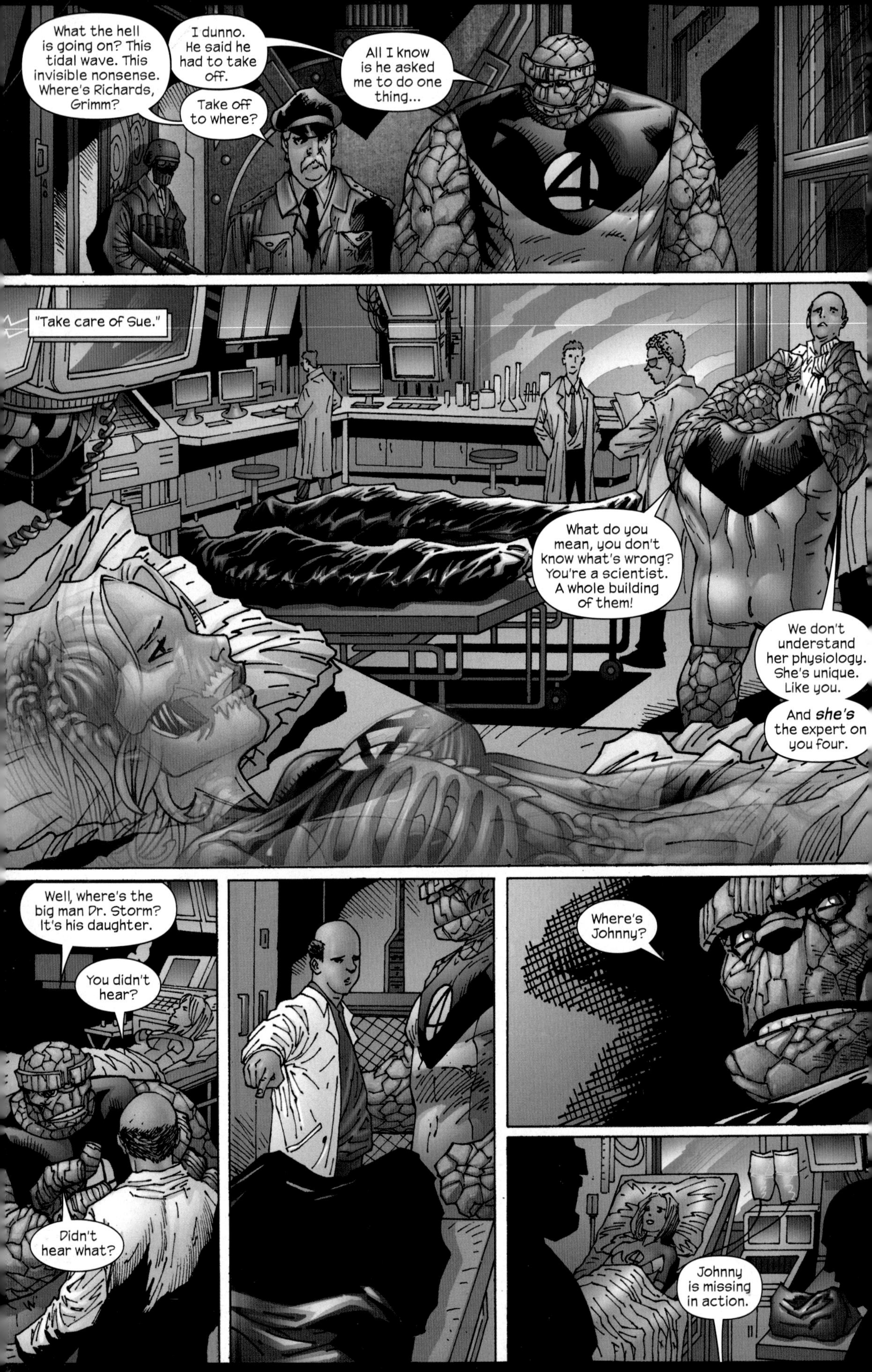
What the hell is going on? This tidal wave. This invisible nonsense. Where's Richards, Grimm?
I dunno. He said he had to take off.
Take off to where?
All I know is he asked me to do one thing...
"Take care of Sue."
What do you mean, you don't know what's wrong? You're a scientist. A whole building of them!
We don't understand her physiology. She's unique. Like you.
And *she's* the expert on you four.
Well, where's the big man Dr. Storm? It's his daughter.
You didn't hear?
Didn't hear what?
Where's Johnny?
Johnny is missing in action.

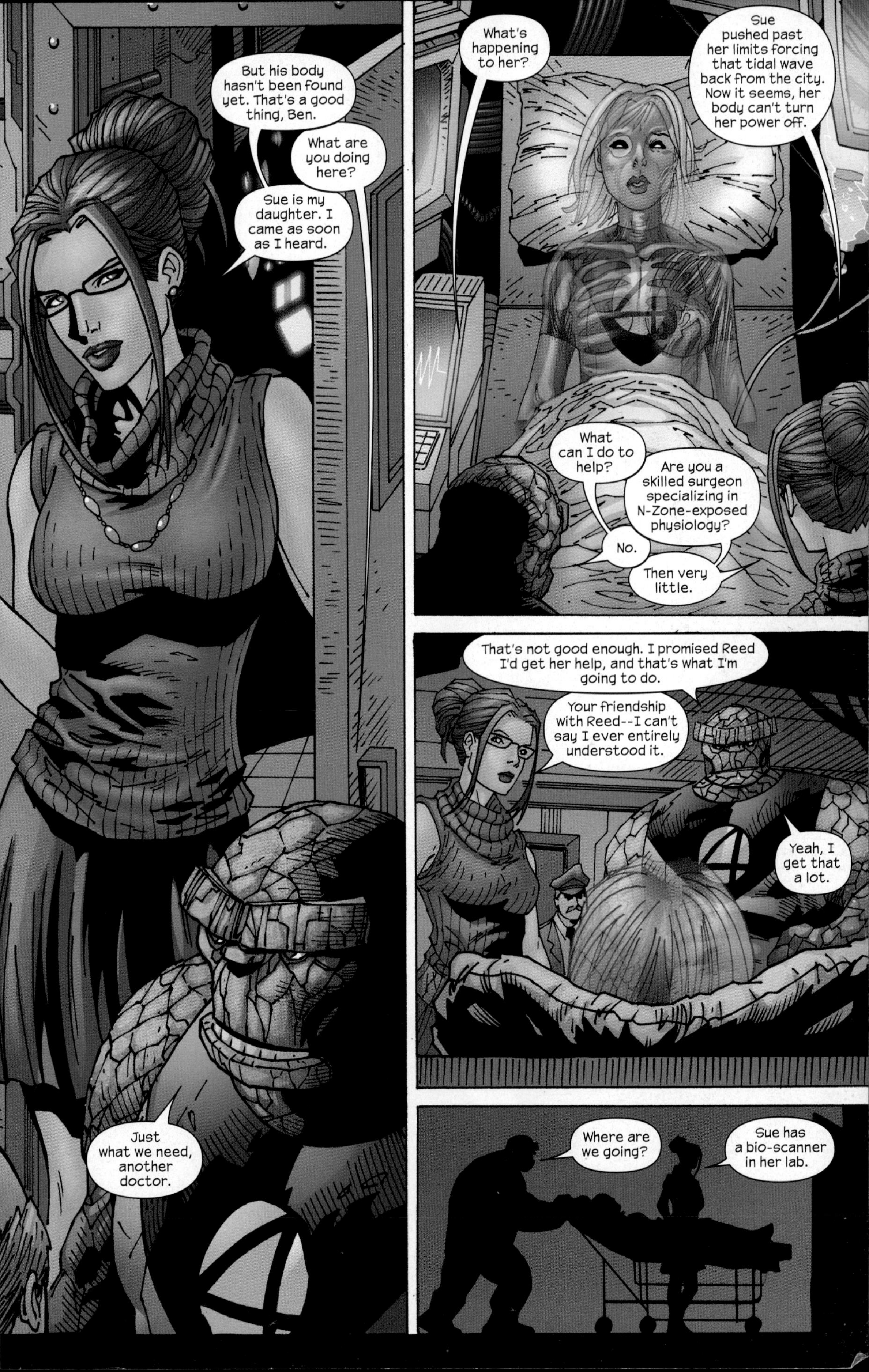
But his body hasn't been found yet. That's a good thing, Ben.
What are you doing here?
Sue is my daughter. I came as soon as I heard.
Just what we need, another doctor.
What's happening to her?
Sue pushed past her limits forcing that tidal wave back from the city. Now it seems, her body can't turn her power off.
What can I do to help?
Are you a skilled surgeon specializing in N-Zone-exposed physiology?
No.
Then very little.
That's not good enough. I promised Reed I'd get her help, and that's what I'm going to do.
Your friendship with Reed--I can't say I ever entirely understood it.
Yeah, I get that a lot.
Where are we going?
Sue has a bio-scanner in her lab.

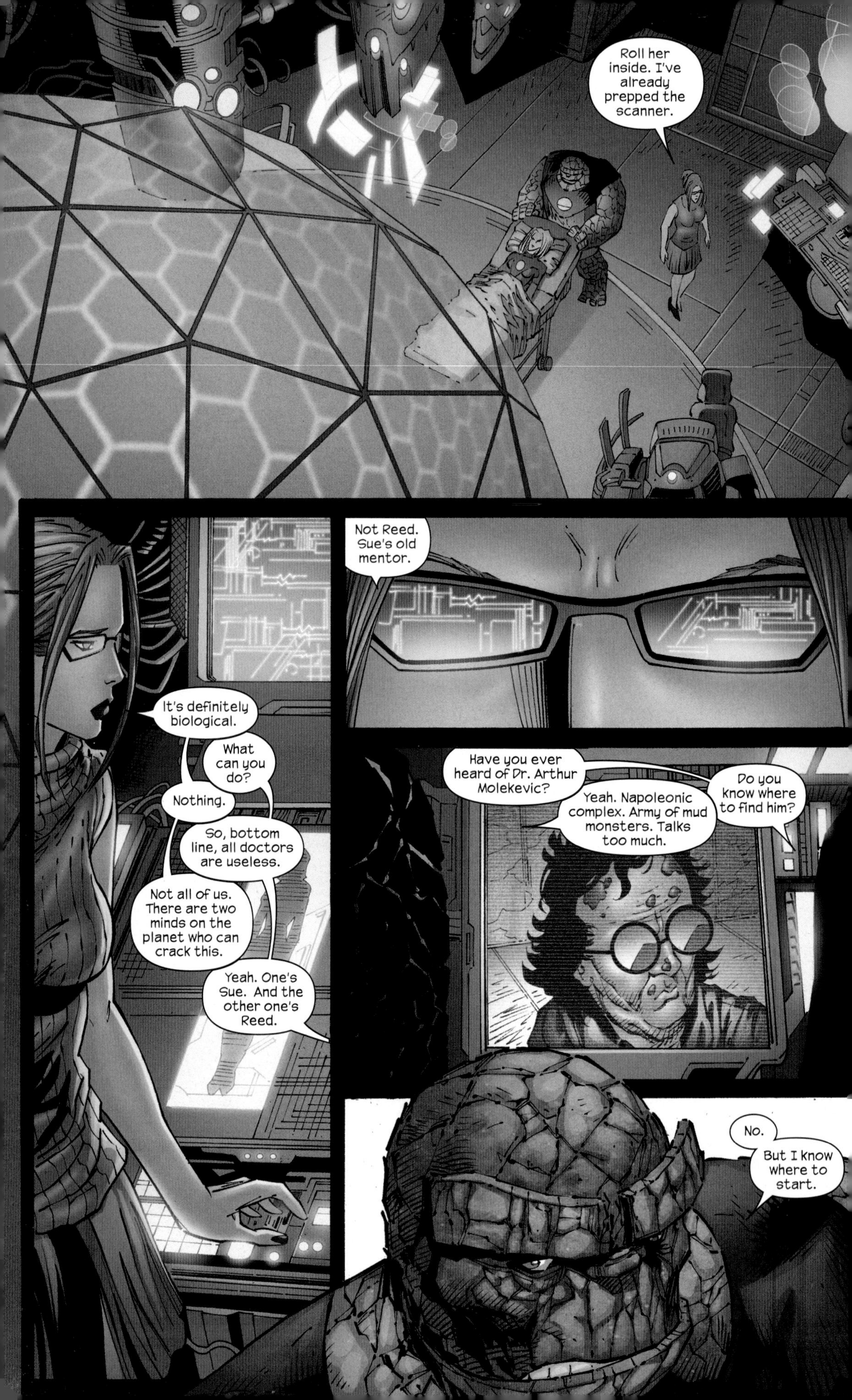

Roll her inside. I've already prepped the scanner.
It's definitely biological.
What can you do?
Nothing.
So, bottom line, all doctors are useless.
Not all of us. There are two minds on the planet who can crack this.
Yeah. One's Sue. And the other one's Reed.
Not Reed. Sue's old mentor.
Have you ever heard of Dr. Arthur Molekevic?
Yeah. Napoleonic complex. Army of mud monsters. Talks too much.
Do you know where to find him?
No.
But I know where to start.

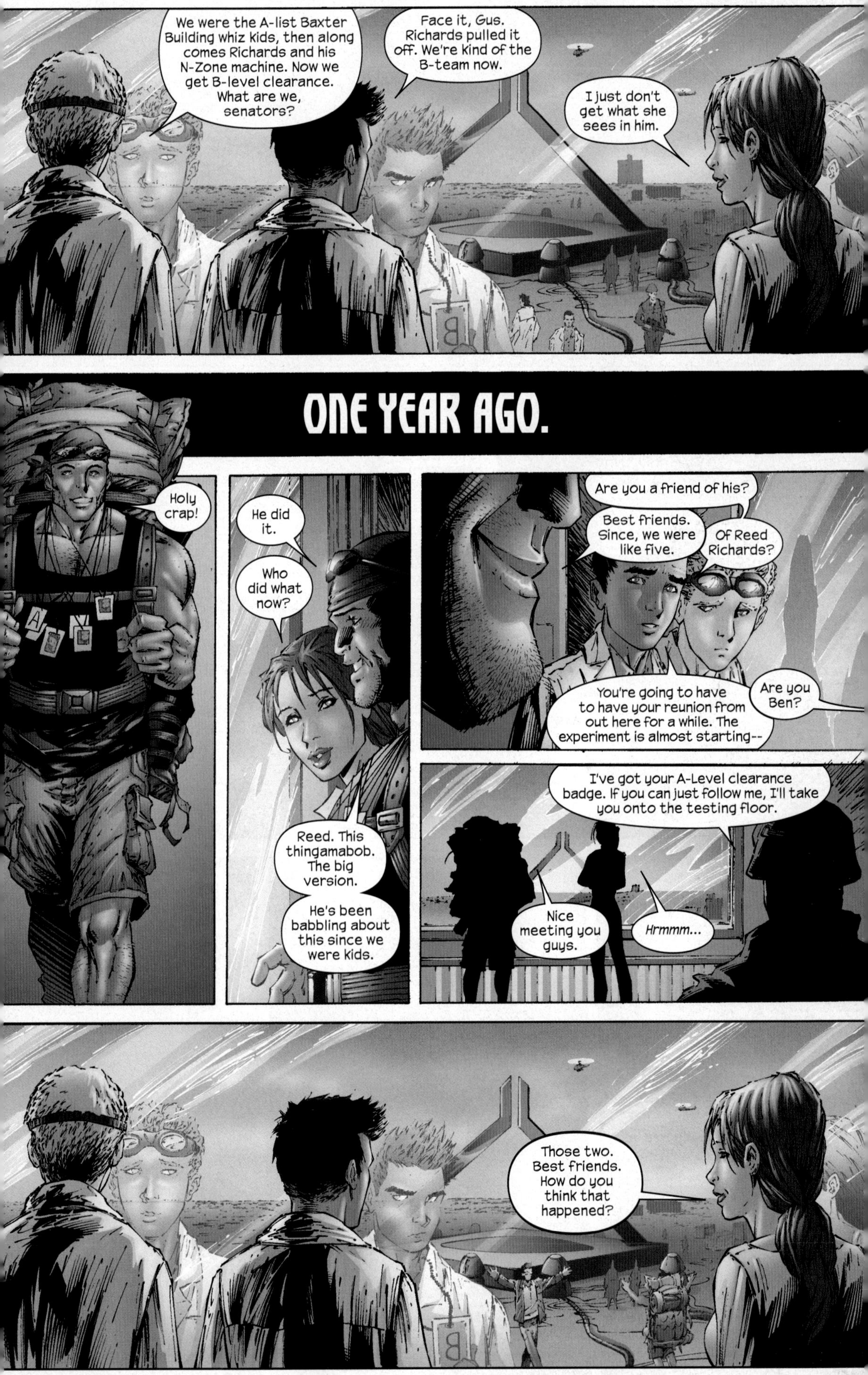
We were the A-list Baxter Building whiz kids, then along comes Richards and his N-Zone machine. Now we get B-level clearance. What are we, senators?
Face it, Gus. Richards pulled it off. We're kind of the B-team now.
I just don't get what she sees in him.
ONE YEAR AGO.
Holy crap!
He did it.
Who did what now?
Reed. This thingamabob. The big version.
He's been babbling about this since we were kids.
Are you a friend of his?
Best friends. Since, we were like five.
Of Reed Richards?
You're going to have to have your reunion from out here for a while. The experiment is almost starting--
Are you Ben?
I've got your A-Level clearance badge. If you can just follow me, I'll take you onto the testing floor.
Nice meeting you guys.
Hrmmm...
Those two. Best friends. How do you think that happened?

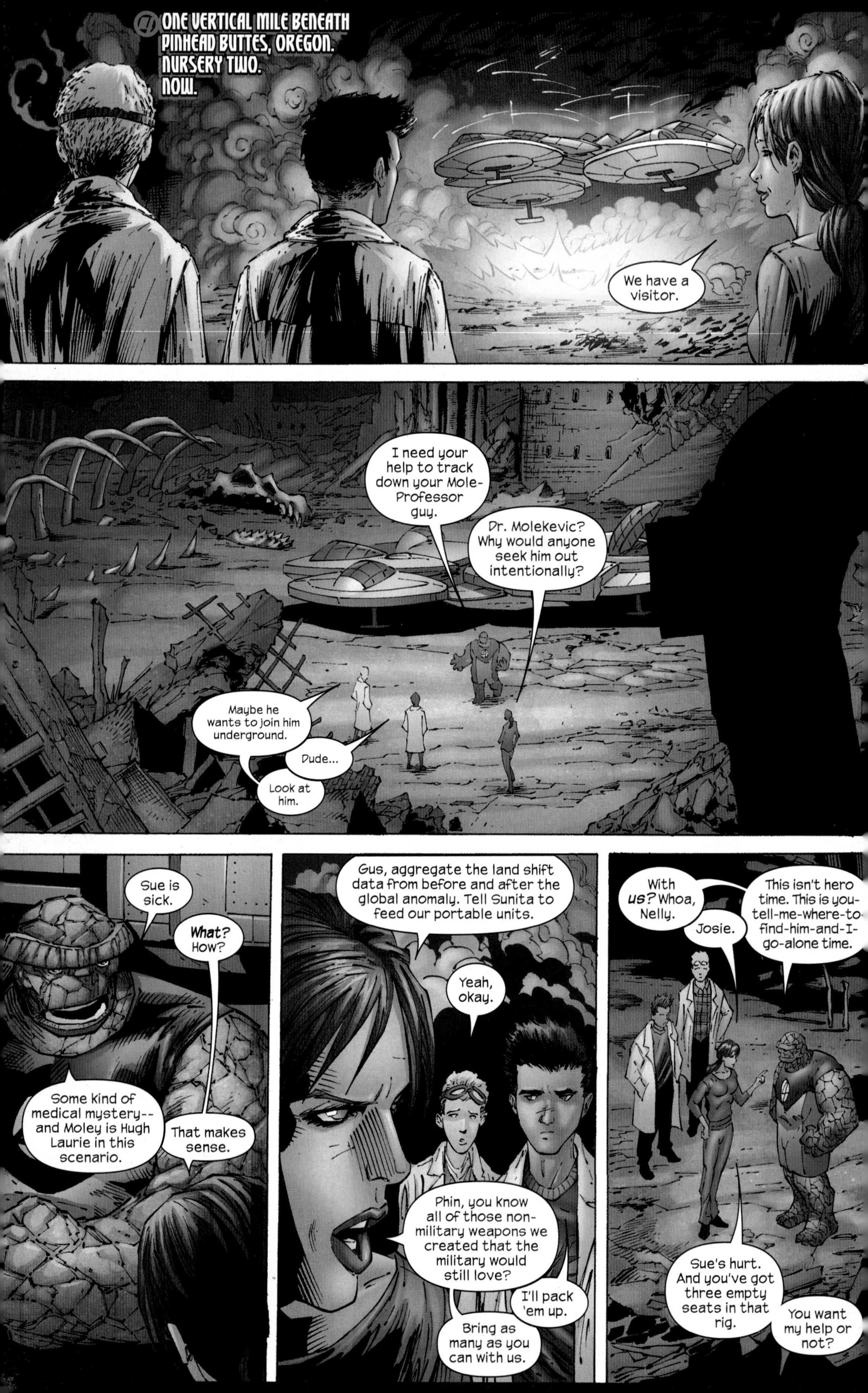
ONE VERTICAL MILE BENEATH PINHEAD BUTTES, OREGON. NURSERY TWO. NOW.
We have a visitor.
I need your help to track down your Mole-Professor guy.
Dr. Molekevic? Why would anyone seek him out intentionally?
Maybe he wants to join him underground.
Dude...
Look at him.
Sue is sick.
What? How?
Some kind of medical mystery-- and Moley is Hugh Laurie in this scenario.
That makes sense.
Gus, aggregate the land shift data from before and after the global anomaly. Tell Sunita to feed our portable units.
Yeah, okay.
Phin, you know all of those non-military weapons we created that the military would still love?
I'll pack 'em up.
Bring as many as you can with us.
With us? Whoa, Nelly.
Josie.
This isn't hero time. This is you-tell-me-where-to-find-him-and-I-go-alone time.
Sue's hurt. And you've got three empty seats in that rig.
You want my help or not?

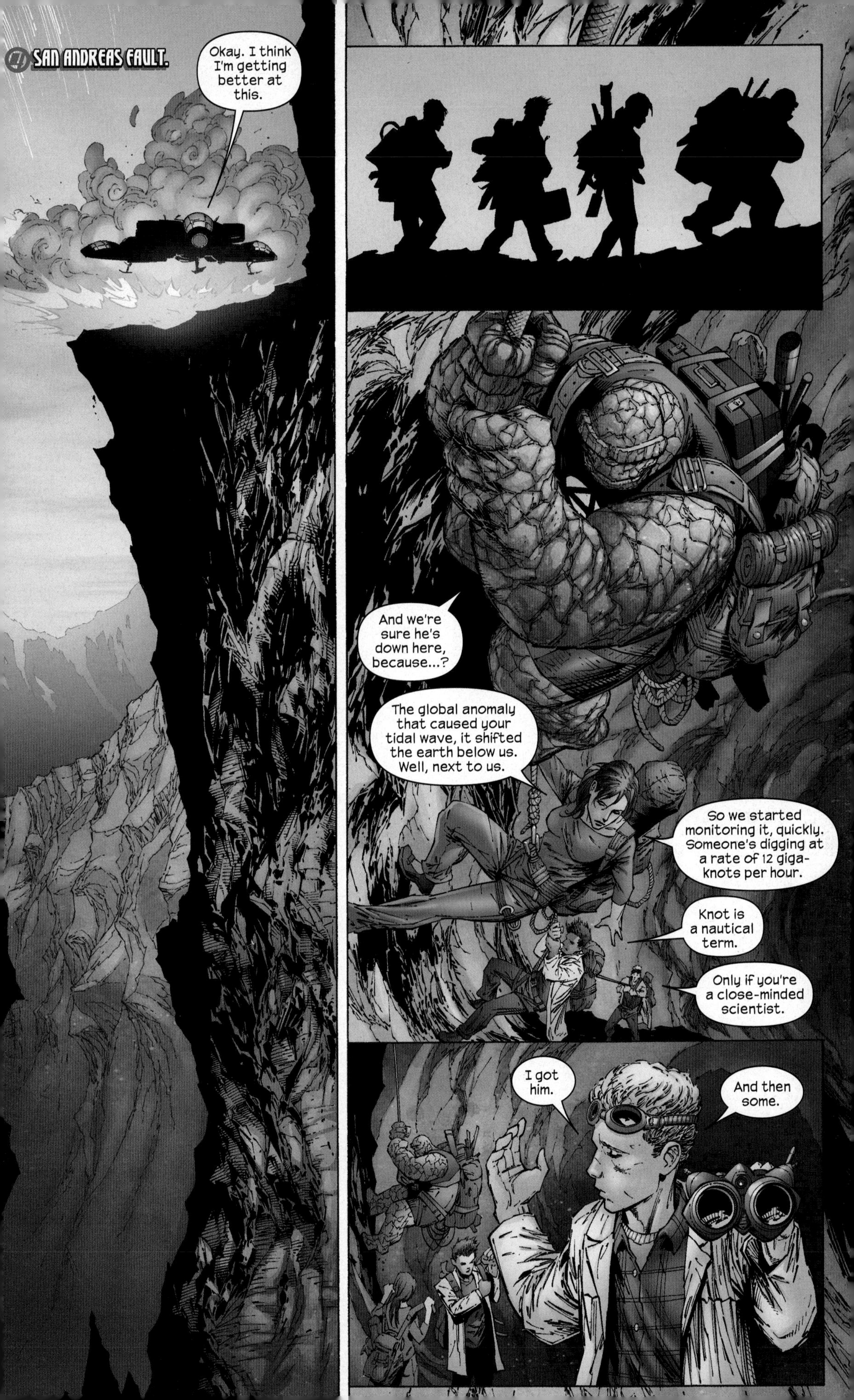
SAN ANDREAS FAULT.
Okay. I think I'm getting better at this.
And we're sure he's down here, because...?
The global anomaly that caused your tidal wave, it shifted the earth below us. Well, next to us.
So we started monitoring it, quickly. Someone's digging at a rate of 12 giga-knots per hour.
Knot is a nautical term.
Only if you're a close-minded scientist.
I got him.
And then some.

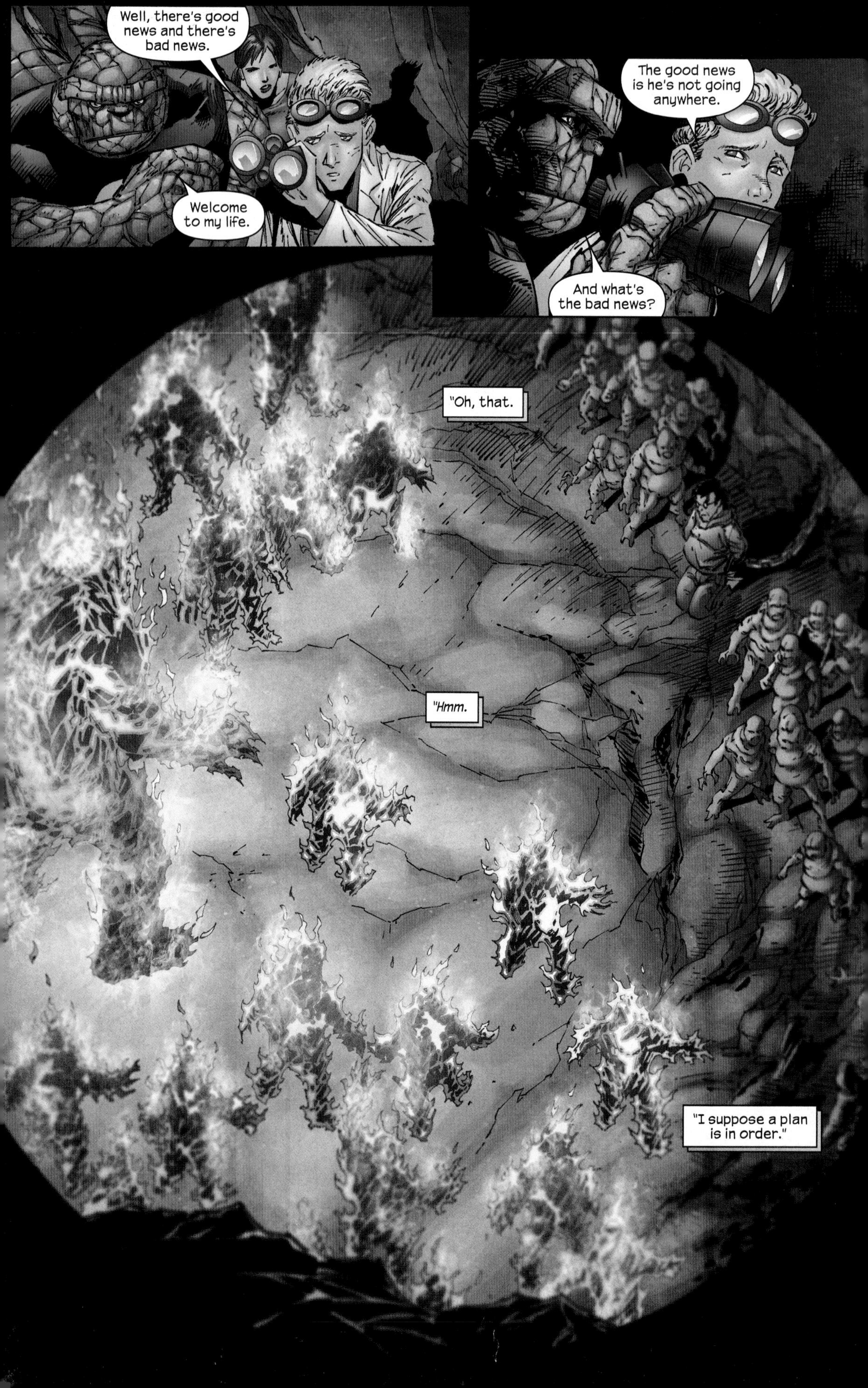
Well, there's good news and there's bad news.
Welcome to my life.
The good news is he's not going anywhere.
And what's the bad news?
"Oh, that.
"Hmm.
"I suppose a plan is in order."

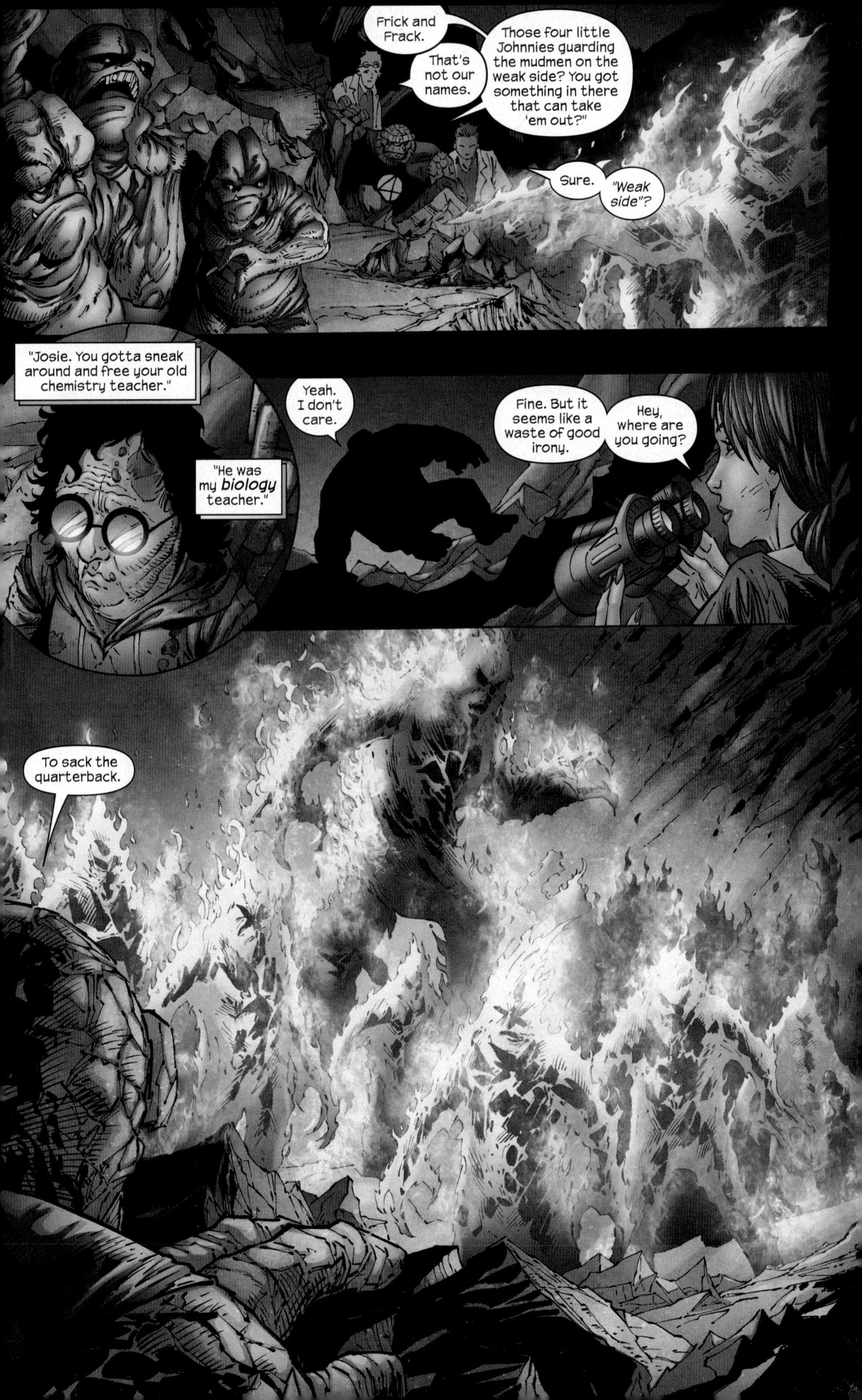
Frick and Frack.
That's not our names.
Those four little Johnnies guarding the mudmen on the weak side? You got something in there that can take 'em out?"
Sure.
"Weak side"?
"Josie. You gotta sneak around and free your old chemistry teacher."
"He was my *biology* teacher."
Yeah. I don't care.
Fine. But it seems like a waste of good irony.
Hey, where are you going?
To sack the quarterback.

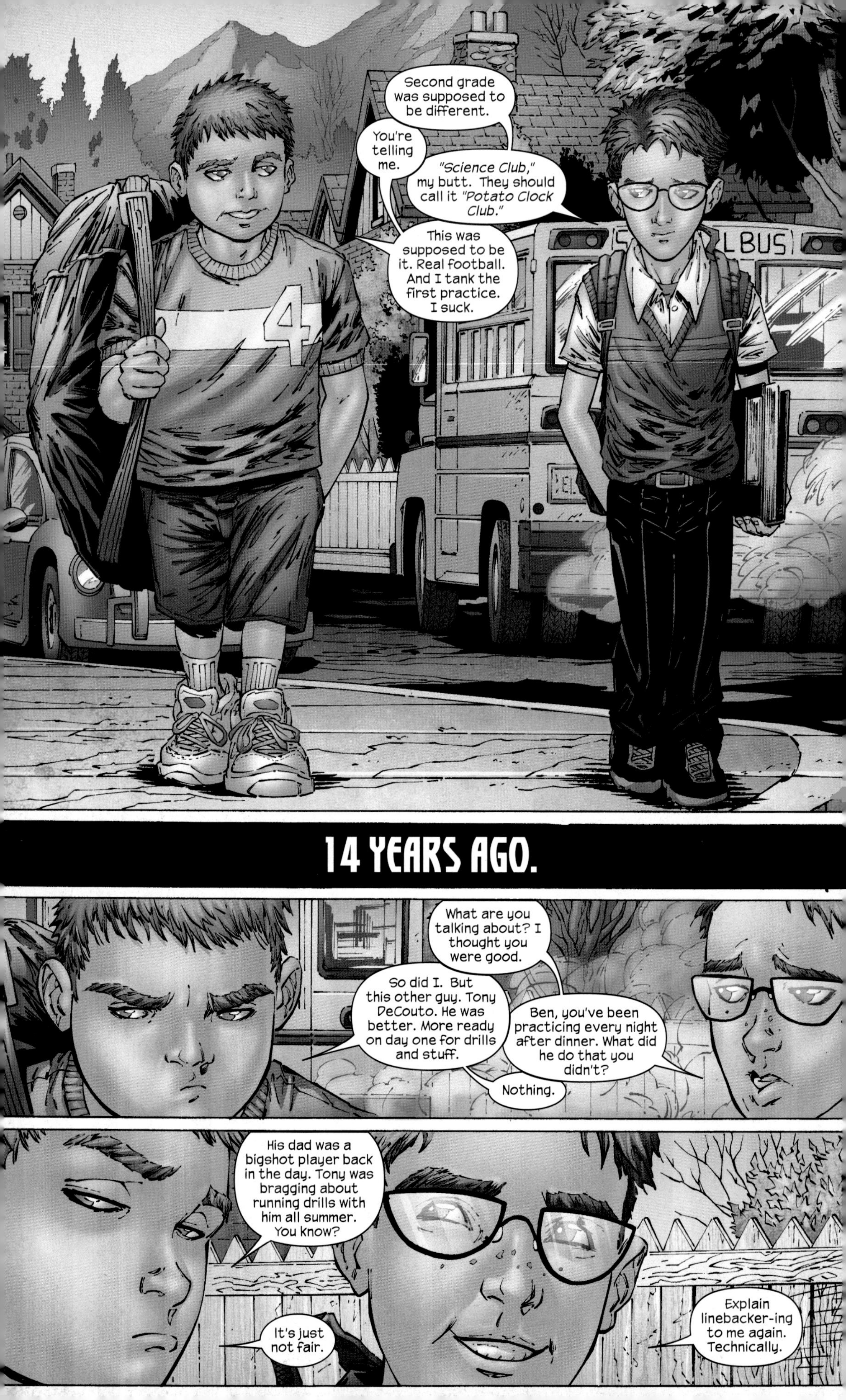

Second grade was supposed to be different.
You're telling me.
"Science Club," my butt. They should call it *"Potato Clock Club."*
This was supposed to be it. Real football. And I tank the first practice. I suck.
LBUS
14 YEARS AGO.
What are you talking about? I thought you were good.
So did I. But this other guy. Tony DeCouto. He was better. More ready on day one for drills and stuff.
Ben, you've been practicing every night after dinner. What did he do that you didn't?
Nothing.
His dad was a bigshot player back in the day. Tony was bragging about running drills with him all summer. You know?
It's just not fair.
Explain linebacker-ing to me again. Technically.

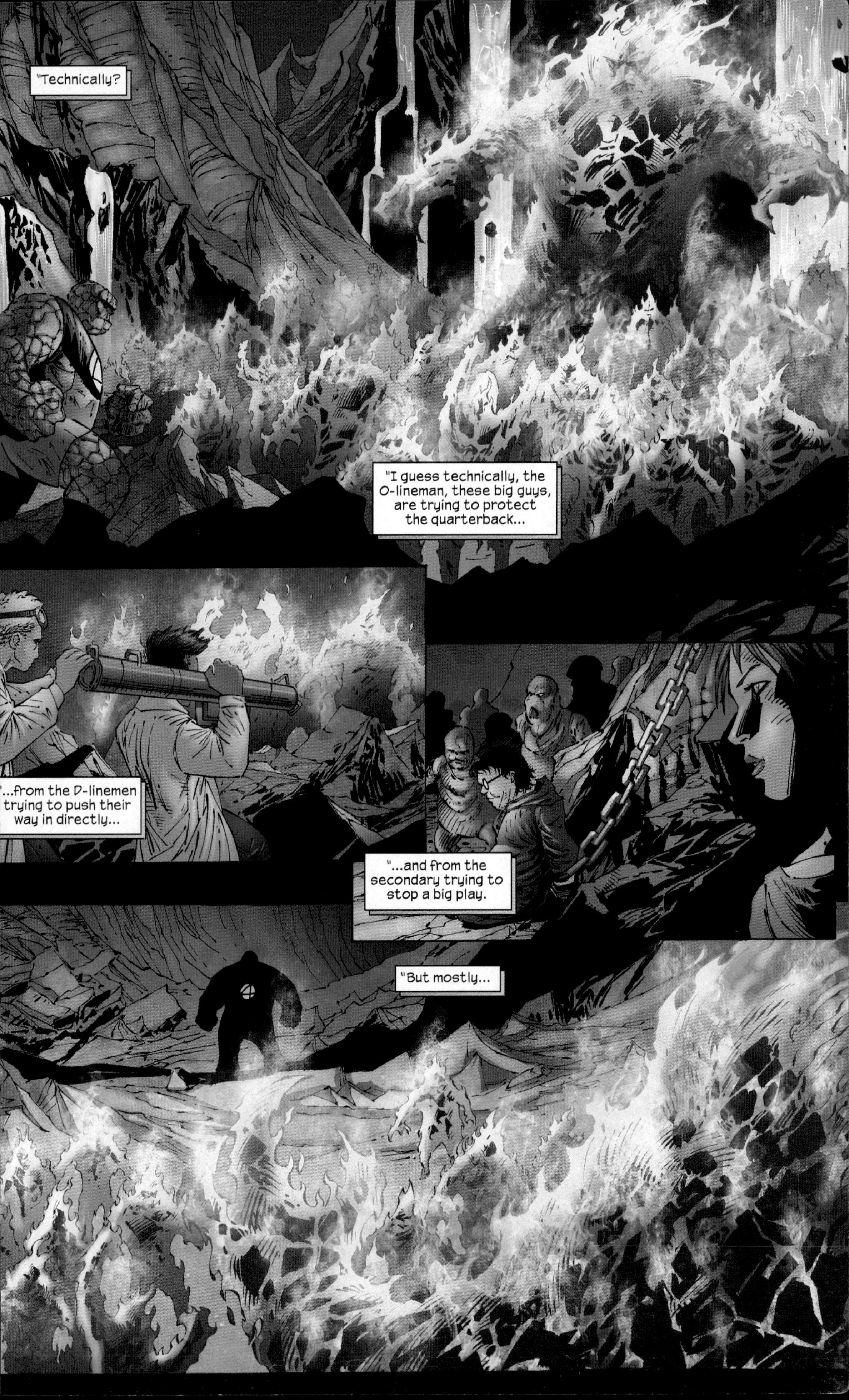
"Technically?
"I guess technically, the O-lineman, these big guys, are trying to protect the quarterback...
"...from the D-linemen trying to push their way in directly...
"...and from the secondary trying to stop a big play.
"But mostly...

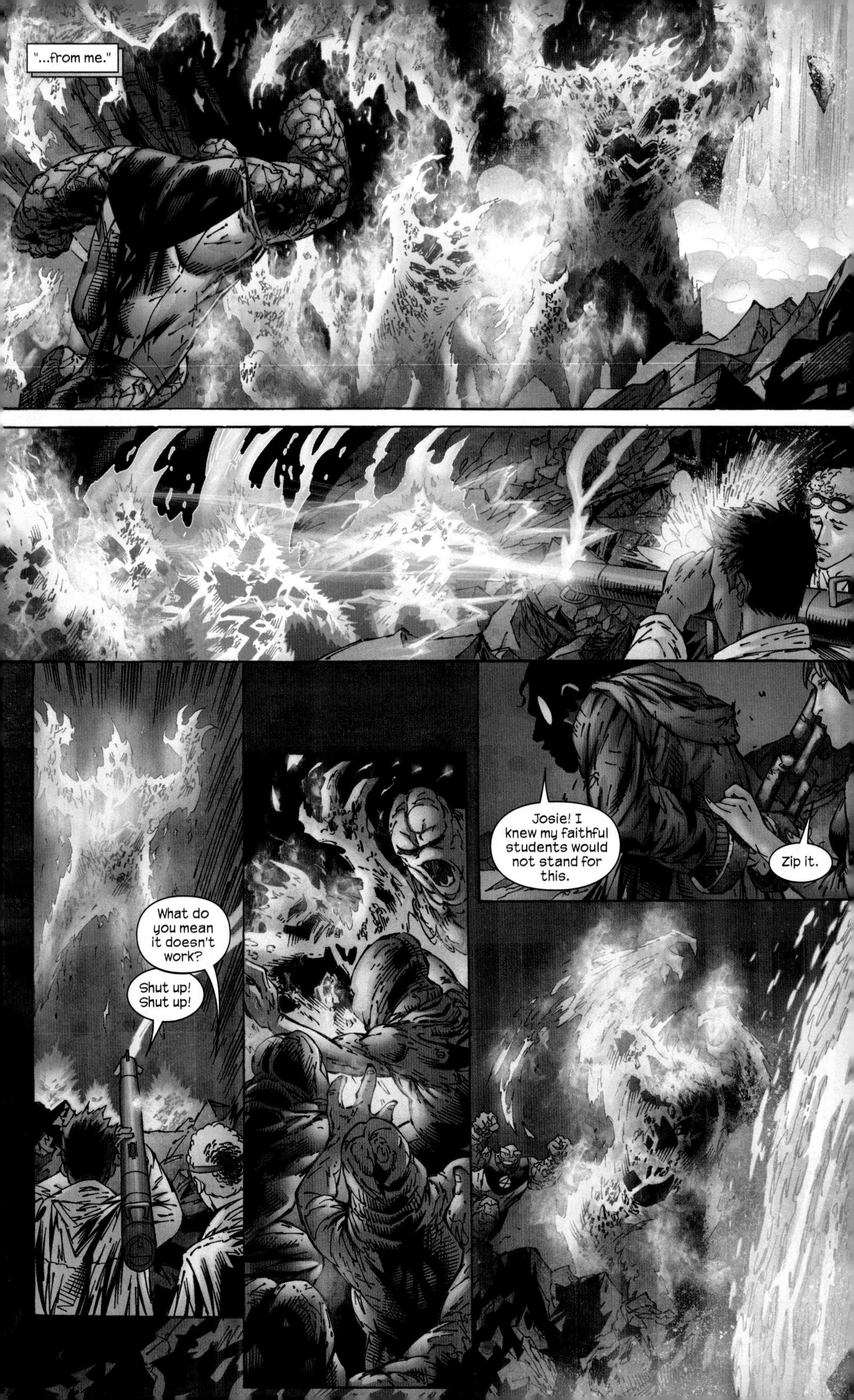
"...from me."
What do you mean it doesn't work?
Shut up! Shut up!
Josie! I knew my faithful students would not stand for this.
Zip it.

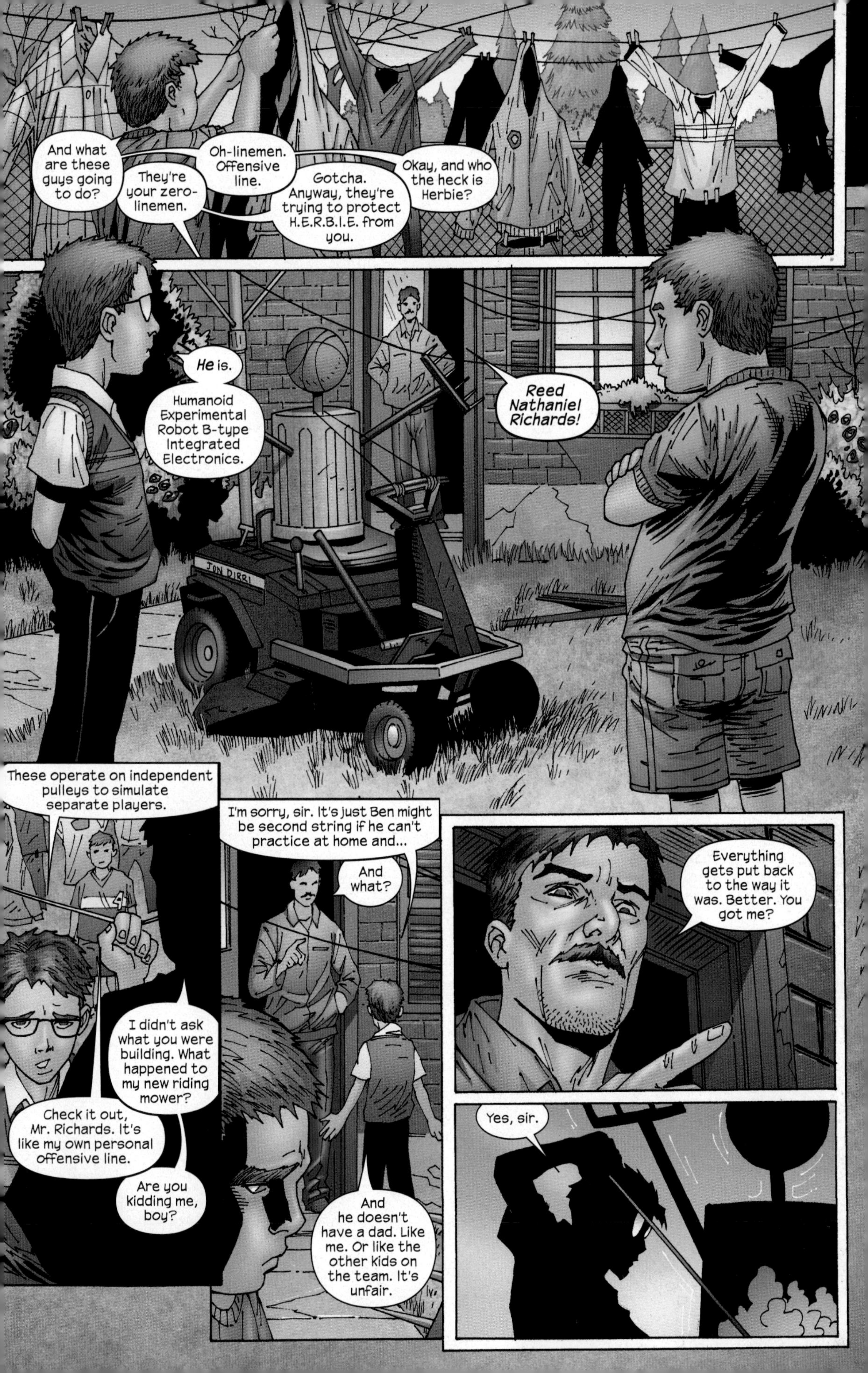
And what are these guys going to do?
Oh-linemen. Offensive line.
They're your zero-linemen.
Gotcha. Anyway, they're trying to protect H.E.R.B.I.E. from you.
Okay, and who the heck is Herbie?
He is.
Humanoid Experimental Robot B-type Integrated Electronics.
Reed Nathaniel Richards!
JON DIRRI
These operate on independent pulleys to simulate separate players.
I didn't ask what you were building. What happened to my new riding mower?
Check it out, Mr. Richards. It's like my own personal offensive line.
Are you kidding me, boy?
I'm sorry, sir. It's just Ben might be second string if he can't practice at home and...
And what?
And he doesn't have a dad. Like me. Or like the other kids on the team. It's unfair.
Everything gets put back to the way it was. Better. You got me?
Yes, sir.

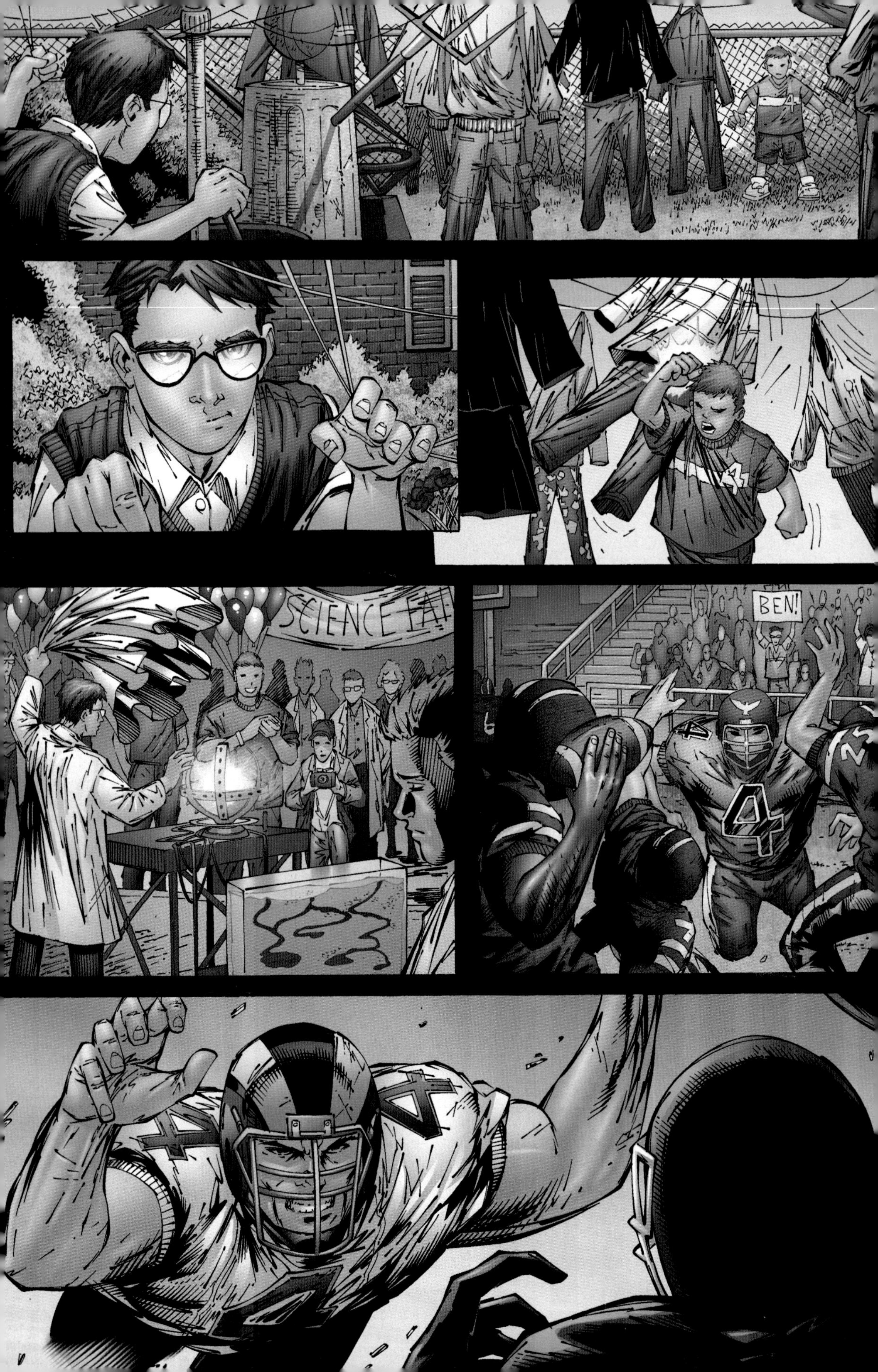
SCIENCE FAI
BEN!

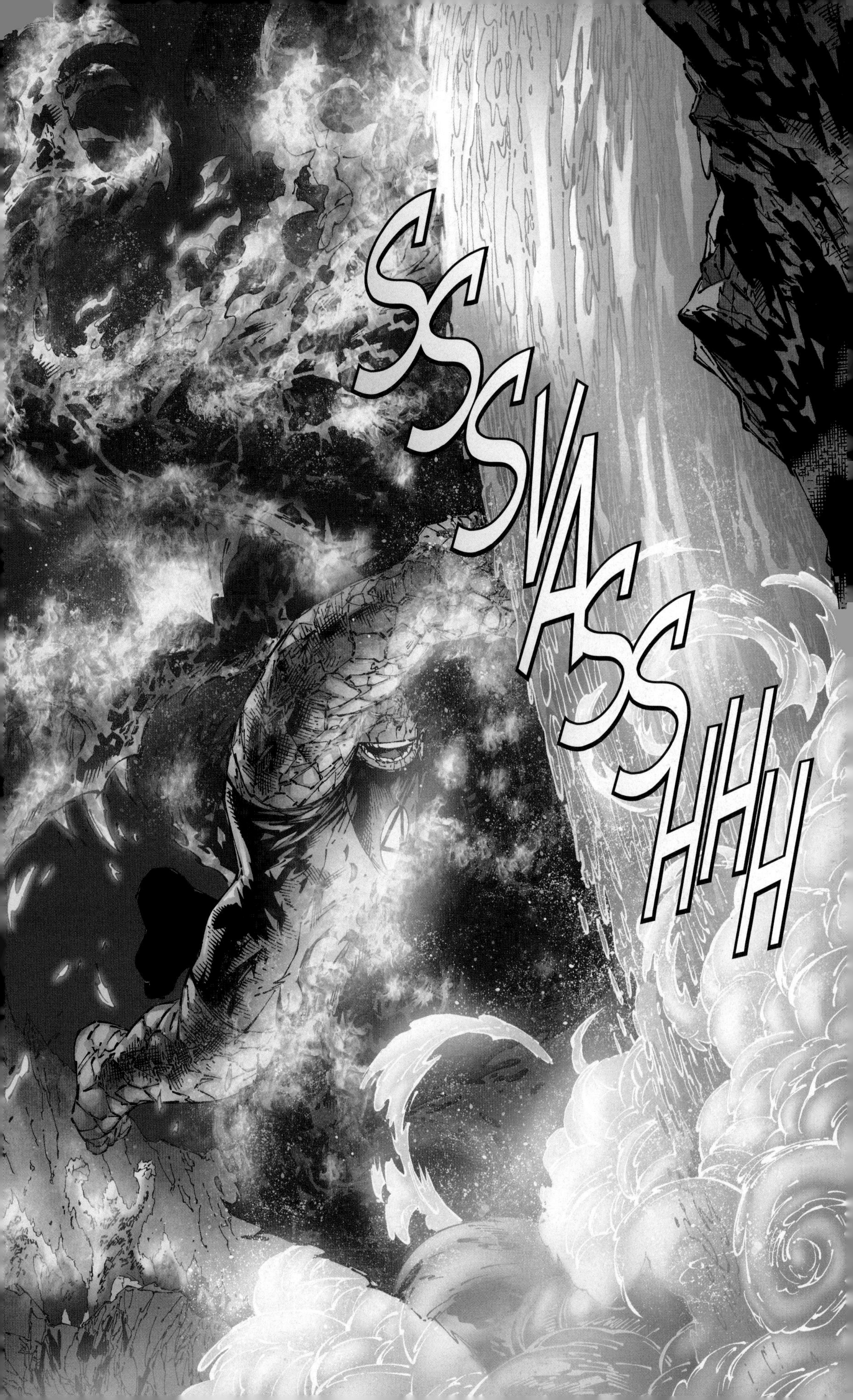
SSSVASSHHH

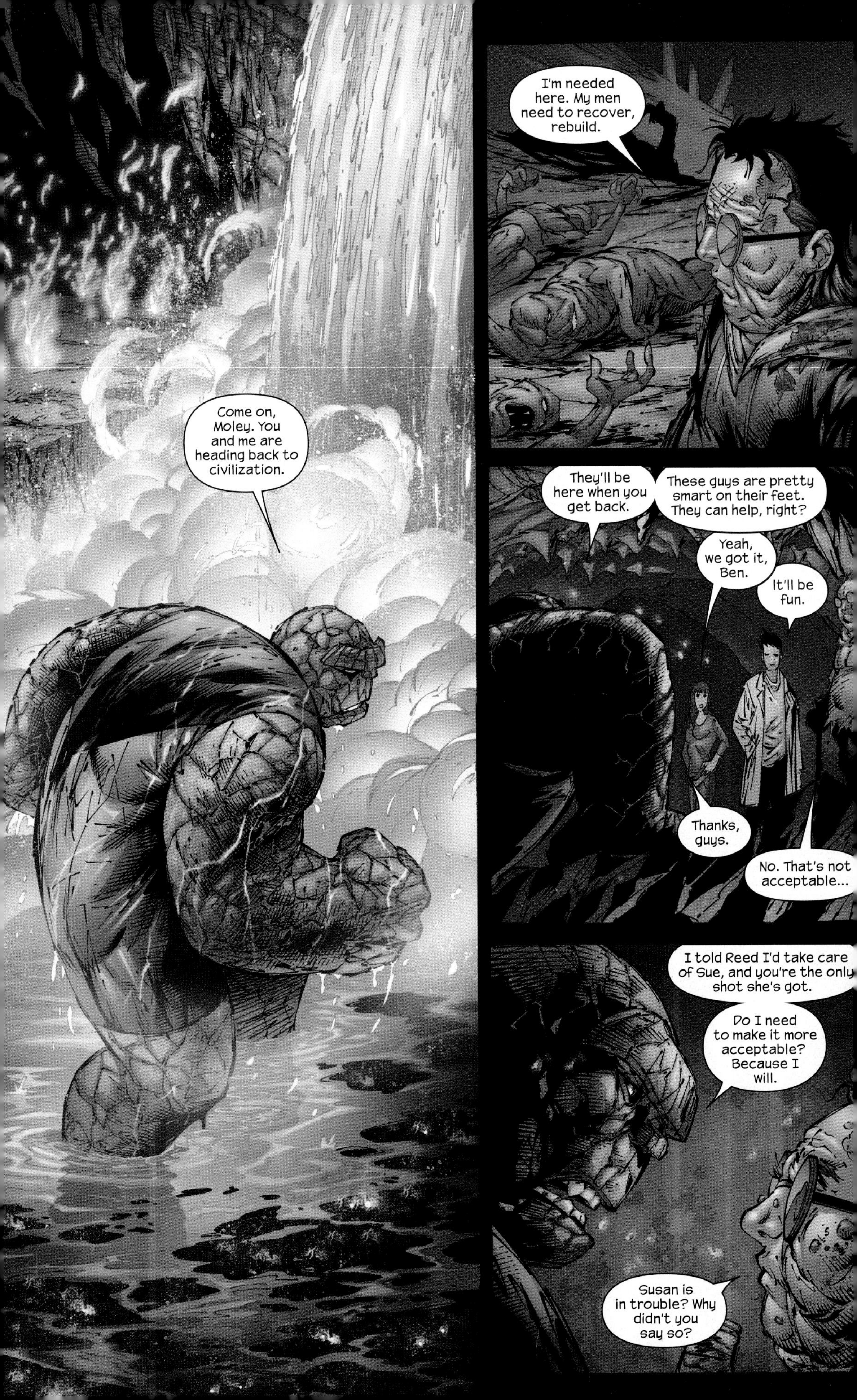
Come on, Moley. You and me are heading back to civilization.
I'm needed here. My men need to recover, rebuild.
They'll be here when you get back.
These guys are pretty smart on their feet. They can help, right?
Yeah, we got it, Ben.
It'll be fun.
Thanks, guys.
No. That's not acceptable...
I told Reed I'd take care of Sue, and you're the only shot she's got.
Do I need to make it more acceptable? Because I will.
Susan is in trouble? Why didn't you say so?

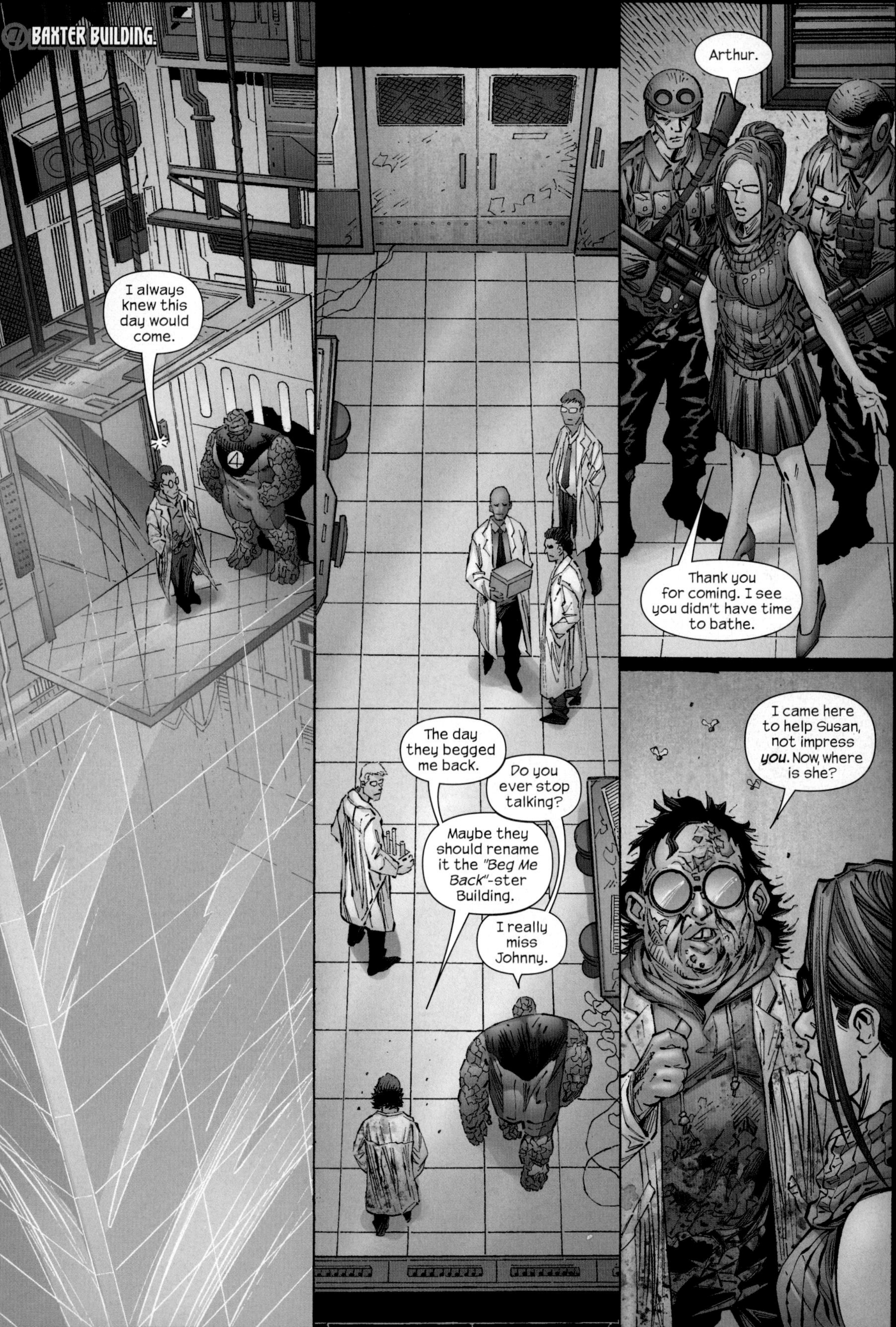
BAXTER BUILDING.
I always knew this day would come.
The day they begged me back.
Do you ever stop talking?
Maybe they should rename it the "Beg Me Back"-ster Building.
I really miss Johnny.
Arthur.
Thank you for coming. I see you didn't have time to bathe.
I came here to help Susan, not impress *you*. Now, where is she?

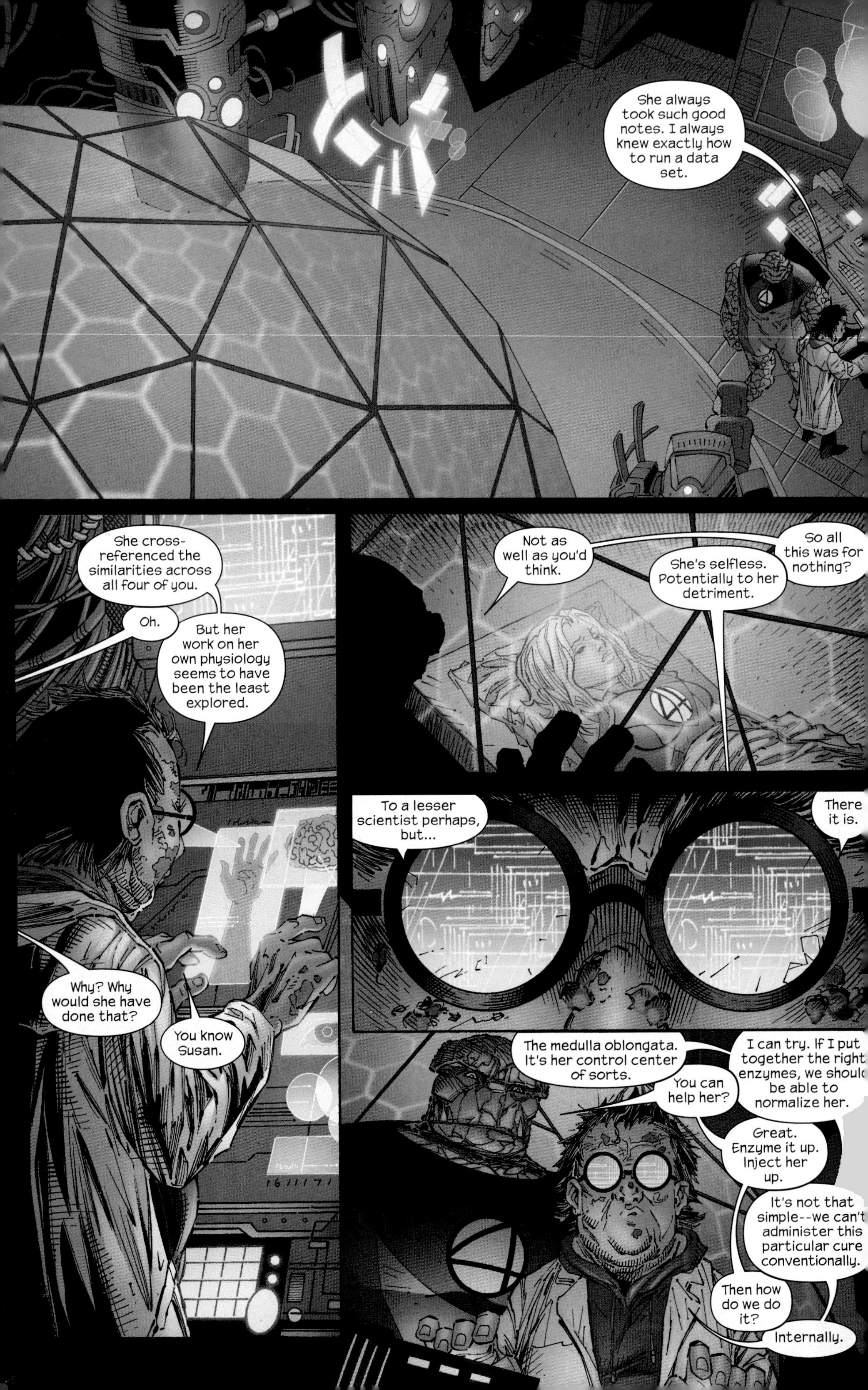
She always took such good notes. I always knew exactly how to run a data set.
She cross-referenced the similarities across all four of you.
Oh.
But her work on her own physiology seems to have been the least explored.
Why? Why would she have done that?
You know Susan.
Not as well as you'd think.
So all this was for nothing?
She's selfless. Potentially to her detriment.
To a lesser scientist perhaps, but...
There it is.
The medulla oblongata. It's her control center of sorts.
You can help her?
I can try. If I put together the right enzymes, we should be able to normalize her.
Great. Enzyme it up. Inject her up.
It's not that simple--we can't administer this particular cure conventionally.
Then how do we do it?
Internally.

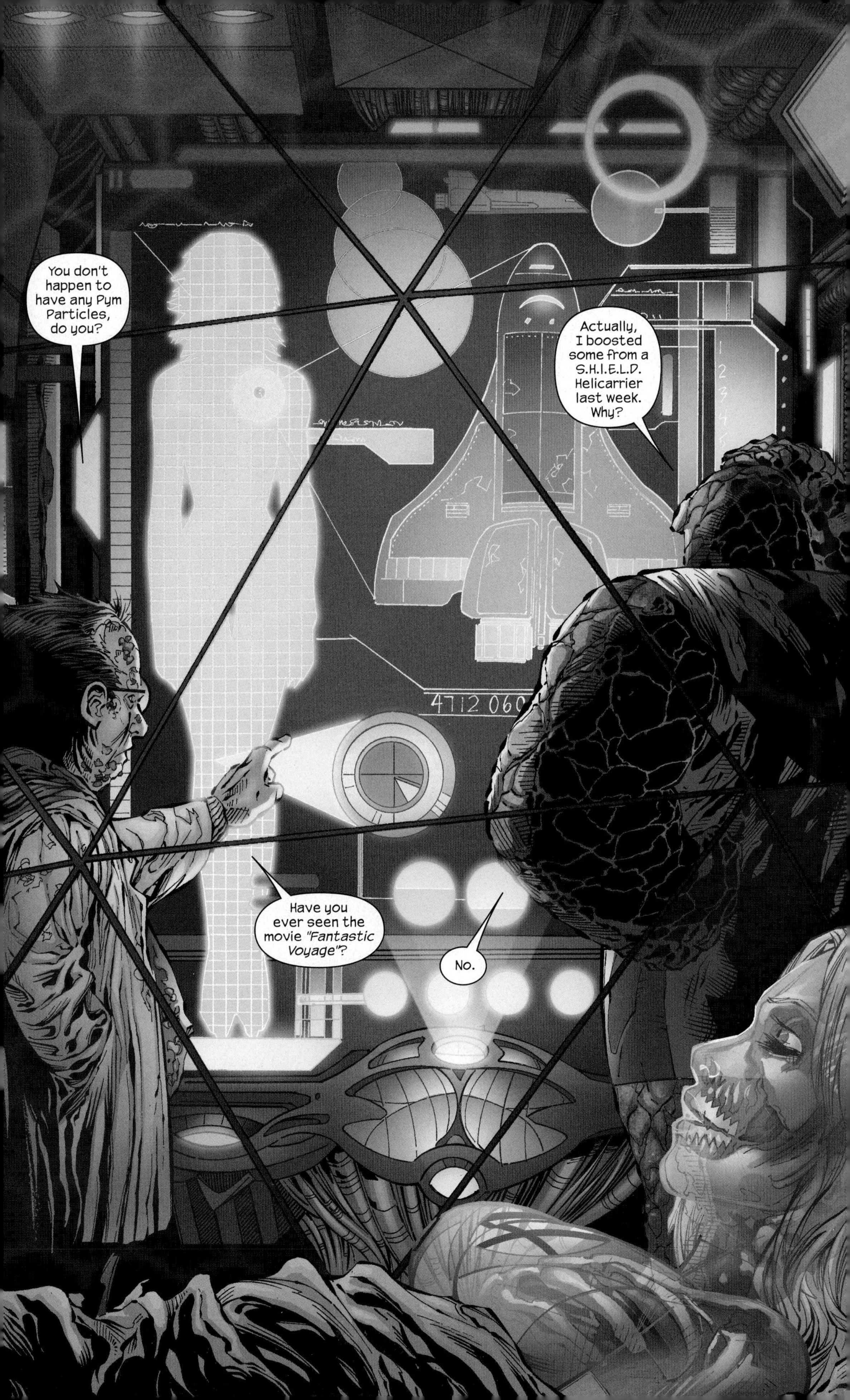

You don't happen to have any Pym Particles, do you?
Actually, I boosted some from a S.H.I.E.L.D. Helicarrier last week. Why?
4712 060
Have you ever seen the movie *"Fantastic Voyage"*?
No.

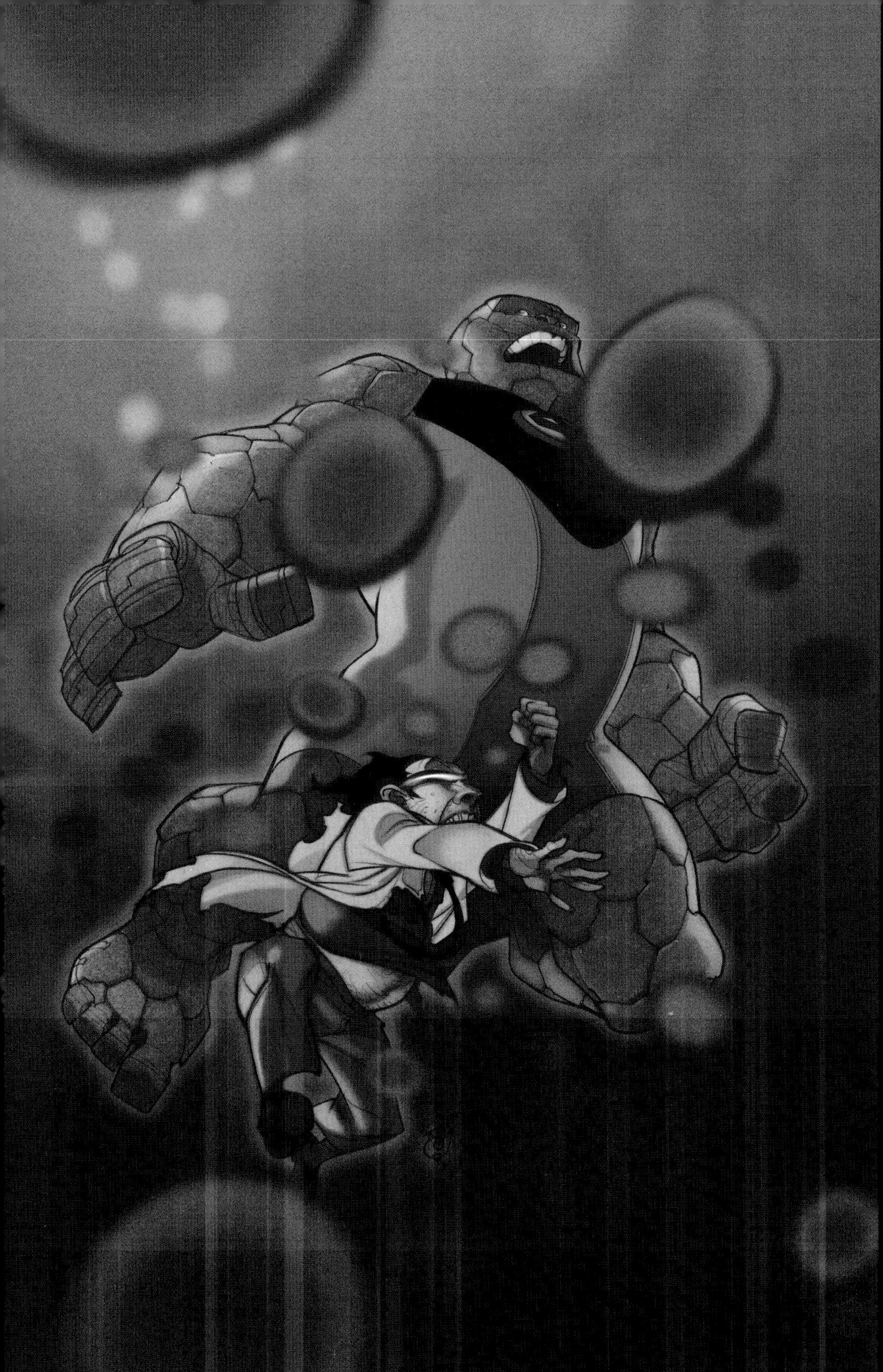

Ultimate Fantastic Four #59

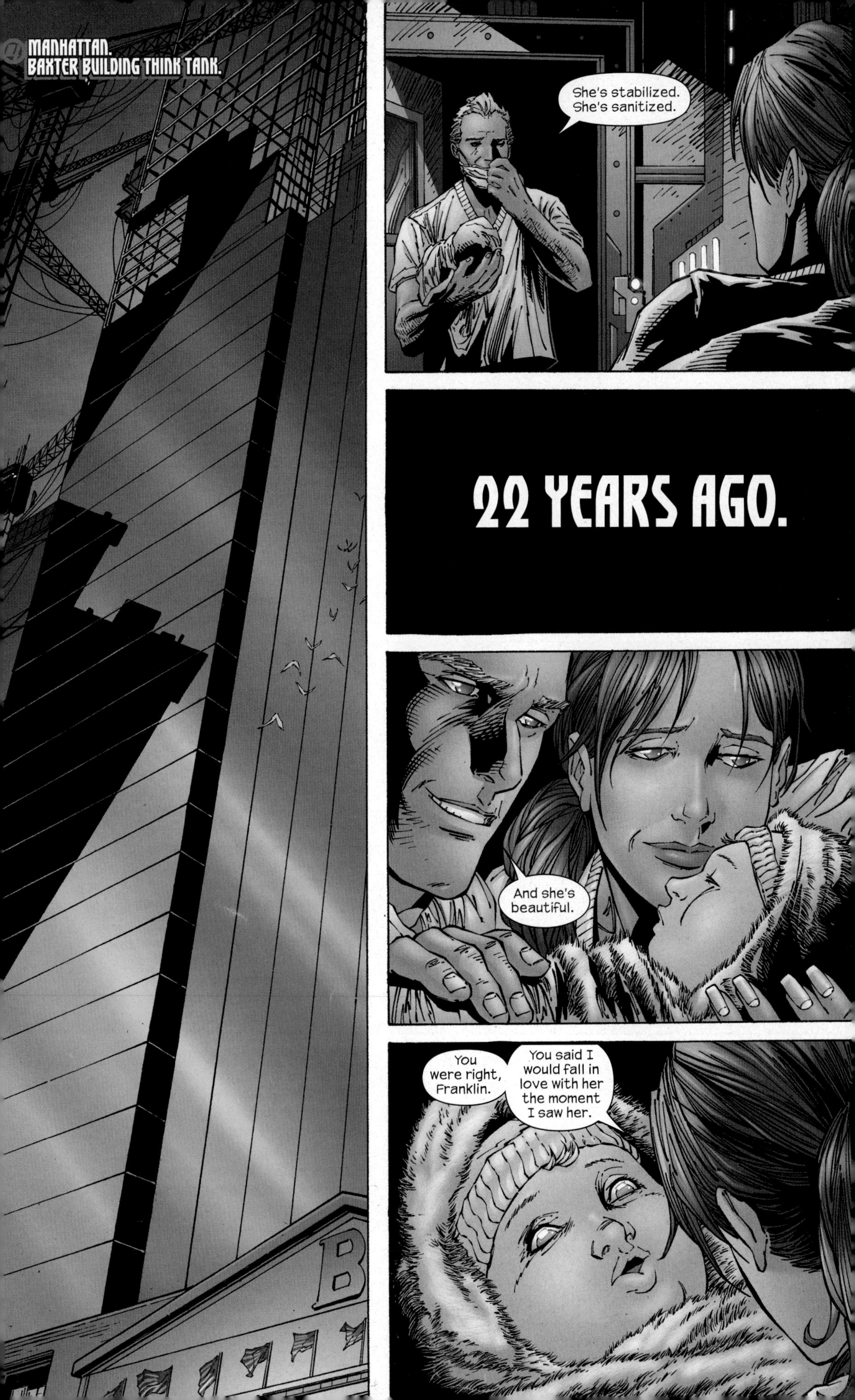
MANHATTAN.
BAXTER BUILDING THINK TANK.
She's stabilized. She's sanitized.
22 YEARS AGO.
And she's beautiful.
You were right, Franklin.
You said I would fall in love with her the moment I saw her.

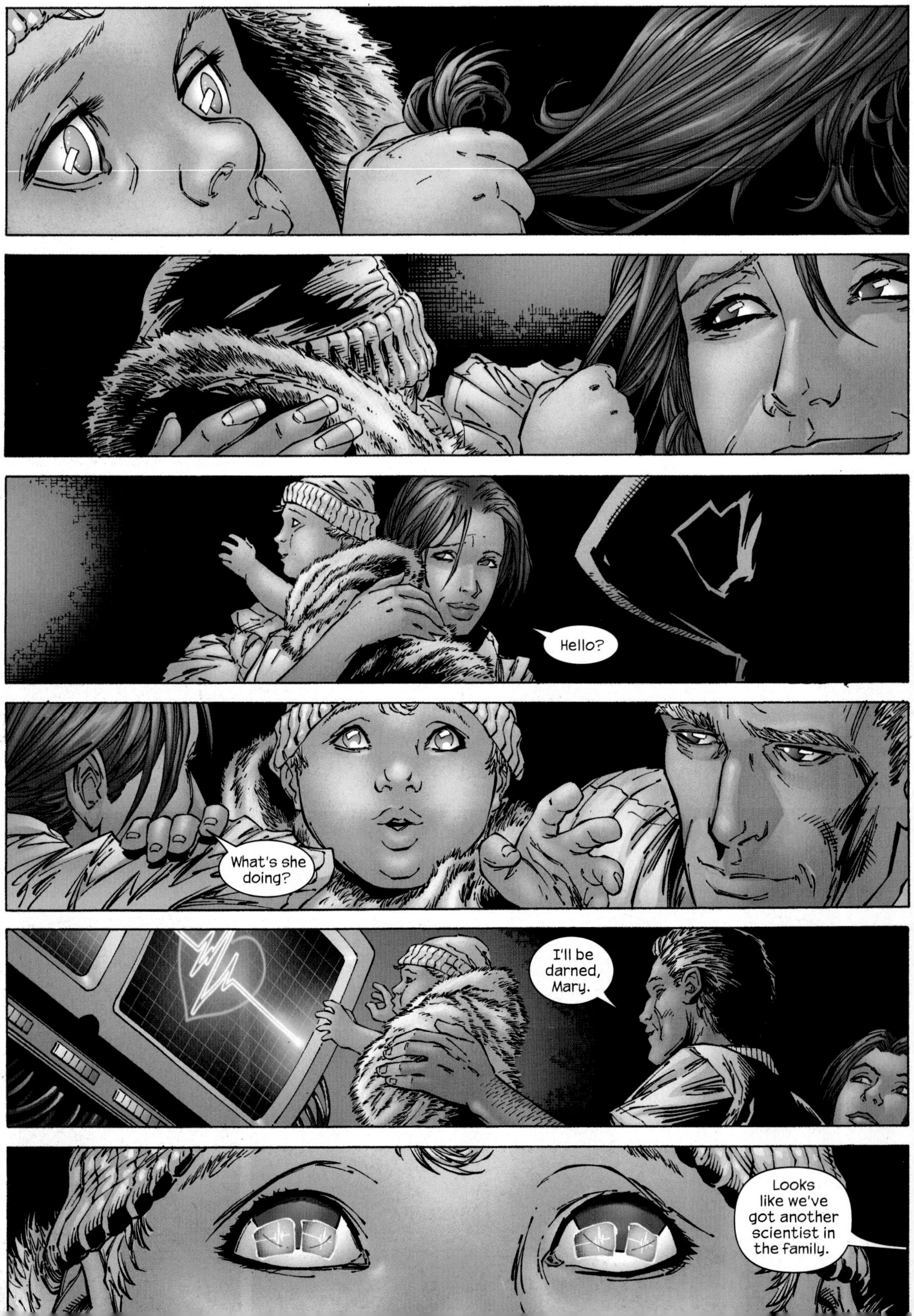
Hello?
What's she doing?
I'll be darned, Mary.
Looks like we've got another scientist in the family.

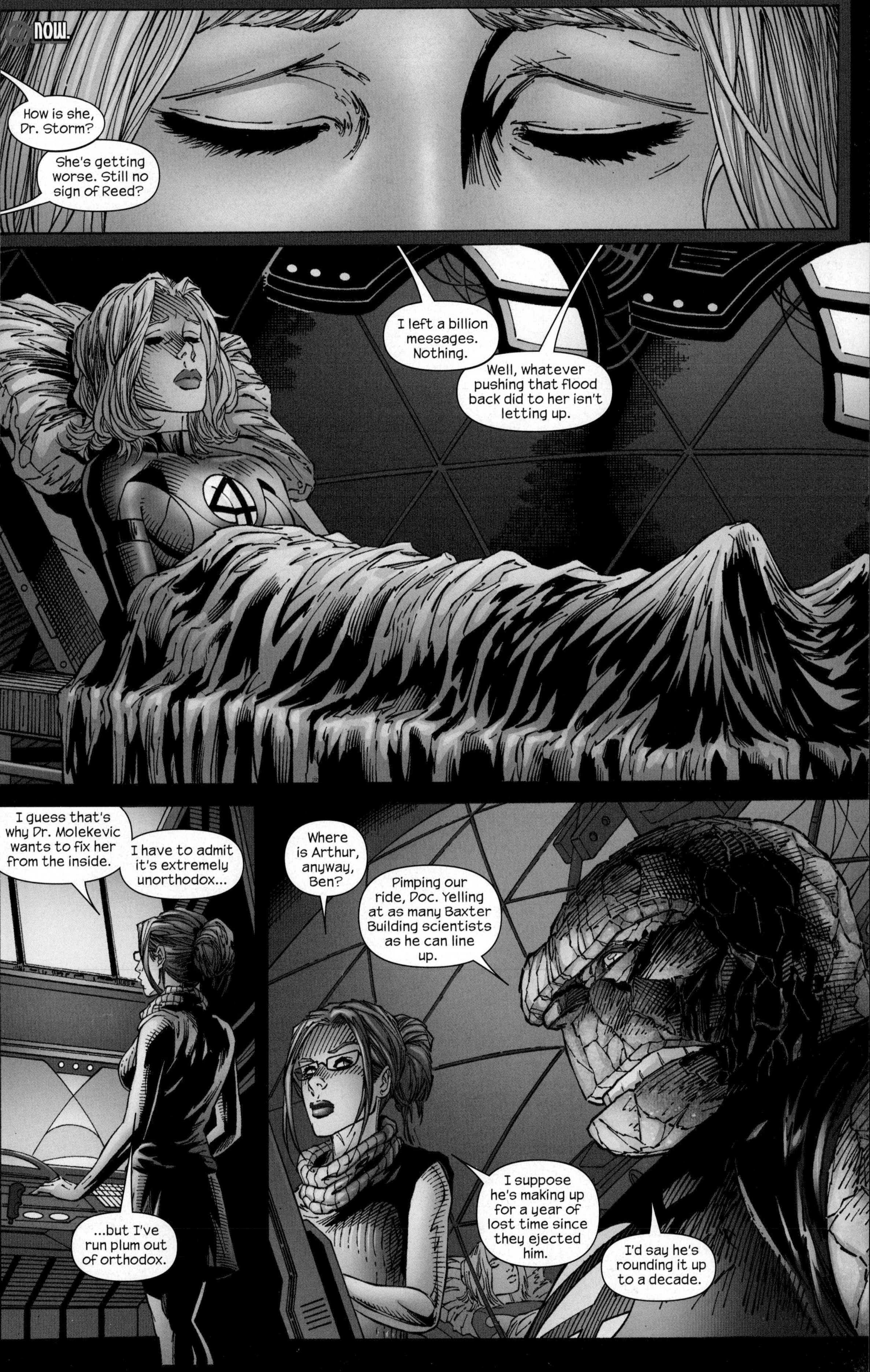
NOW.
How is she, Dr. Storm?
She's getting worse. Still no sign of Reed?
I left a billion messages. Nothing.
Well, whatever pushing that flood back did to her isn't letting up.
I guess that's why Dr. Molekevic wants to fix her from the inside.
I have to admit it's extremely unorthodox...
...but I've run plum out of orthodox.
Where is Arthur, anyway, Ben?
Pimping our ride, Doc. Yelling at as many Baxter Building scientists as he can line up.
I suppose he's making up for a year of lost time since they ejected him.
I'd say he's rounding it up to a decade.

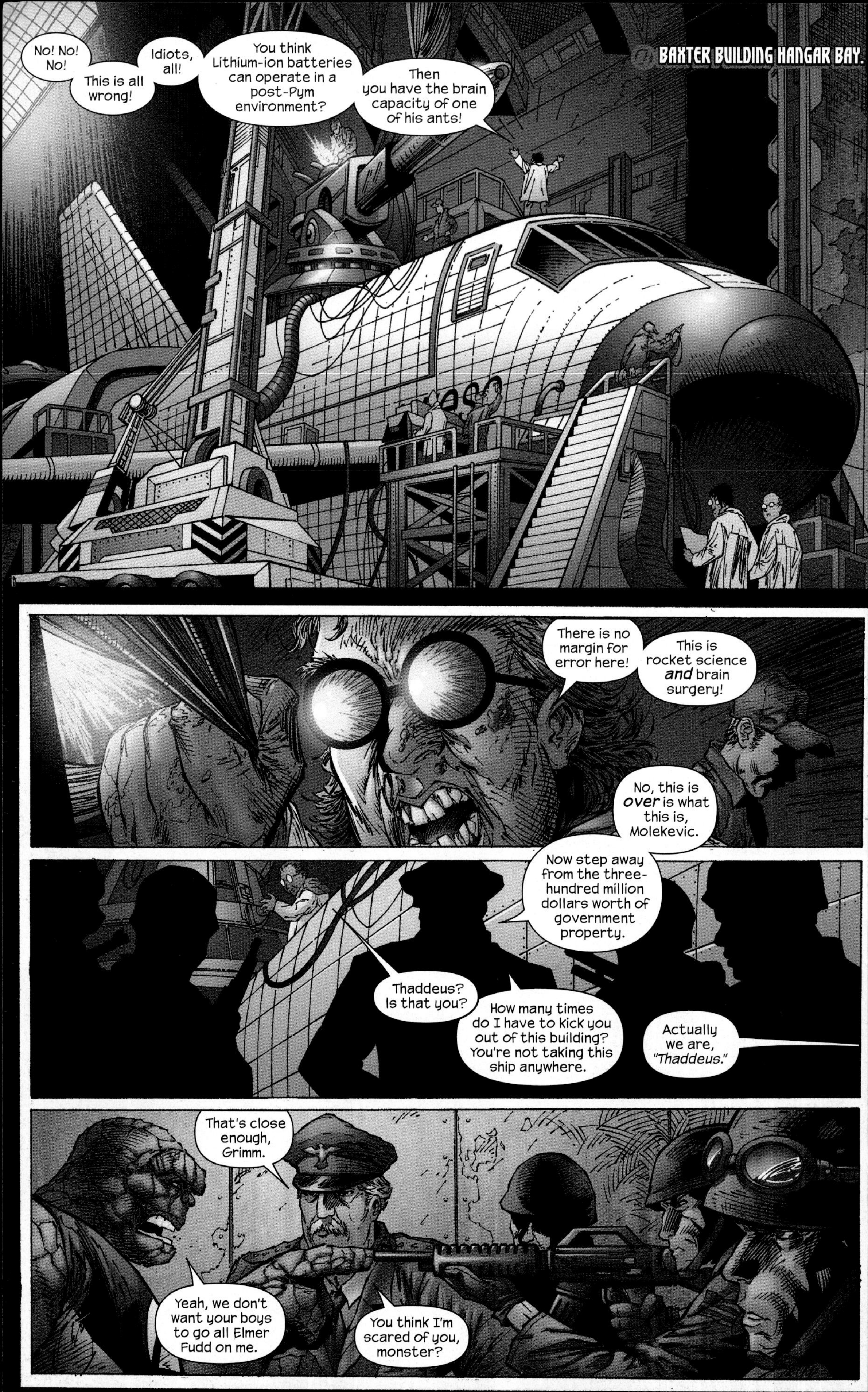
BAXTER BUILDING HANGAR BAY.
No! No! No!
This is all wrong!
Idiots, all!
You think Lithium-ion batteries can operate in a post-Pym environment?
Then you have the brain capacity of one of his ants!
There is no margin for error here!
This is rocket science *and* brain surgery!
No, this is *over* is what this is, Molekevic.
Now step away from the three-hundred million dollars worth of government property.
Thaddeus? Is that you?
How many times do I have to kick you out of this building? You're not taking this ship anywhere.
Actually we are, "Thaddeus."
That's close enough, Grimm.
Yeah, we don't want your boys to go all Elmer Fudd on me.
You think I'm scared of you, monster?

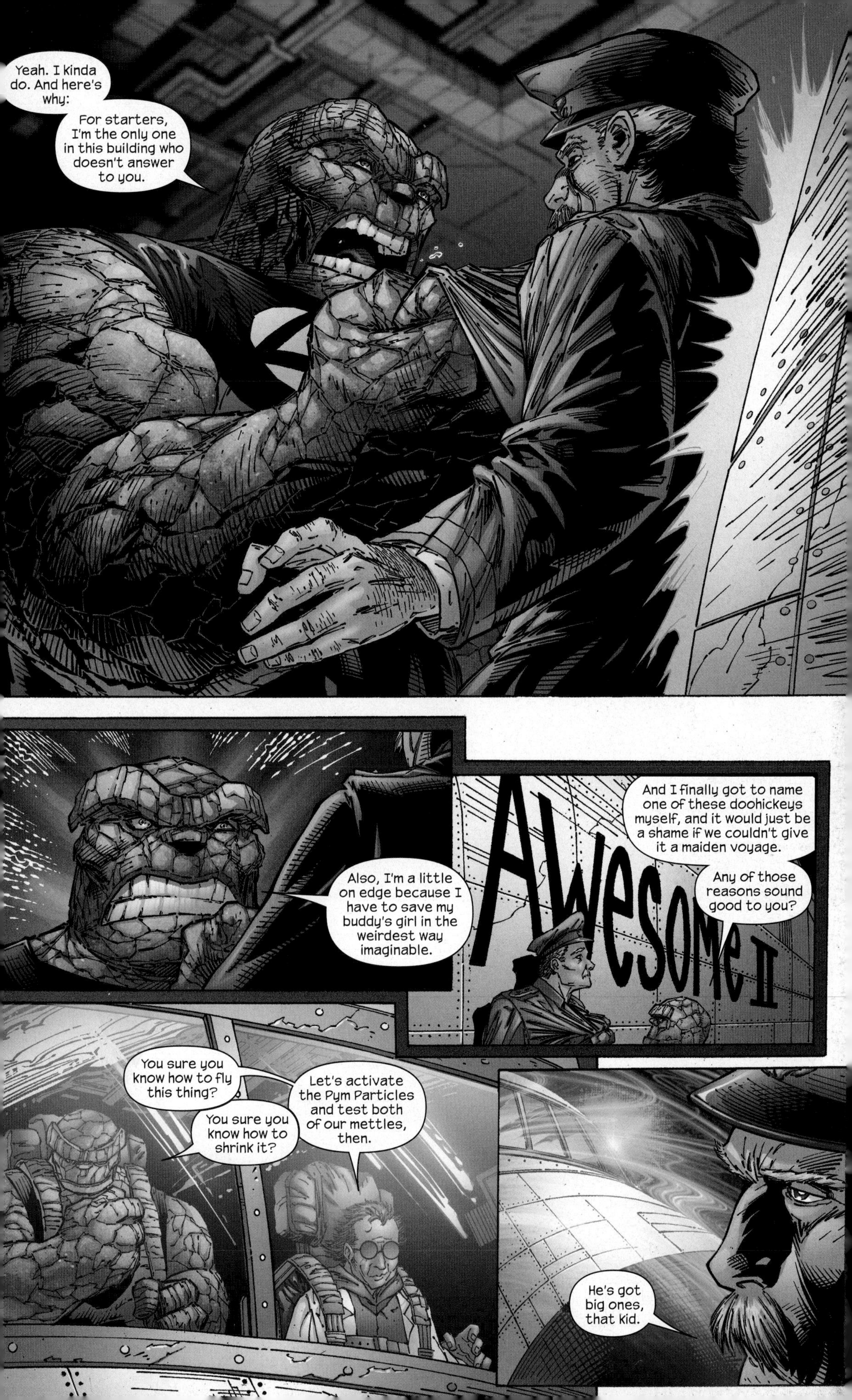
Yeah. I kinda do. And here's why:
For starters, I'm the only one in this building who doesn't answer to you.
Also, I'm a little on edge because I have to save my buddy's girl in the weirdest way imaginable.
And I finally got to name one of these doohickeys myself, and it would just be a shame if we couldn't give it a maiden voyage.
Any of those reasons sound good to you?
Awesome II
You sure you know how to fly this thing?
You sure you know how to shrink it?
Let's activate the Pym Particles and test both of our mettles, then.
He's got big ones, that kid.

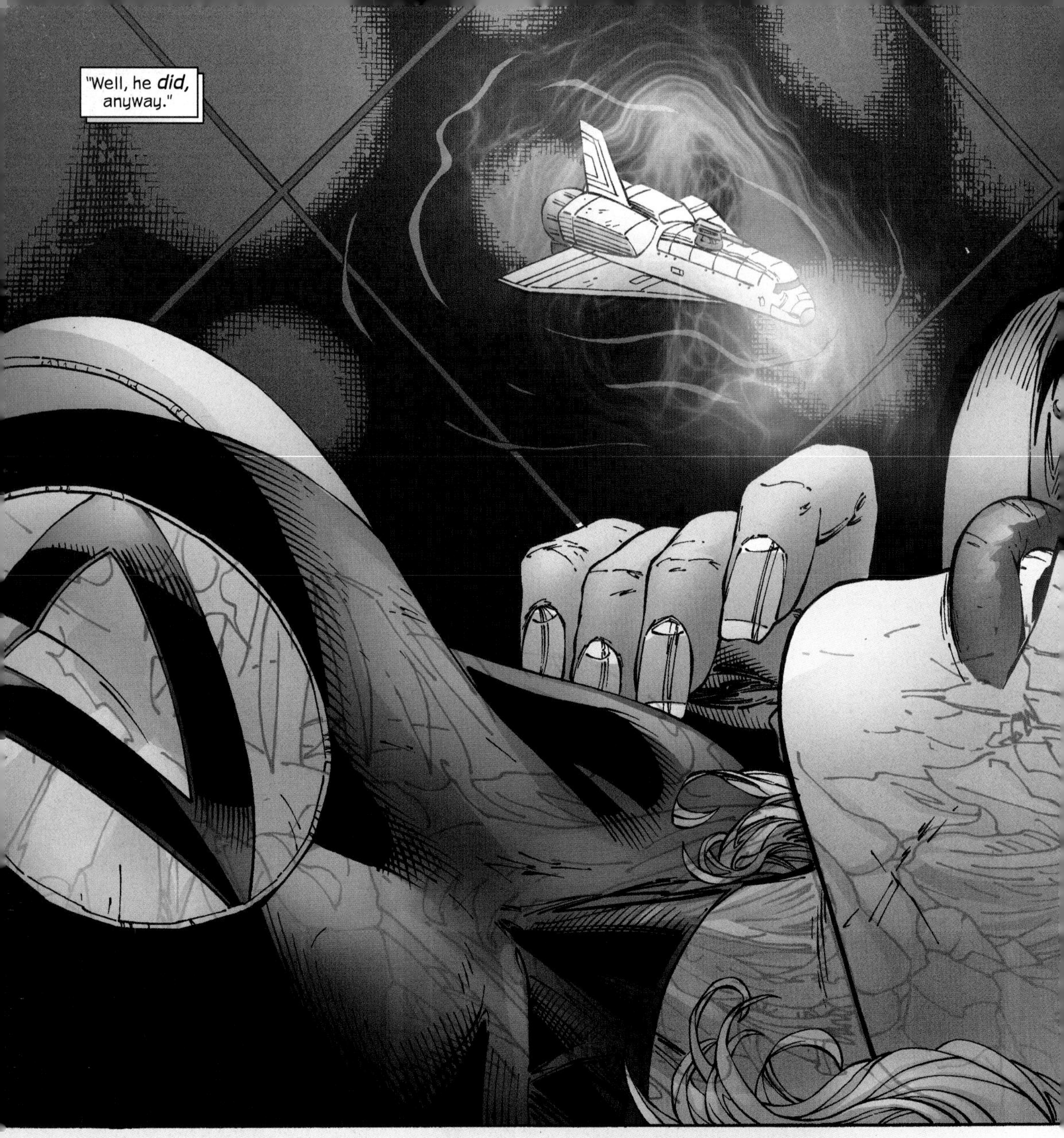
"Well, he did, anyway."

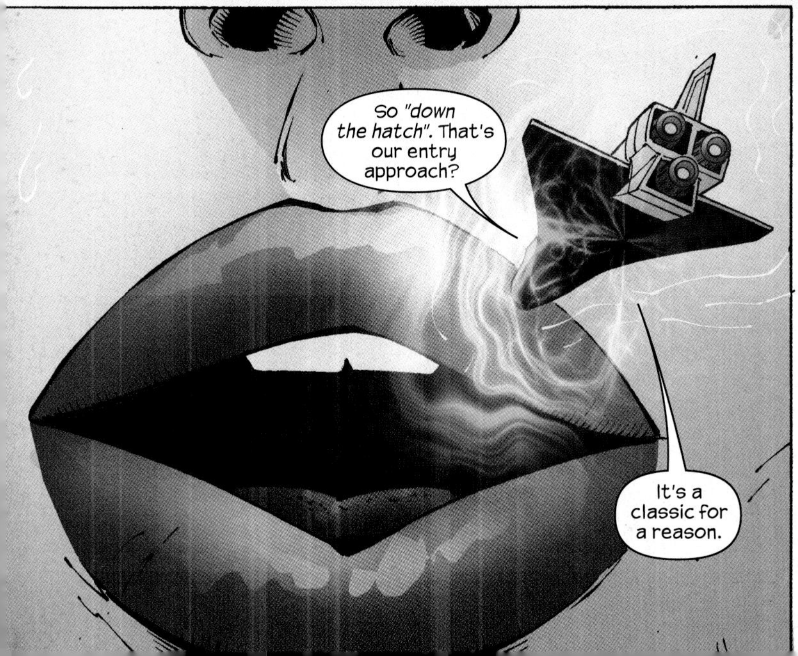
So "down the hatch". That's our entry approach?
It's a classic for a reason.

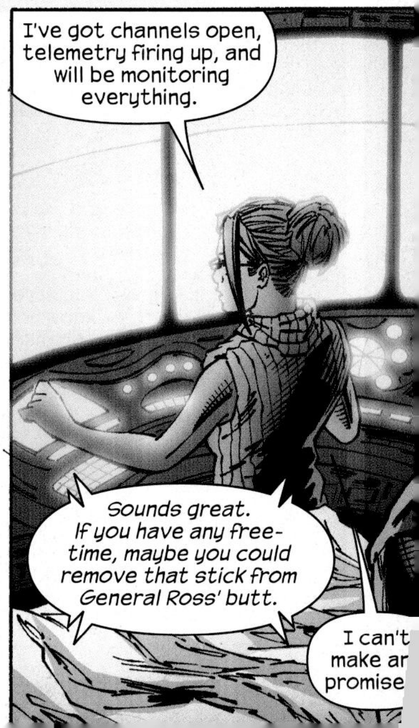
I've got channels open, telemetry firing up, and will be monitoring everything.
Sounds great. If you have any free-time, maybe you could remove that stick from General Ross' butt.

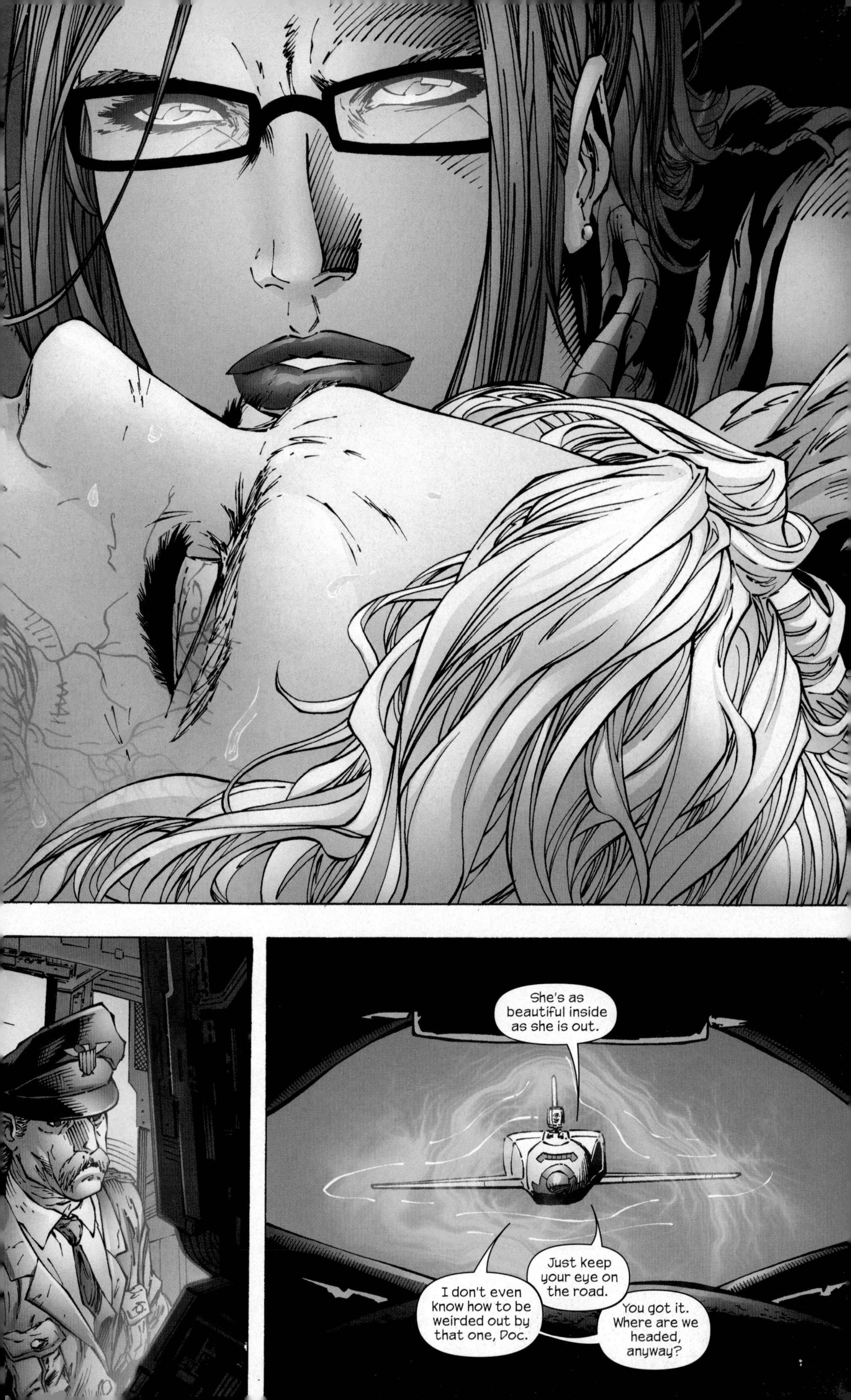
She's as beautiful inside as she is out.
I don't even know how to be weirded out by that one, Doc.
Just keep your eye on the road.
You got it. Where are we headed, anyway?

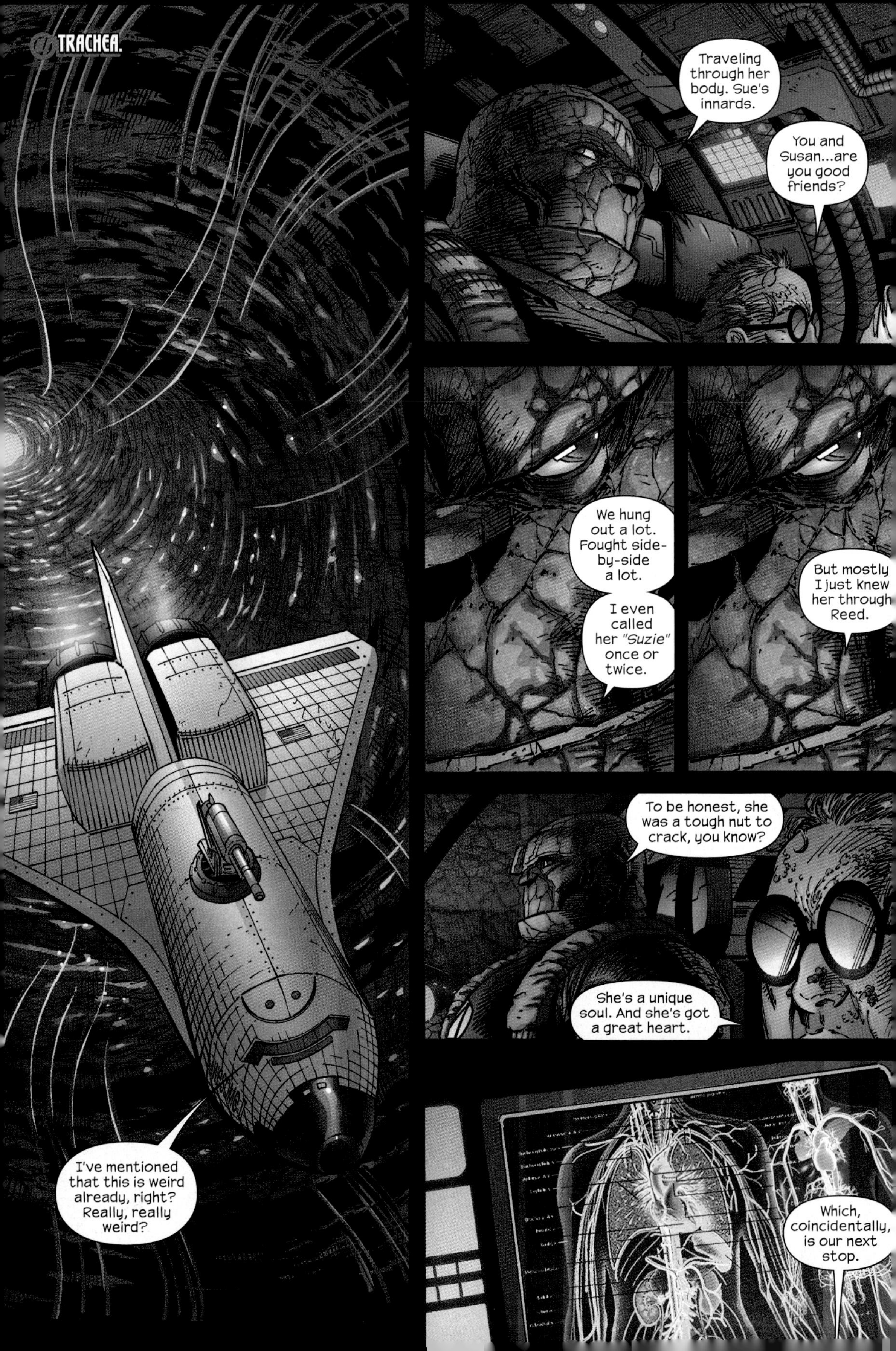
TRACHEA.
I've mentioned that this is weird already, right? Really, really weird?
Traveling through her body. Sue's innards.
You and Susan...are you good friends?
We hung out a lot. Fought side-by-side a lot.
I even called her "Suzie" once or twice.
But mostly I just knew her through Reed.
To be honest, she was a tough nut to crack, you know?
She's a unique soul. And she's got a great heart.
Which, coincidentally, is our next stop.

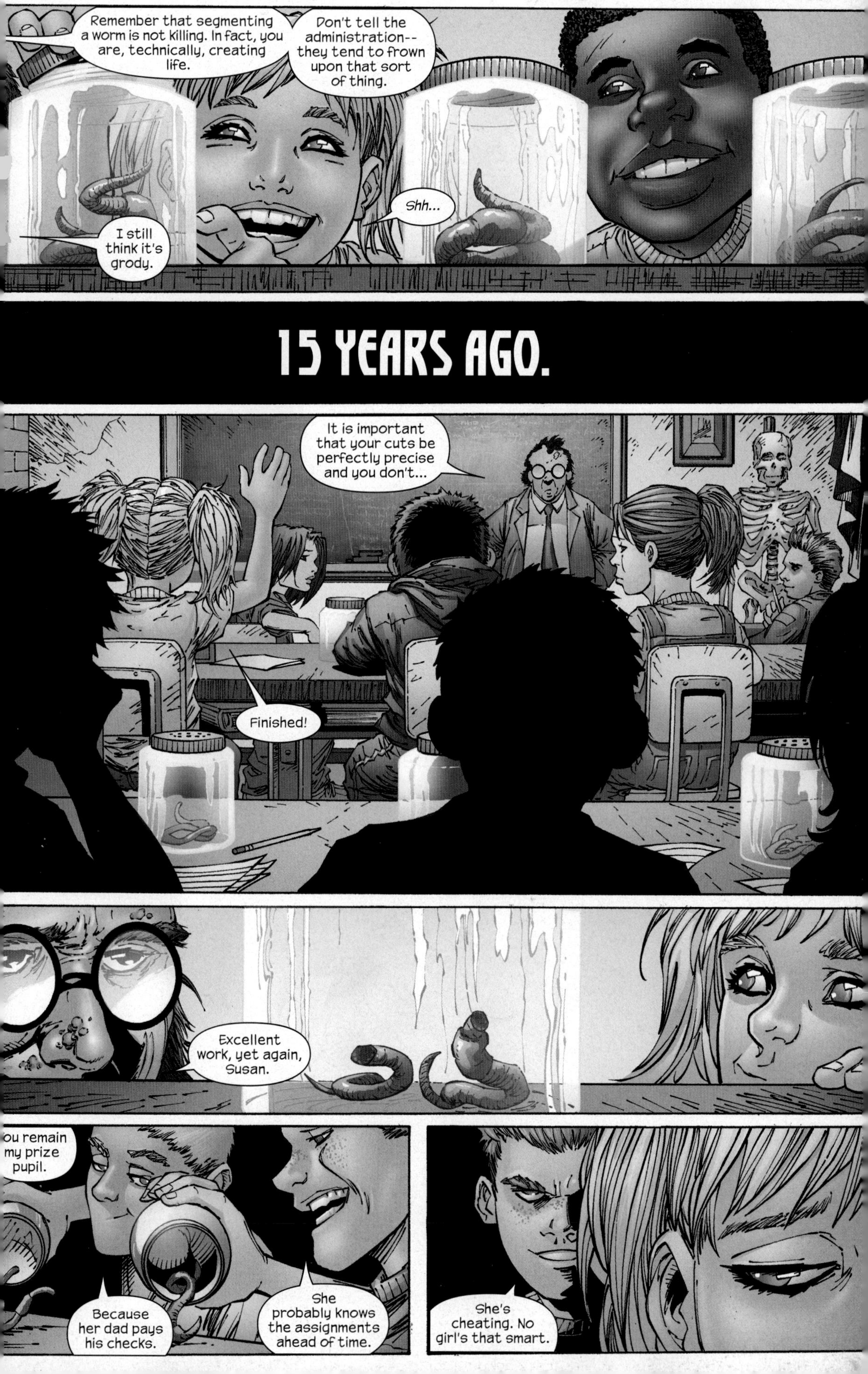
Remember that segmenting a worm is not killing. In fact, you are, technically, creating life.
Don't tell the administration-- they tend to frown upon that sort of thing.
I still think it's grody.
Shh...
15 YEARS AGO.
It is important that your cuts be perfectly precise and you don't...
Finished!
Excellent work, yet again, Susan.
ou remain my prize pupil.
Because her dad pays his checks.
She probably knows the assignments ahead of time.
She's cheating. No girl's that smart.

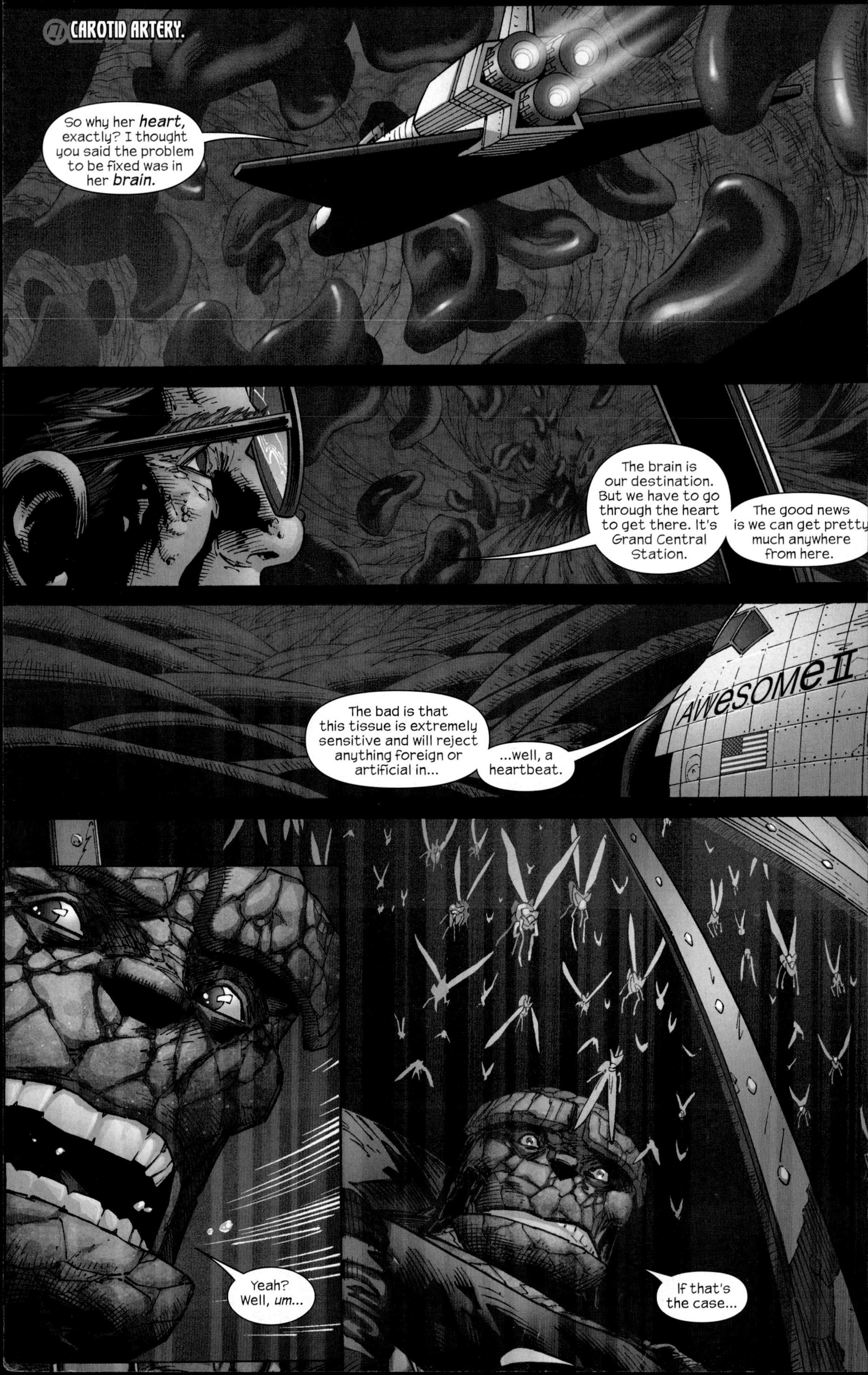
CAROTID ARTERY.
So why her heart, exactly? I thought you said the problem to be fixed was in her brain.
The brain is our destination. But we have to go through the heart to get there. It's Grand Central Station.
The good news is we can get pretty much anywhere from here.
The bad is that this tissue is extremely sensitive and will reject anything foreign or artificial in...
...well, a heartbeat.
AWESOME II
Yeah? Well, um...
If that's the case...

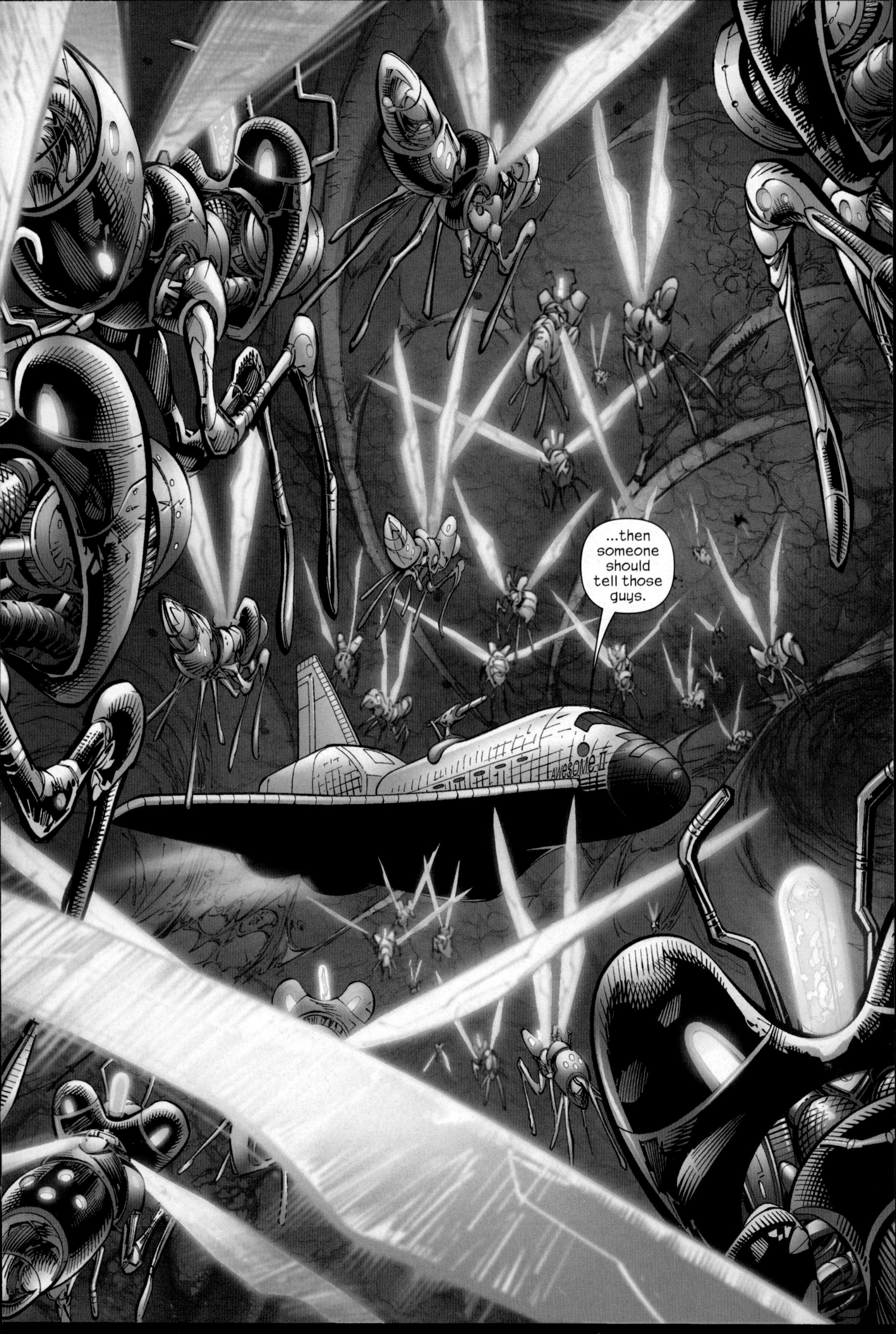
...then someone should tell those guys.
AWESOME II

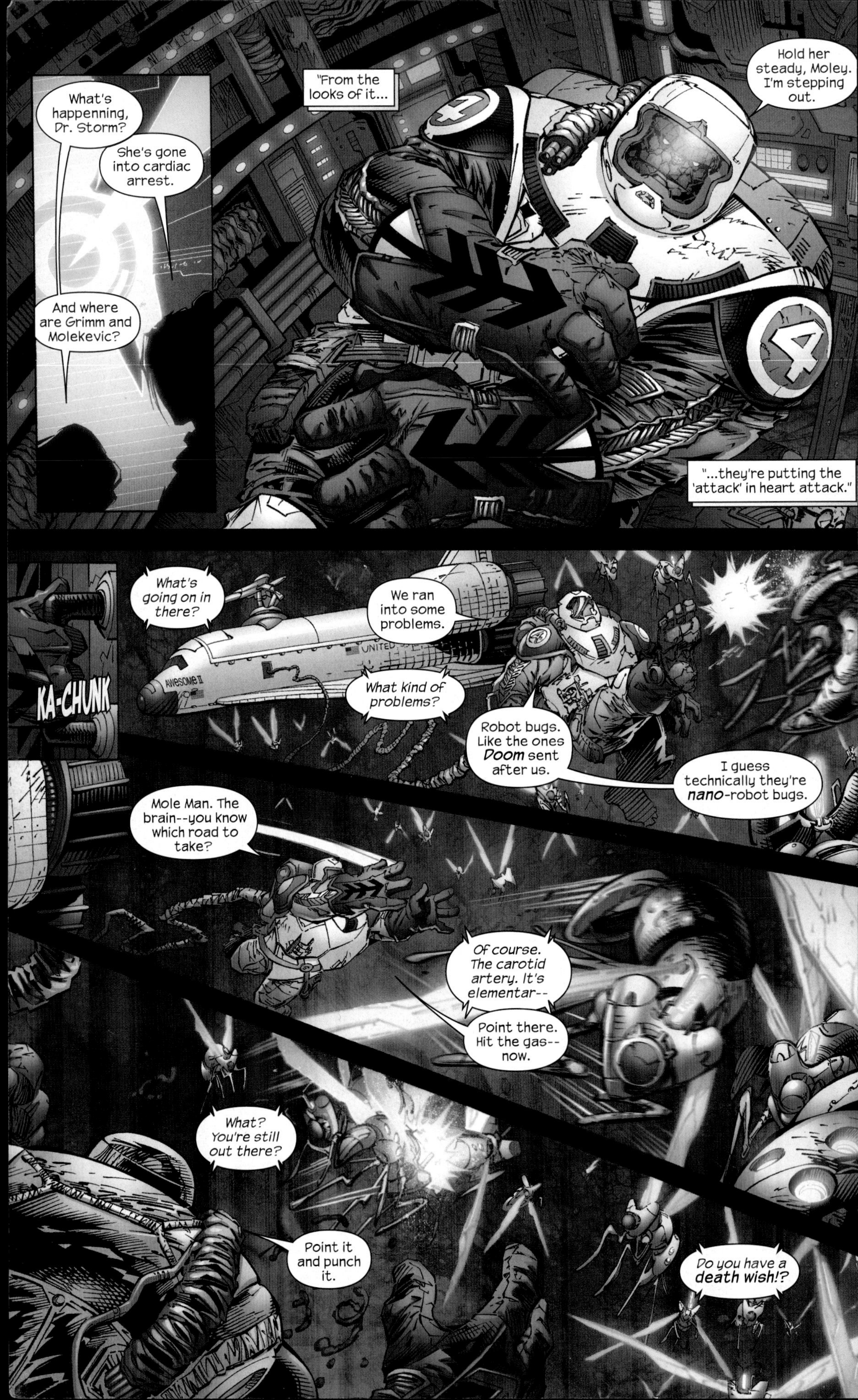

What's happenning, Dr. Storm?
She's gone into cardiac arrest.
And where are Grimm and Molekevic?
"From the looks of it...
Hold her steady, Moley. I'm stepping out.
"...they're putting the 'attack' in heart attack."
What's going on in there?
We ran into some problems.
KA-CHUNK
What kind of problems?
Robot bugs. Like the ones Doom sent after us.
I guess technically they're nano-robot bugs.
Mole Man. The brain--you know which road to take?
Of course. The carotid artery. It's elementar--
Point there. Hit the gas--now.
What? You're still out there?
Point it and punch it.
Do you have a death wish!?

9 MONTHS AGO.

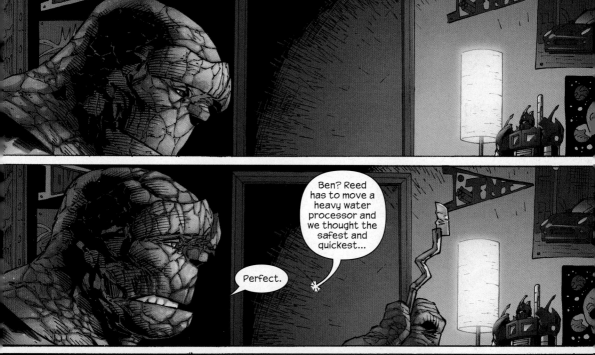

Ben? Reed has to move a heavy water processor and we thought the safest and quickest...

Perfect.

...hey.

I'm sorry, I didn't think you'd be...

It's okay.

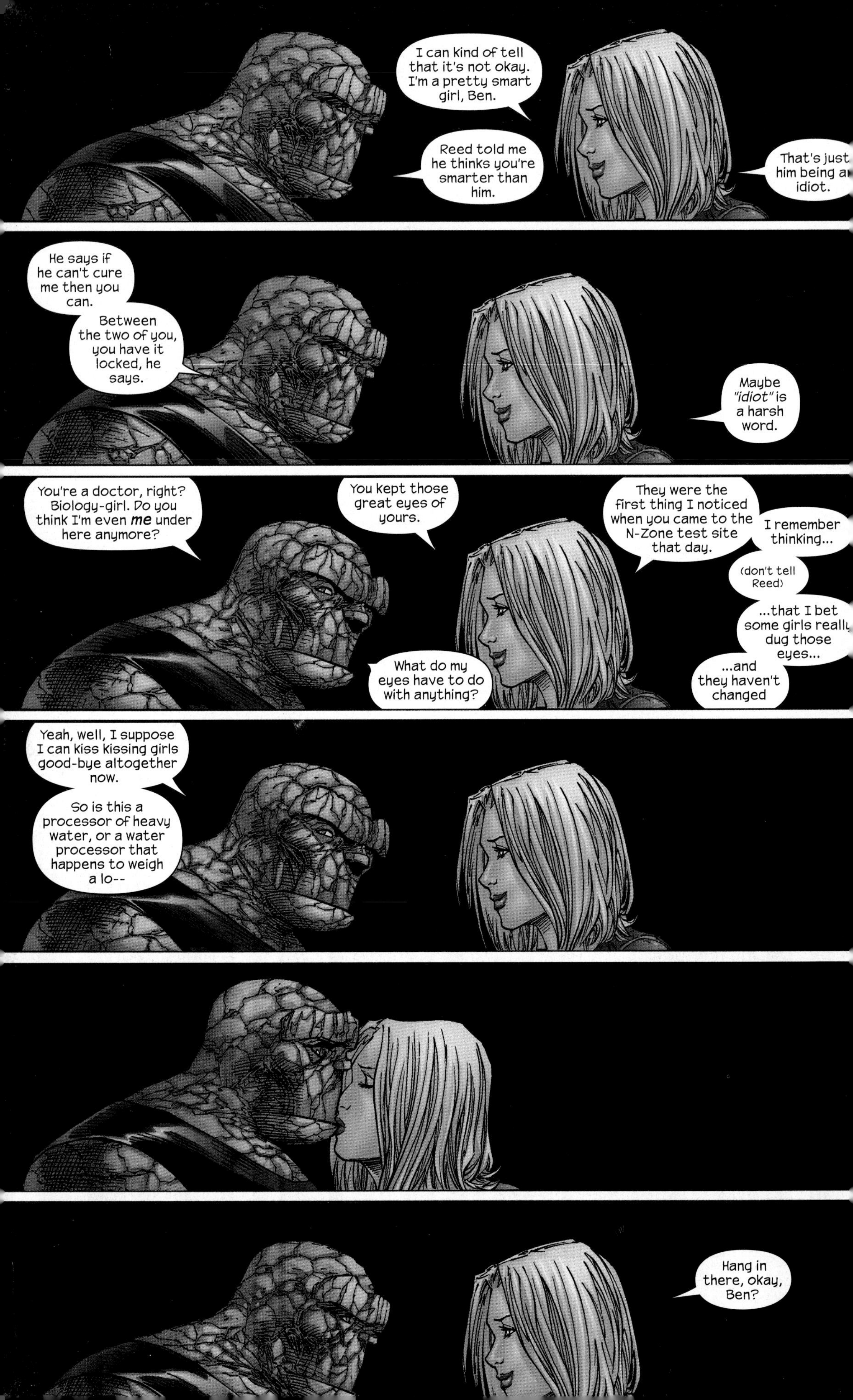
I can kind of tell that it's not okay. I'm a pretty smart girl, Ben.
Reed told me he thinks you're smarter than him.
That's just him being an idiot.
He says if he can't cure me then you can.
Between the two of you, you have it locked, he says.
Maybe "idiot" is a harsh word.
You're a doctor, right? Biology-girl. Do you think I'm even **me** under here anymore?
You kept those great eyes of yours.
They were the first thing I noticed when you came to the N-Zone test site that day.
I remember thinking...
(don't tell Reed)
...that I bet some girls really dug those eyes...
What do my eyes have to do with anything?
...and they haven't changed
Yeah, well, I suppose I can kiss kissing girls good-bye altogether now.
So is this a processor of heavy water, or a water processor that happens to weigh a lo--
Hang in there, okay, Ben?

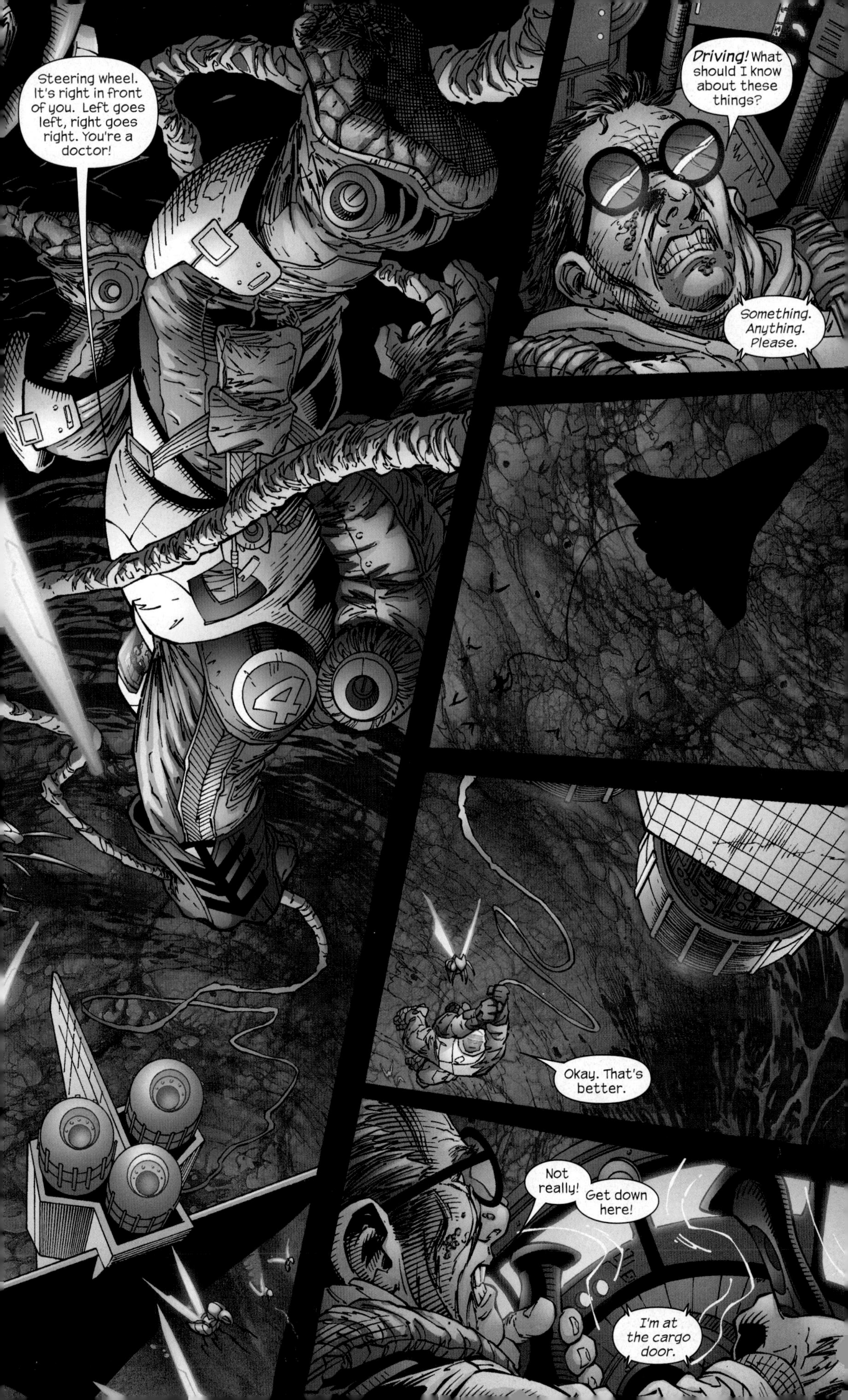
Steering wheel. It's right in front of you. Left goes left, right goes right. You're a doctor!
Driving! What should I know about these things?
Something. Anything. Please.
Okay. That's better.
Not really!
Get down here!
I'm at the cargo door.

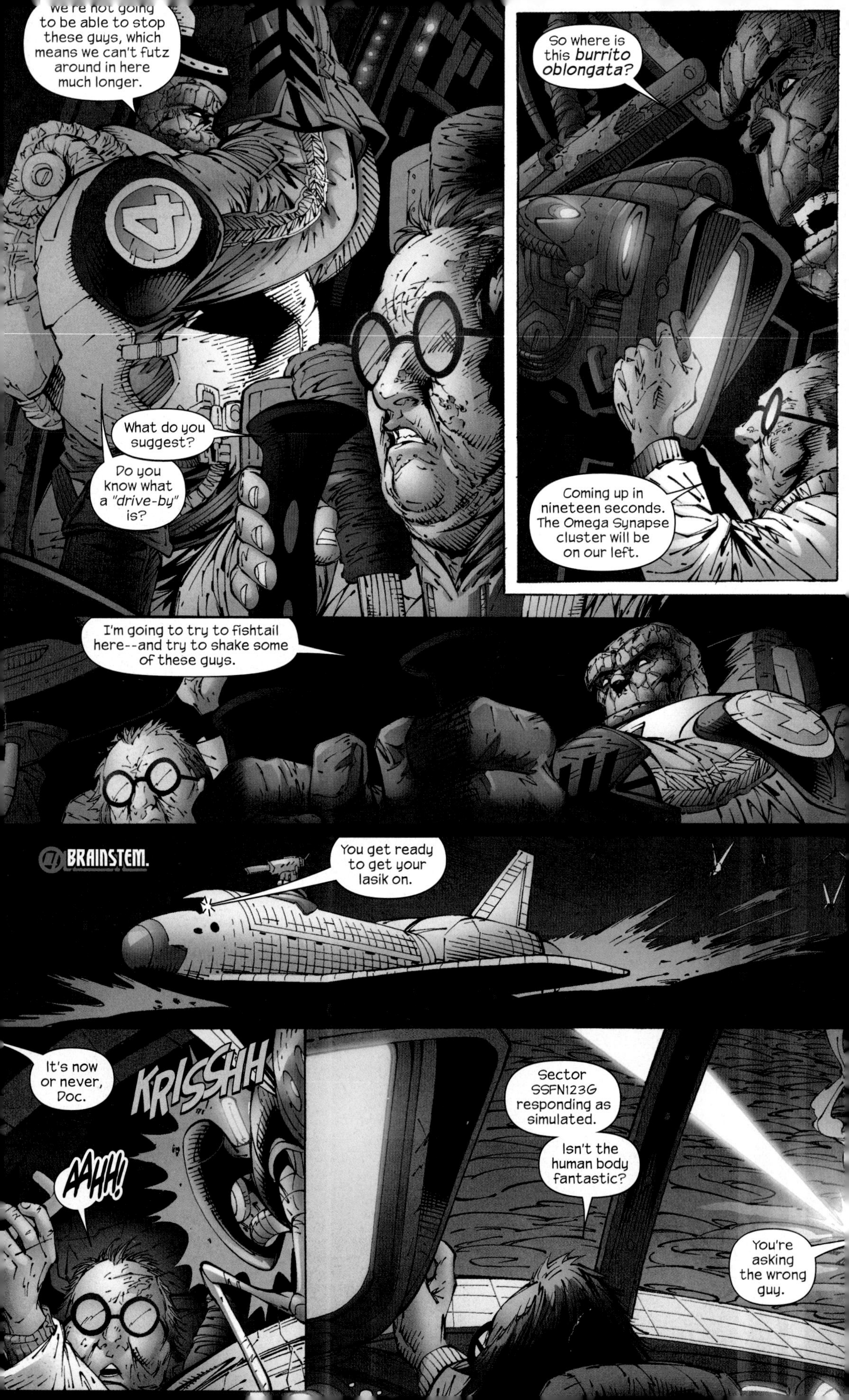
We're not going to be able to stop these guys, which means we can't futz around in here much longer.
So where is this *burrito oblongata?*
What do you suggest?
Do you know what a "*drive-by*" is?
Coming up in nineteen seconds. The Omega Synapse cluster will be on our left.
I'm going to try to fishtail here--and try to shake some of these guys.
BRAINSTEM.
You get ready to get your lasik on.
It's now or never, Doc.
KRISSHH
AAHH!
Sector SSFN123G responding as simulated.
Isn't the human body fantastic?
You're asking the wrong guy.

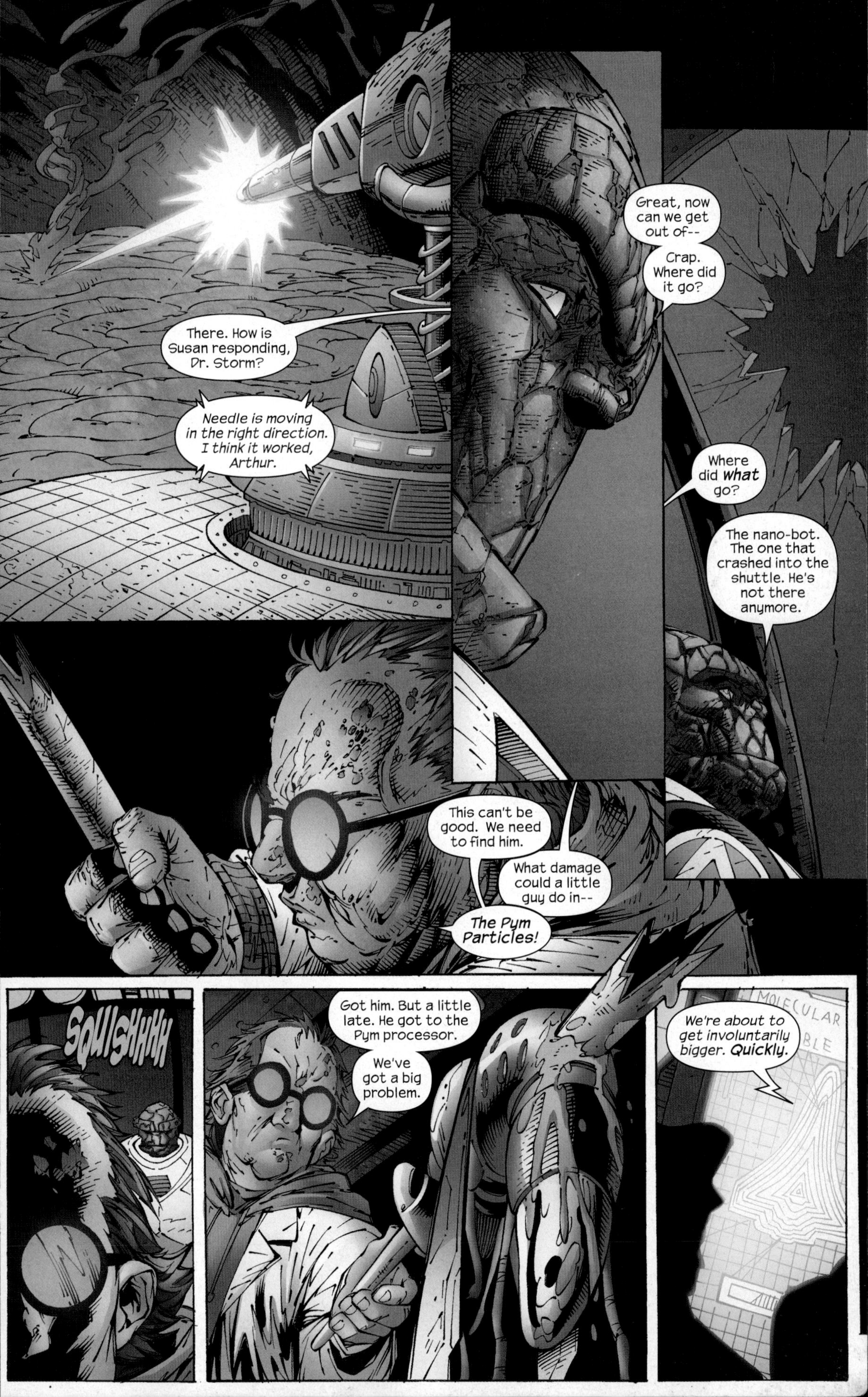

Great, now can we get out of--
Crap. Where did it go?
There. How is Susan responding, Dr. Storm?
Needle is moving in the right direction. I think it worked, Arthur.
Where did ***what*** go?
The nano-bot. The one that crashed into the shuttle. He's not there anymore.
This can't be good. We need to find him.
What damage could a little guy do in--
The Pym Particles!
SQUISHHHH
Got him. But a little late. He got to the Pym processor.
We've got a big problem.
*We're about to get involuntarily bigger. **Quickly**.*

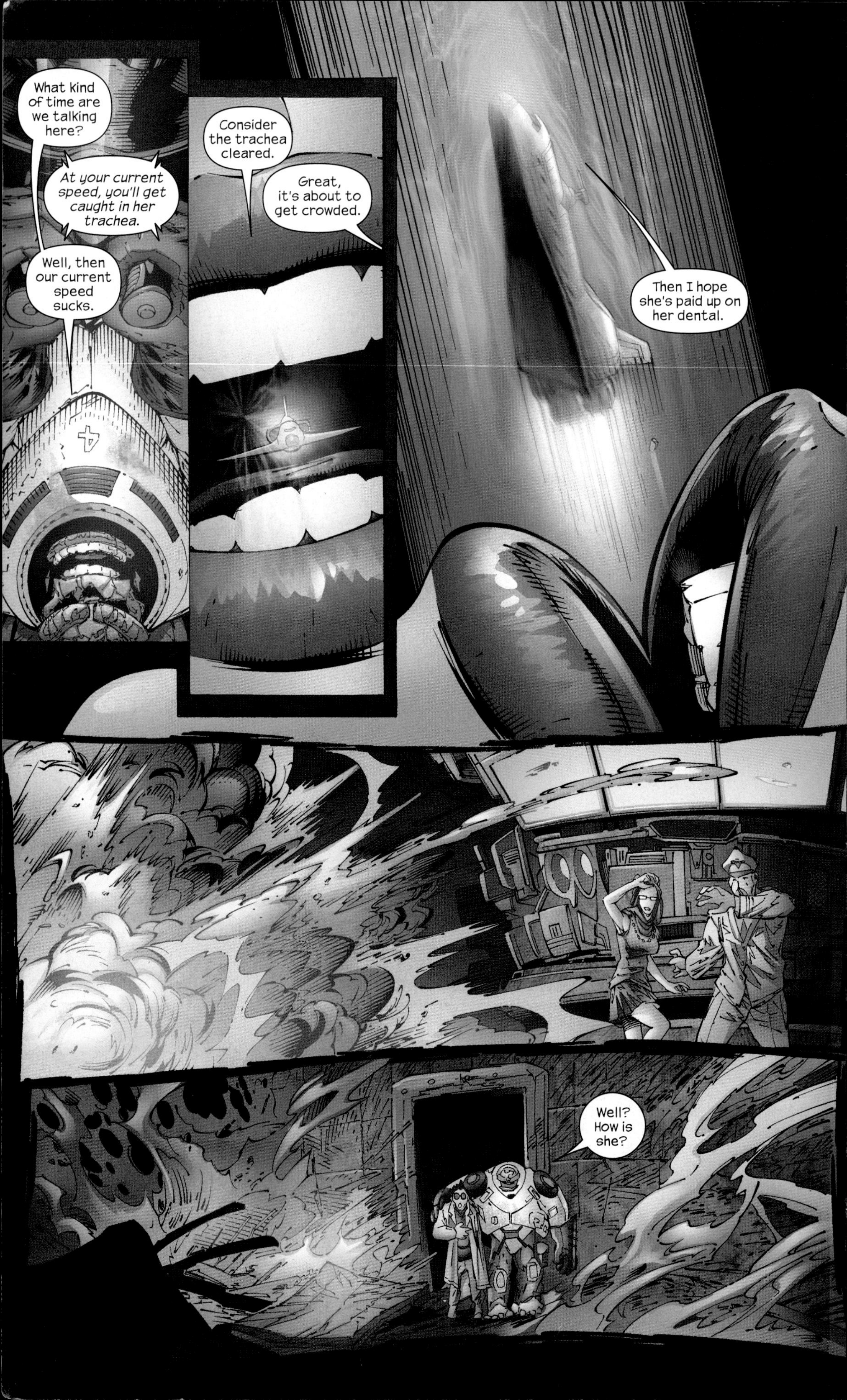
What kind of time are we talking here?
At your current speed, you'll get caught in her trachea.
Well, then our current speed sucks.
Consider the trachea cleared.
Great, it's about to get crowded.
Then I hope she's paid up on her dental.
Well? How is she?

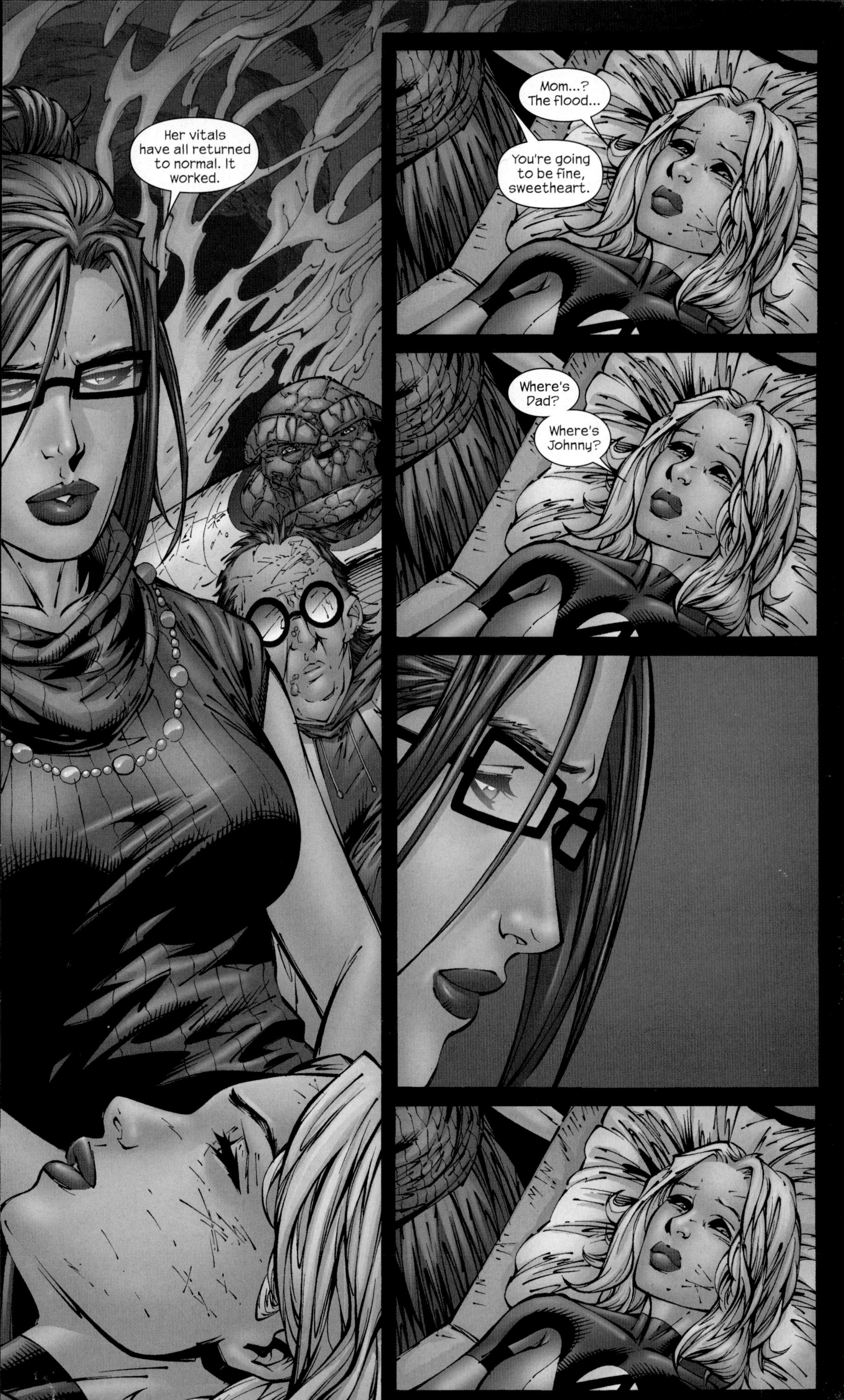
Her vitals have all returned to normal. It worked.
Mom...? The flood...
You're going to be fine, sweetheart.
Where's Dad?
Where's Johnny?

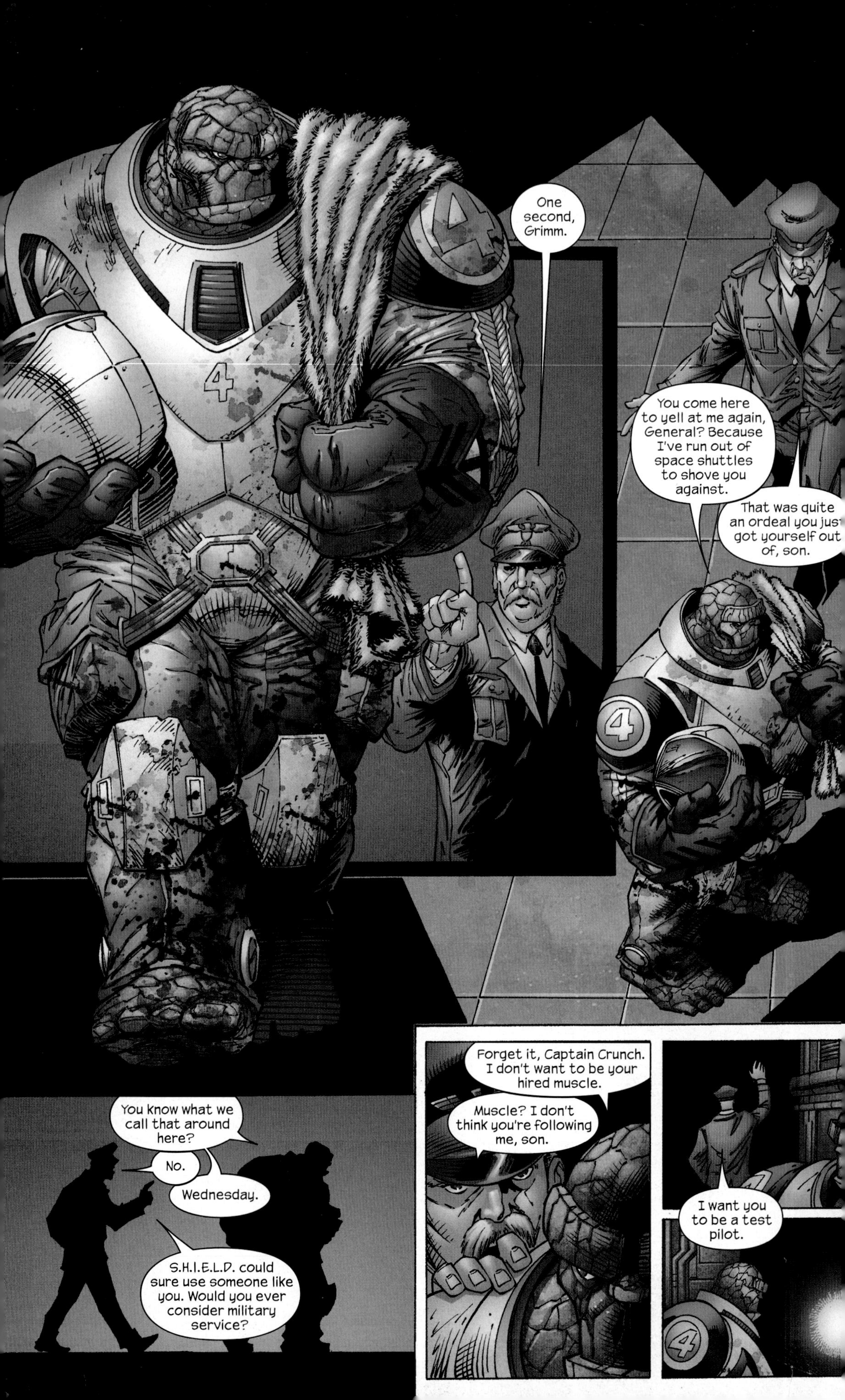
One second, Grimm.
You come here to yell at me again, General? Because I've run out of space shuttles to shove you against.
That was quite an ordeal you just got yourself out of, son.
You know what we call that around here?
No.
Wednesday.
S.H.I.E.L.D. could sure use someone like you. Would you ever consider military service?
Forget it, Captain Crunch. I don't want to be your hired muscle.
Muscle? I don't think you're following me, son.
I want you to be a test pilot.

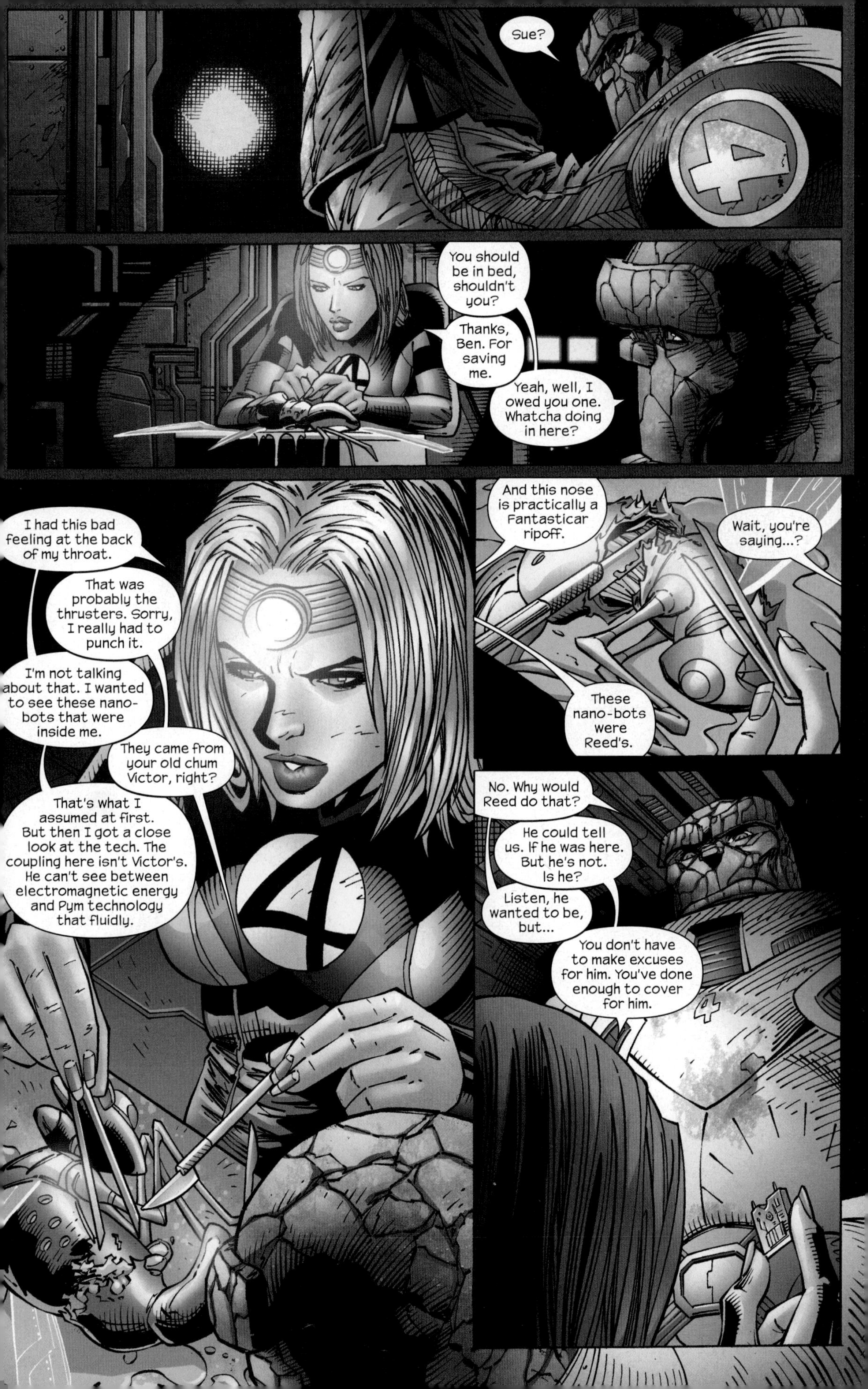
Sue?
You should be in bed, shouldn't you?
Thanks, Ben. For saving me.
Yeah, well, I owed you one. Whatcha doing in here?
I had this bad feeling at the back of my throat.
That was probably the thrusters. Sorry, I really had to punch it.
I'm not talking about that. I wanted to see these nano-bots that were inside me.
They came from your old chum Victor, right?
That's what I assumed at first. But then I got a close look at the tech. The coupling here isn't Victor's. He can't see between electromagnetic energy and Pym technology that fluidly.
And this nose is practically a Fantasticar ripoff.
Wait, you're saying...?
These nano-bots were Reed's.
No. Why would Reed do that?
He could tell us. If he was here. But he's not. Is he?
Listen, he wanted to be, but...
You don't have to make excuses for him. You've done enough to cover for him.

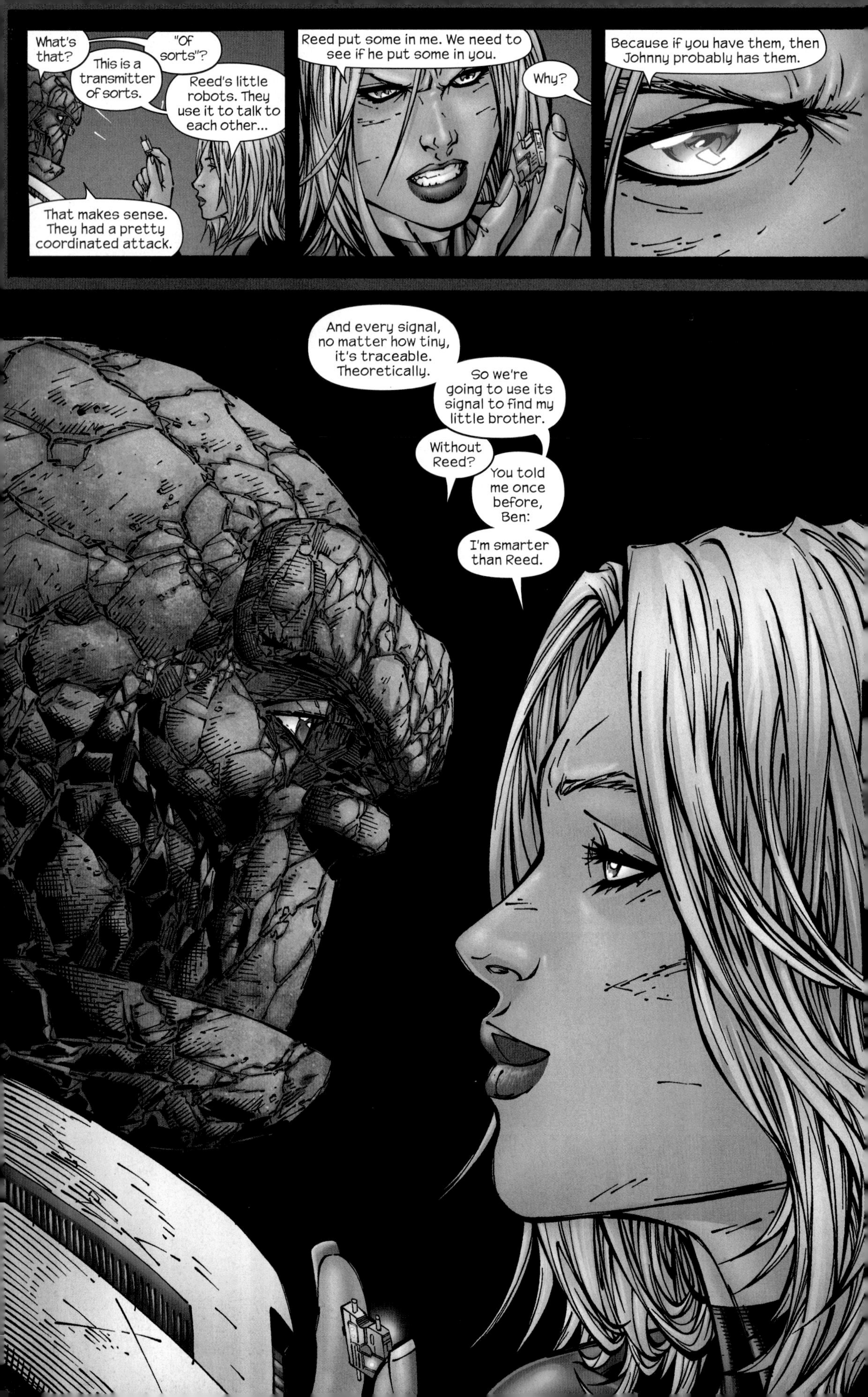

What's that?
This is a transmitter of sorts.
"Of sorts"?
Reed's little robots. They use it to talk to each other...
That makes sense. They had a pretty coordinated attack.
Reed put some in me. We need to see if he put some in you.
Why?
Because if you have them, then Johnny probably has them.
And every signal, no matter how tiny, it's traceable. Theoretically.
So we're going to use its signal to find my little brother.
Without Reed?
You told me once before, Ben:
I'm smarter than Reed.

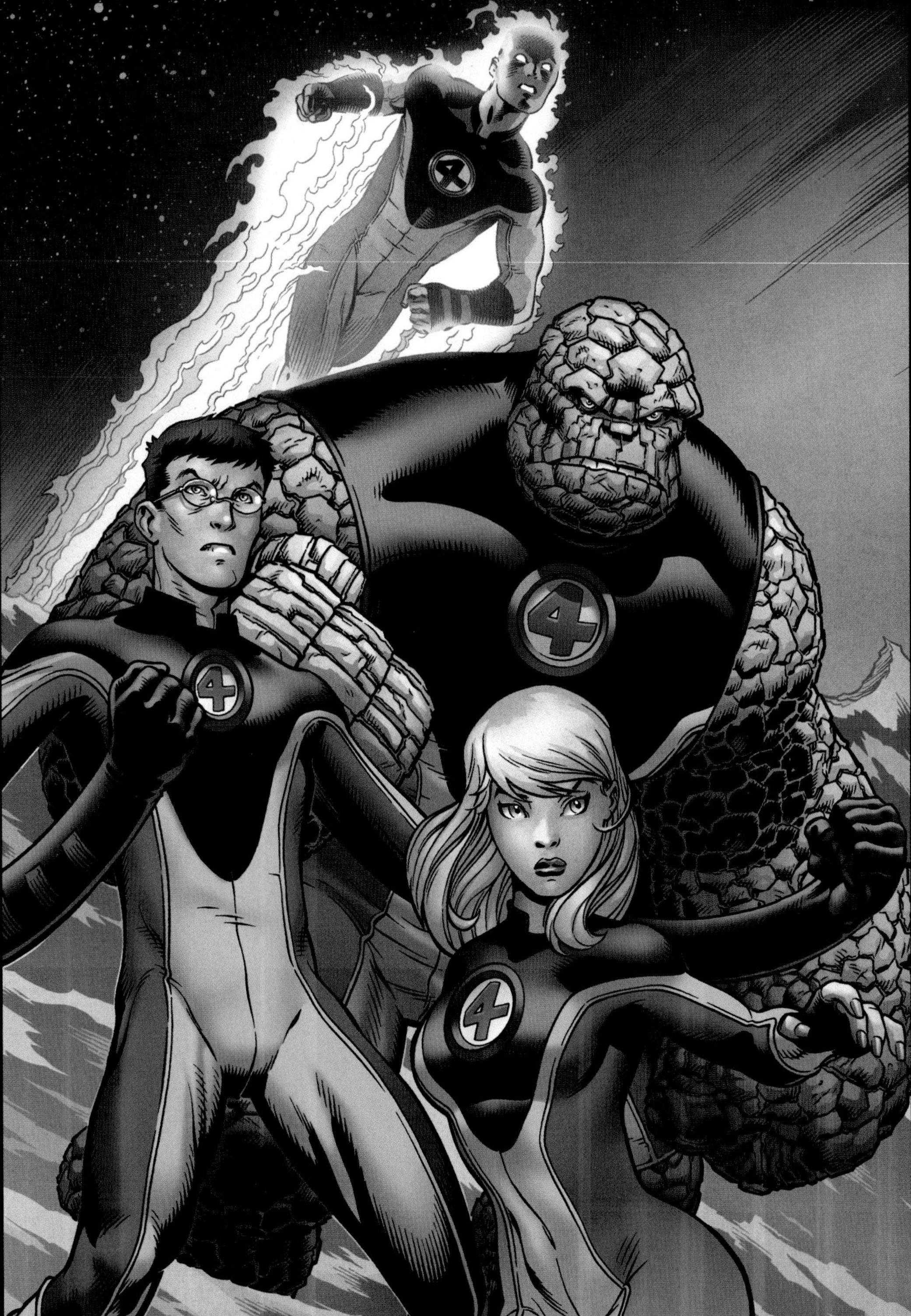

ULTIMATE FANTASTIC FOUR #60

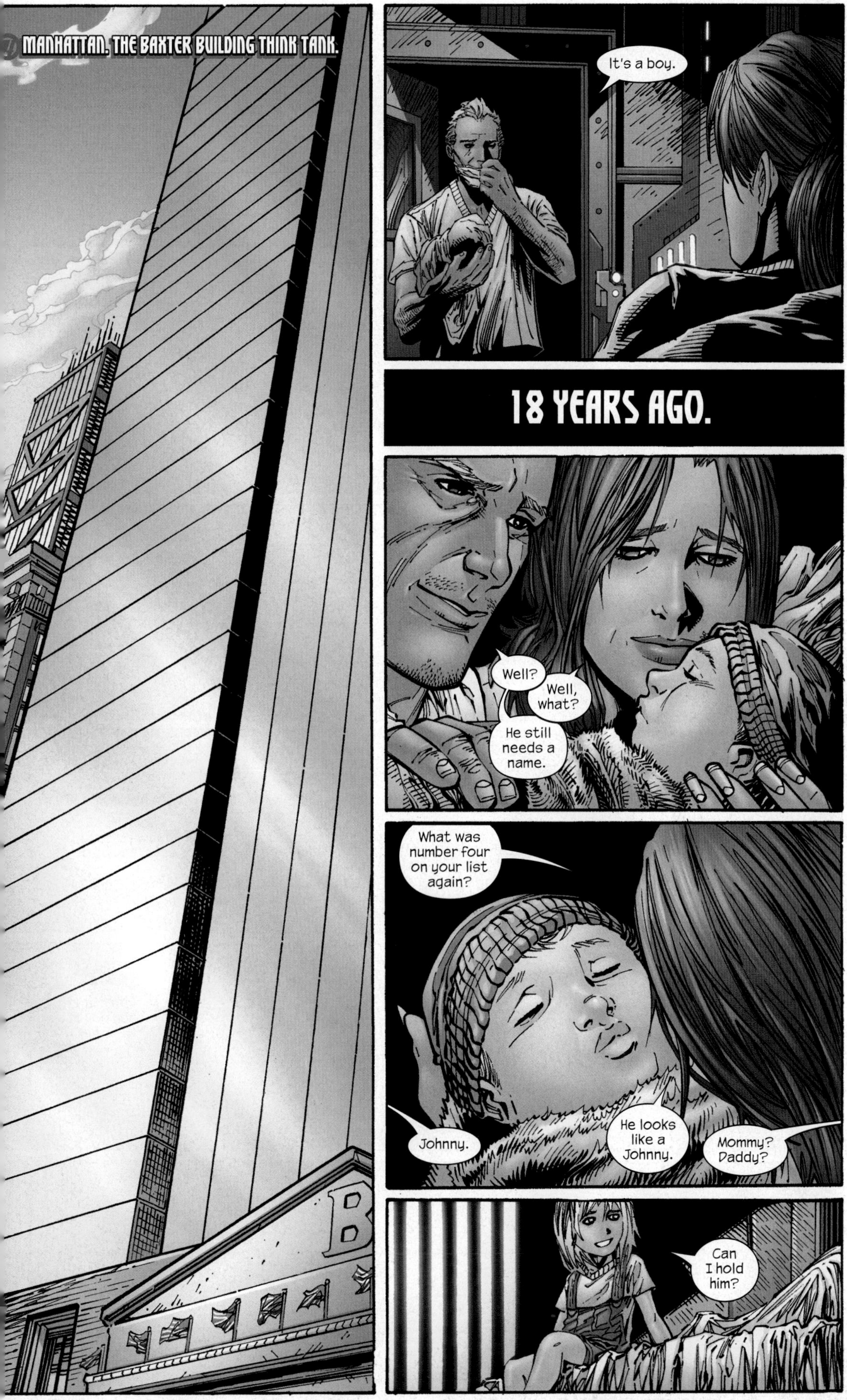
MANHATTAN. THE BAXTER BUILDING THINK TANK.
It's a boy.
18 YEARS AGO.
Well?
Well, what?
He still needs a name.
What was number four on your list again?
Johnny.
He looks like a Johnny.
Mommy? Daddy?
Can I hold him?

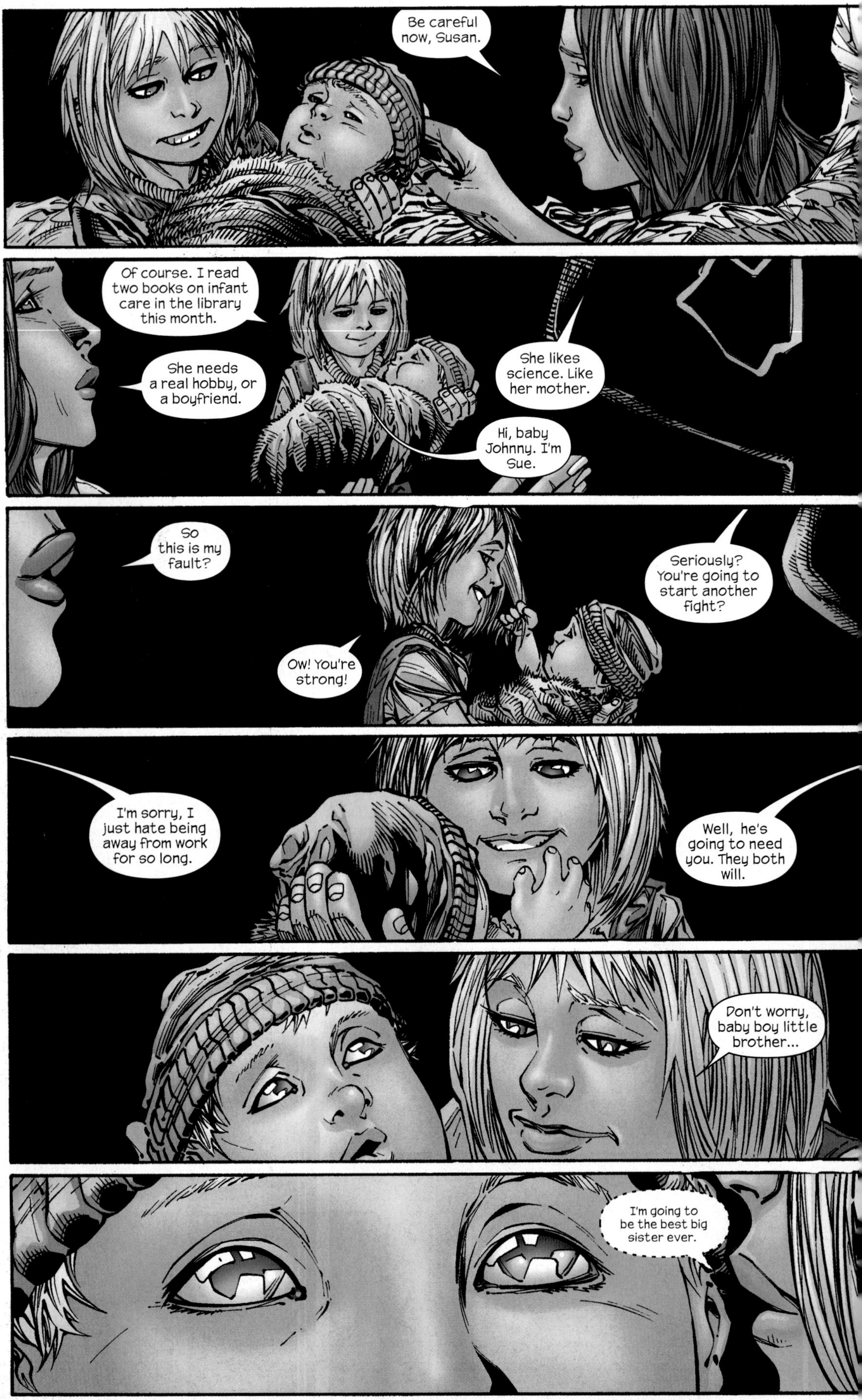
Be careful now, Susan.
Of course. I read two books on infant care in the library this month.
She needs a real hobby, or a boyfriend.
She likes science. Like her mother.
Hi, baby Johnny. I'm Sue.
So this is my fault?
Seriously? You're going to start another fight?
Ow! You're strong!
I'm sorry, I just hate being away from work for so long.
Well, he's going to need you. They both will.
Don't worry, baby boy little brother...
I'm going to be the best big sister ever.

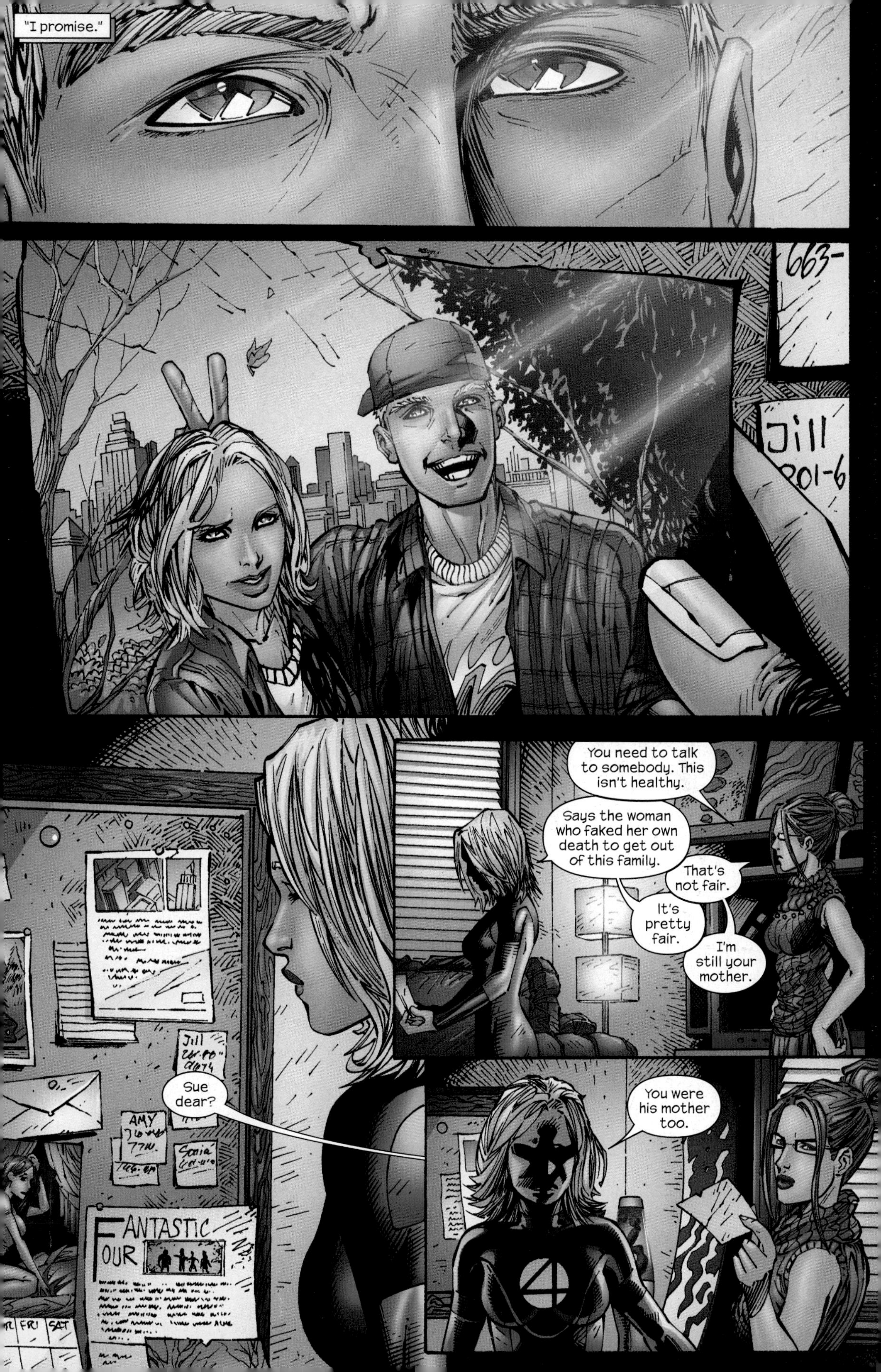
"I promise."
663-
Jill
201-6
You need to talk to somebody. This isn't healthy.
Says the woman who faked her own death to get out of this family.
That's not fair.
It's pretty fair.
I'm still your mother.
Sue dear?
You were his mother too.
FANTASTIC FOUR

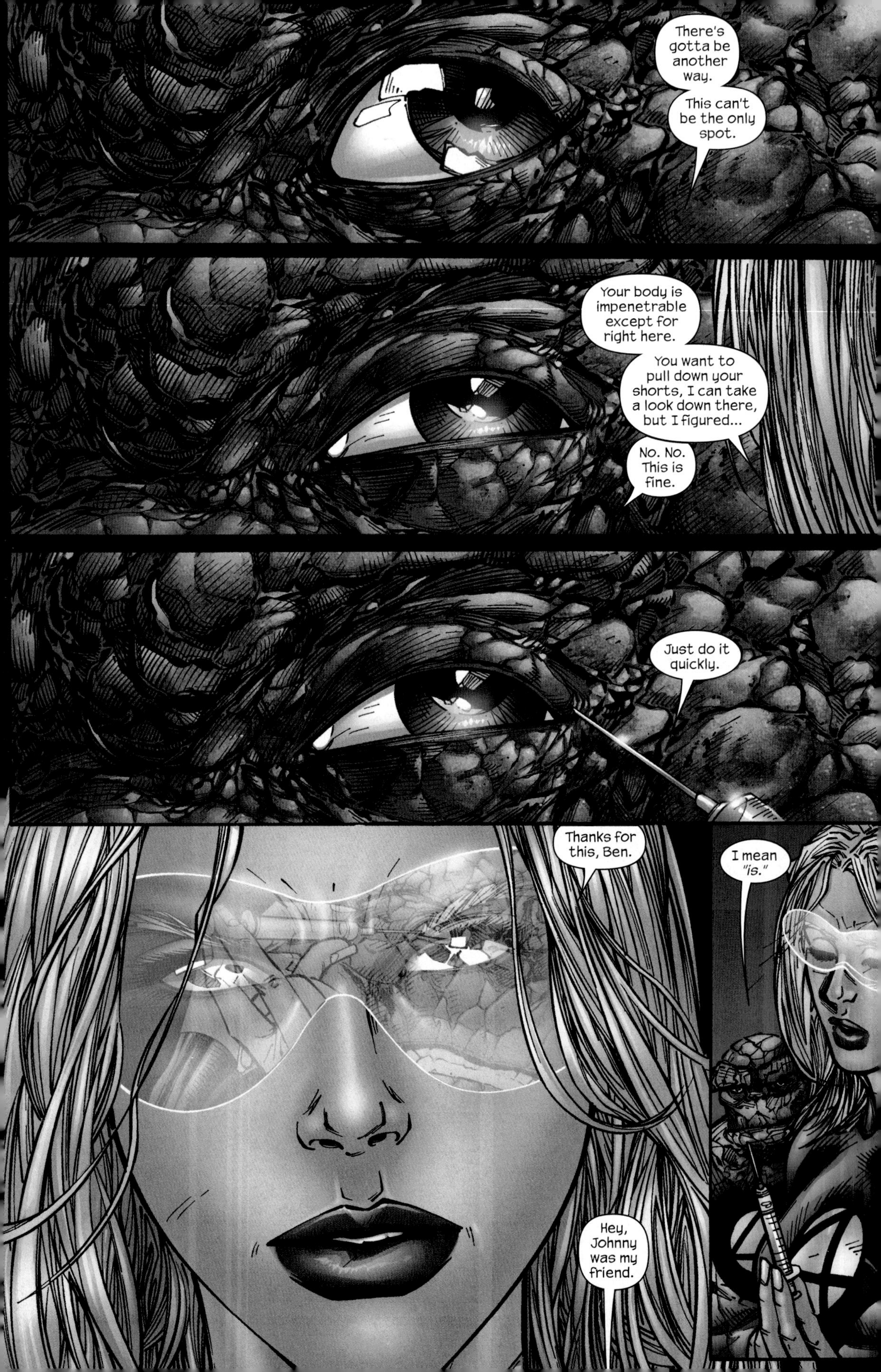
There's gotta be another way.
This can't be the only spot.
Your body is impenetrable except for right here.
You want to pull down your shorts, I can take a look down there, but I figured...
No. No. This is fine.
Just do it quickly.
Thanks for this, Ben.
Hey, Johnny was my friend.
I mean "is."

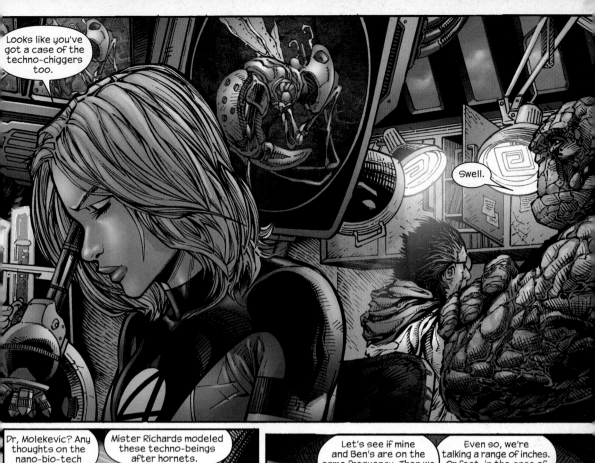

Looks like you've got a case of the techno-chiggers too.

Swell.

Dr, Molekevic? Any thoughts on the nano-bio-tech of it all?

Mister Richards modeled these techno-beings after hornets.

What's of interest to us is their hive-mentality communication method.

So they do talk to each other?

Within the same host, yes, but who knows if they can talk inter-body.

Let's see if mine and Ben's are on the same frequency. Then we can assume Johnny's are as well.

Even so, we're talking a range of inches. Or feet, in the case of this enlarged one.

So we upgrade their equipment to boost the signal. What would they need?

An antenna. Two to six million times as powerful as this one.

I don't suppose you know where we can find that.

No...

...but your mother might.

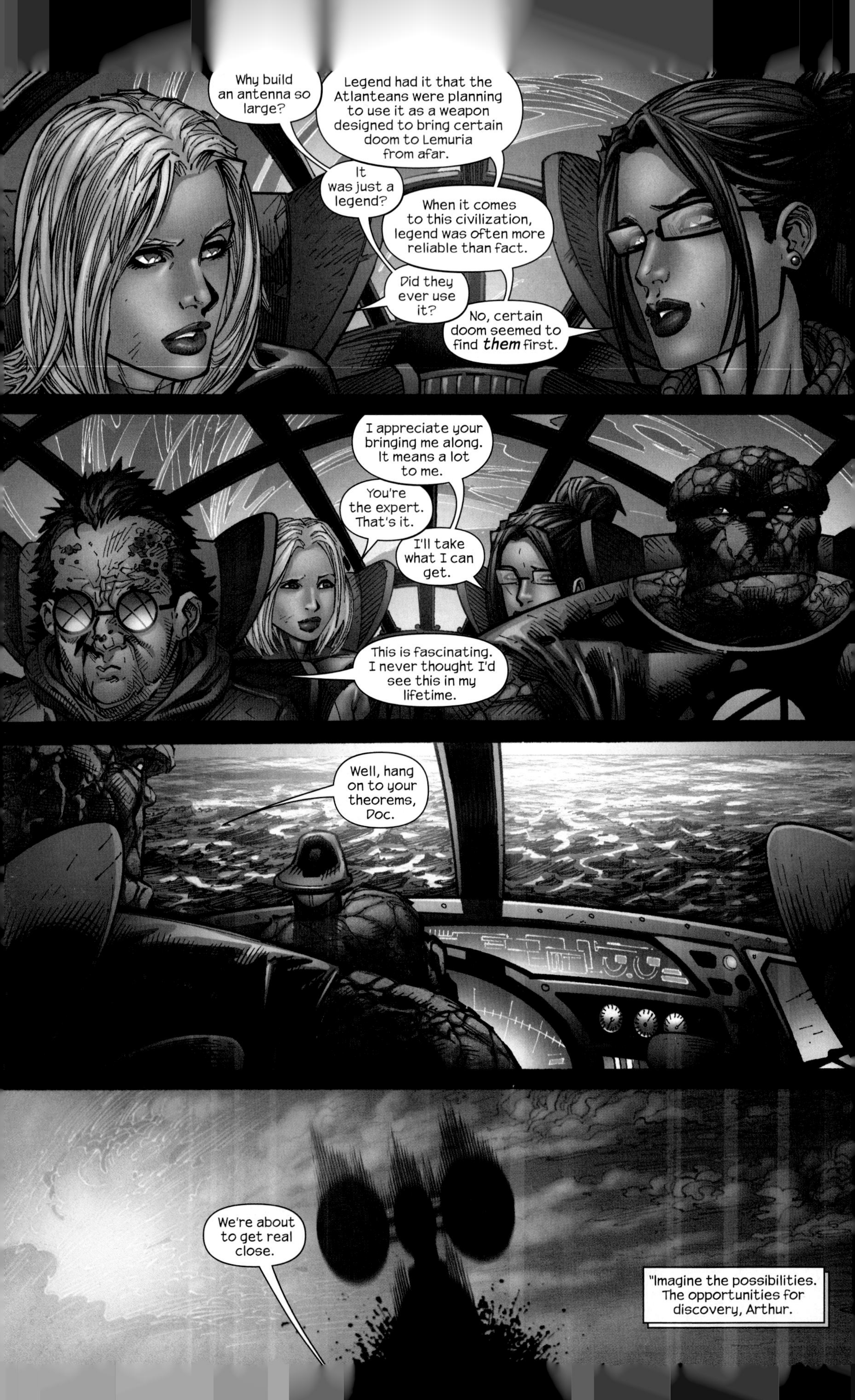
Why build an antenna so large?
Legend had it that the Atlanteans were planning to use it as a weapon designed to bring certain doom to Lemuria from afar.
It was just a legend?
When it comes to this civilization, legend was often more reliable than fact.
Did they ever use it?
No, certain doom seemed to find *them* first.
I appreciate your bringing me along. It means a lot to me.
You're the expert. That's it.
I'll take what I can get.
This is fascinating. I never thought I'd see this in my lifetime.
Well, hang on to your theorems, Doc.
We're about to get real close.
"Imagine the possibilities. The opportunities for discovery, Arthur.

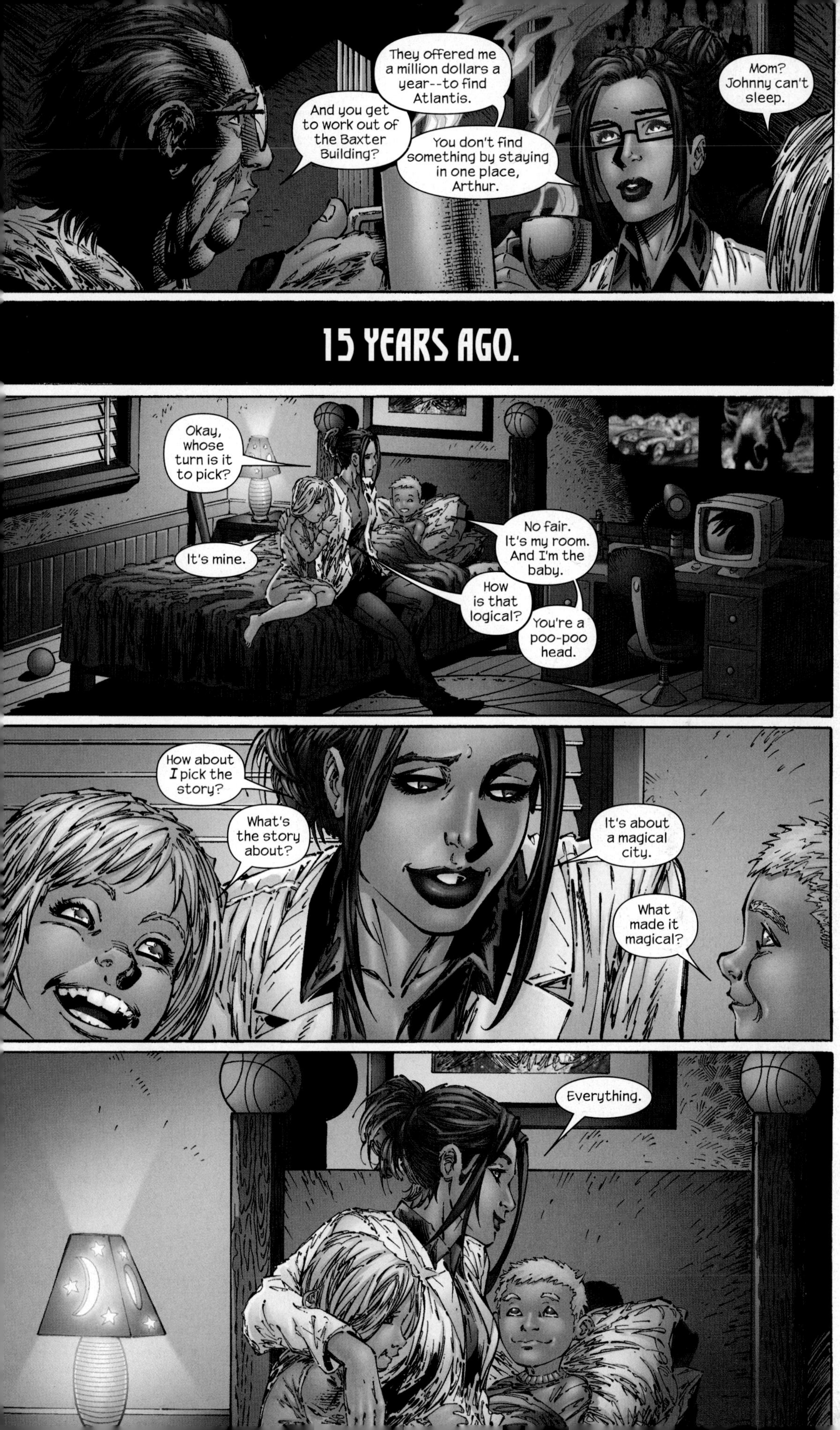
And you get to work out of the Baxter Building?
They offered me a million dollars a year--to find Atlantis.
You don't find something by staying in one place, Arthur.
Mom? Johnny can't sleep.
15 YEARS AGO.
Okay, whose turn is it to pick?
It's mine.
No fair. It's my room. And I'm the baby.
How is that logical?
You're a poo-poo head.
How about I pick the story?
What's the story about?
It's about a magical city.
What made it magical?
Everything.

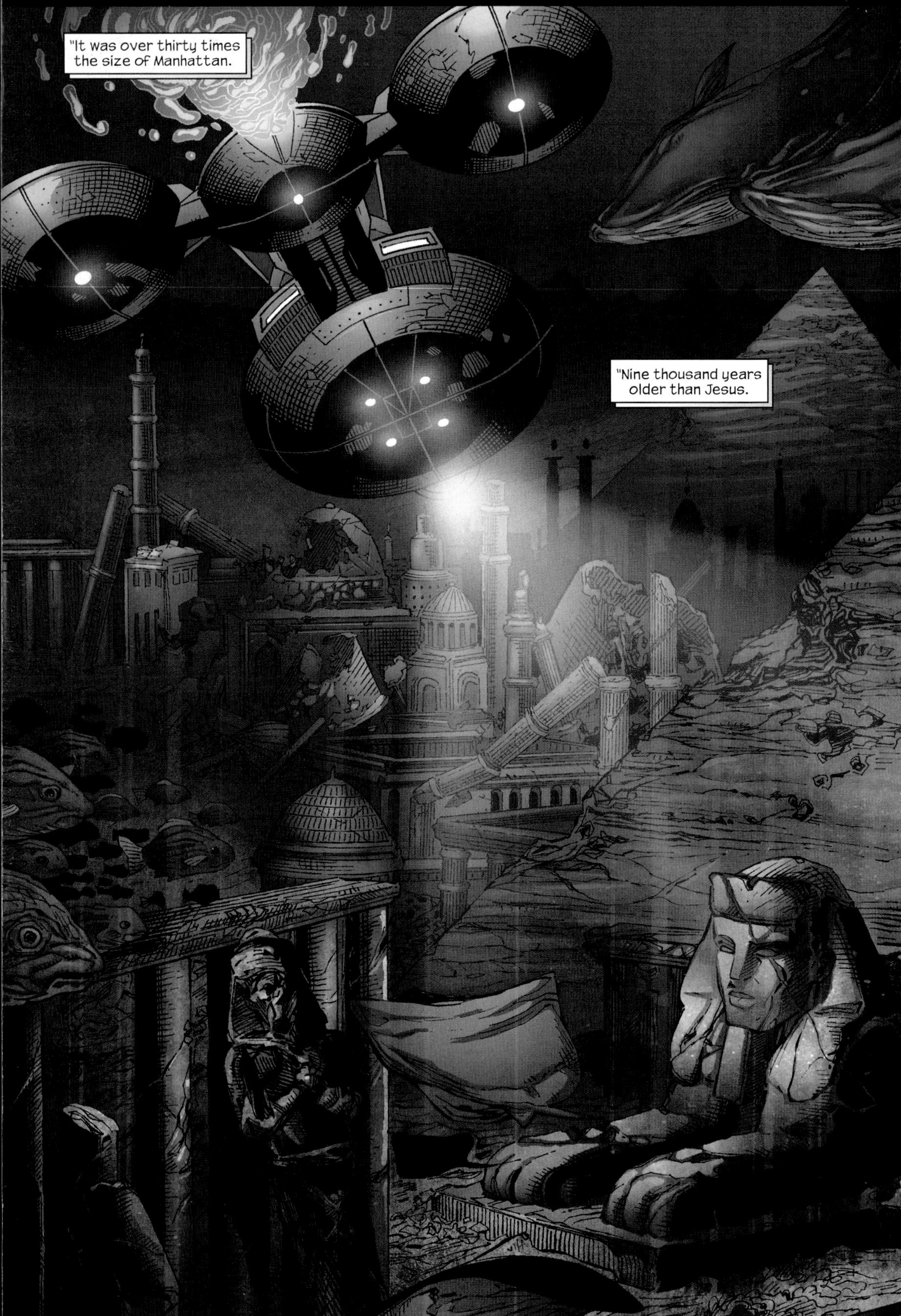
"It was over thirty times the size of Manhattan.
"Nine thousand years older than Jesus.

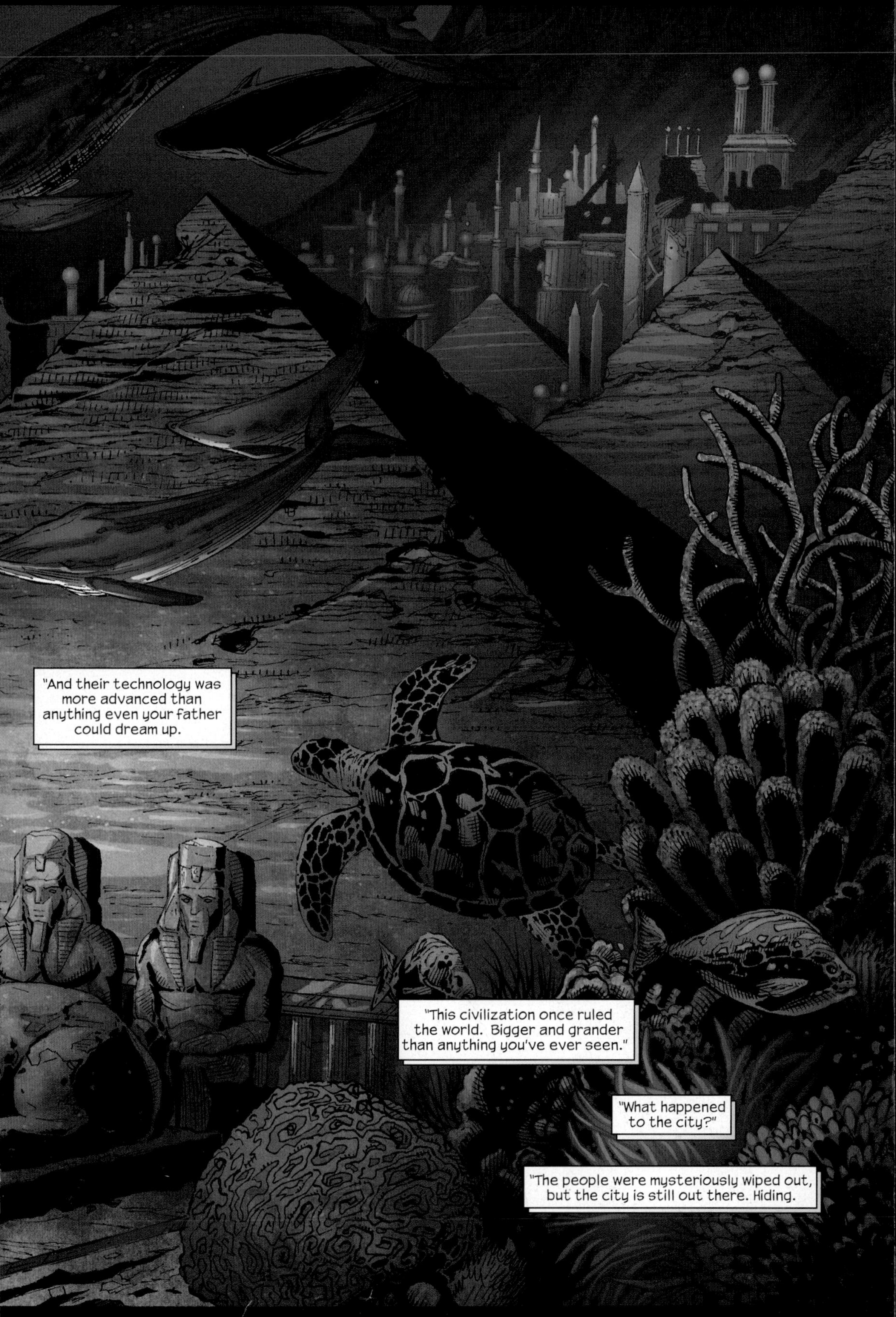
"And their technology was more advanced than anything even your father could dream up.
"This civilization once ruled the world. Bigger and grander than anything you've ever seen."
"What happened to the city?"
"The people were mysteriously wiped out, but the city is still out there. Hiding.

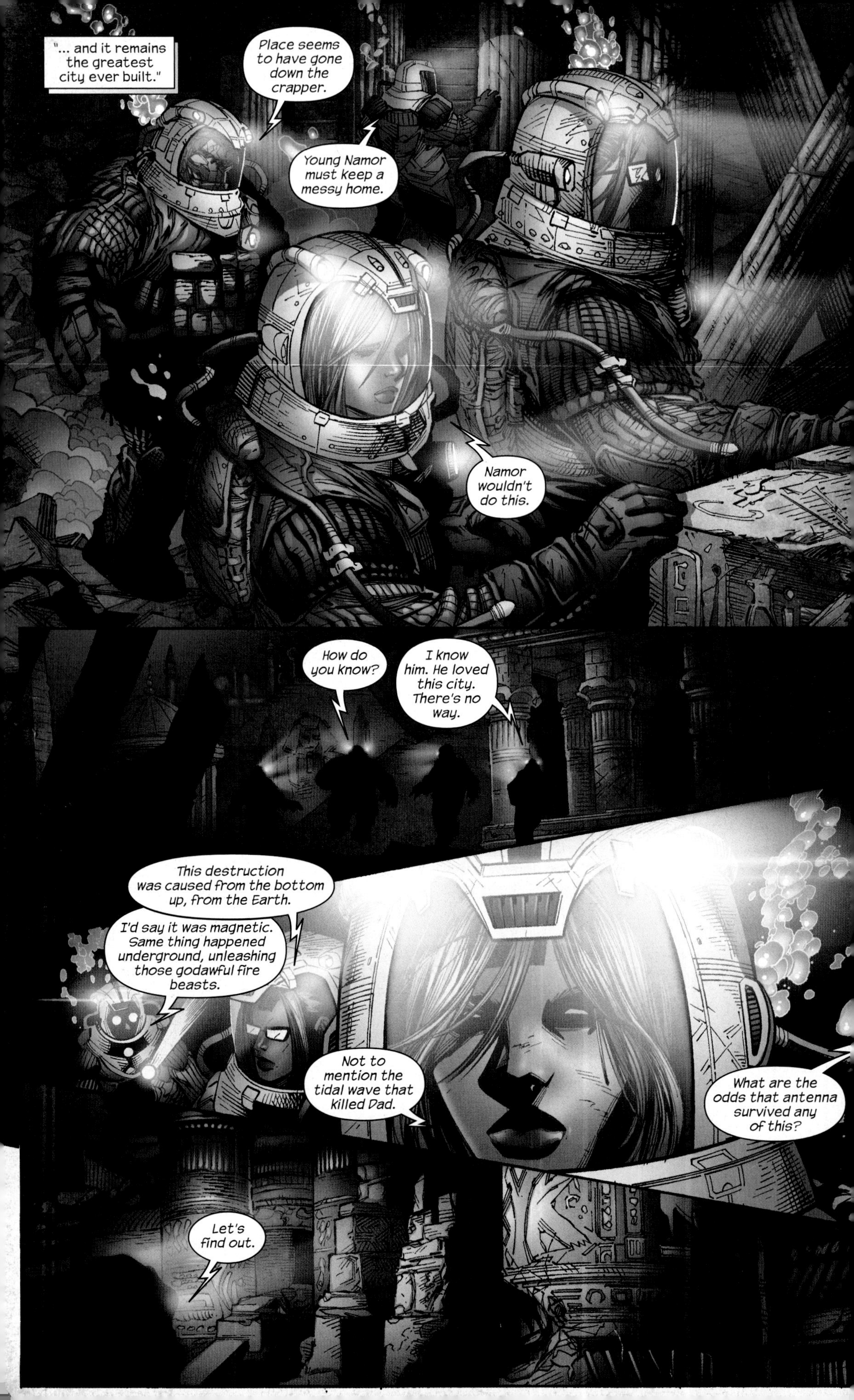
"... and it remains the greatest city ever built."
Place seems to have gone down the crapper.
Young Namor must keep a messy home.
Namor wouldn't do this.
How do you know?
I know him. He loved this city. There's no way.
This destruction was caused from the bottom up, from the Earth.
I'd say it was magnetic. Same thing happened underground, unleashing those godawful fire beasts.
Not to mention the tidal wave that killed Dad.
What are the odds that antenna survived any of this?
Let's find out.

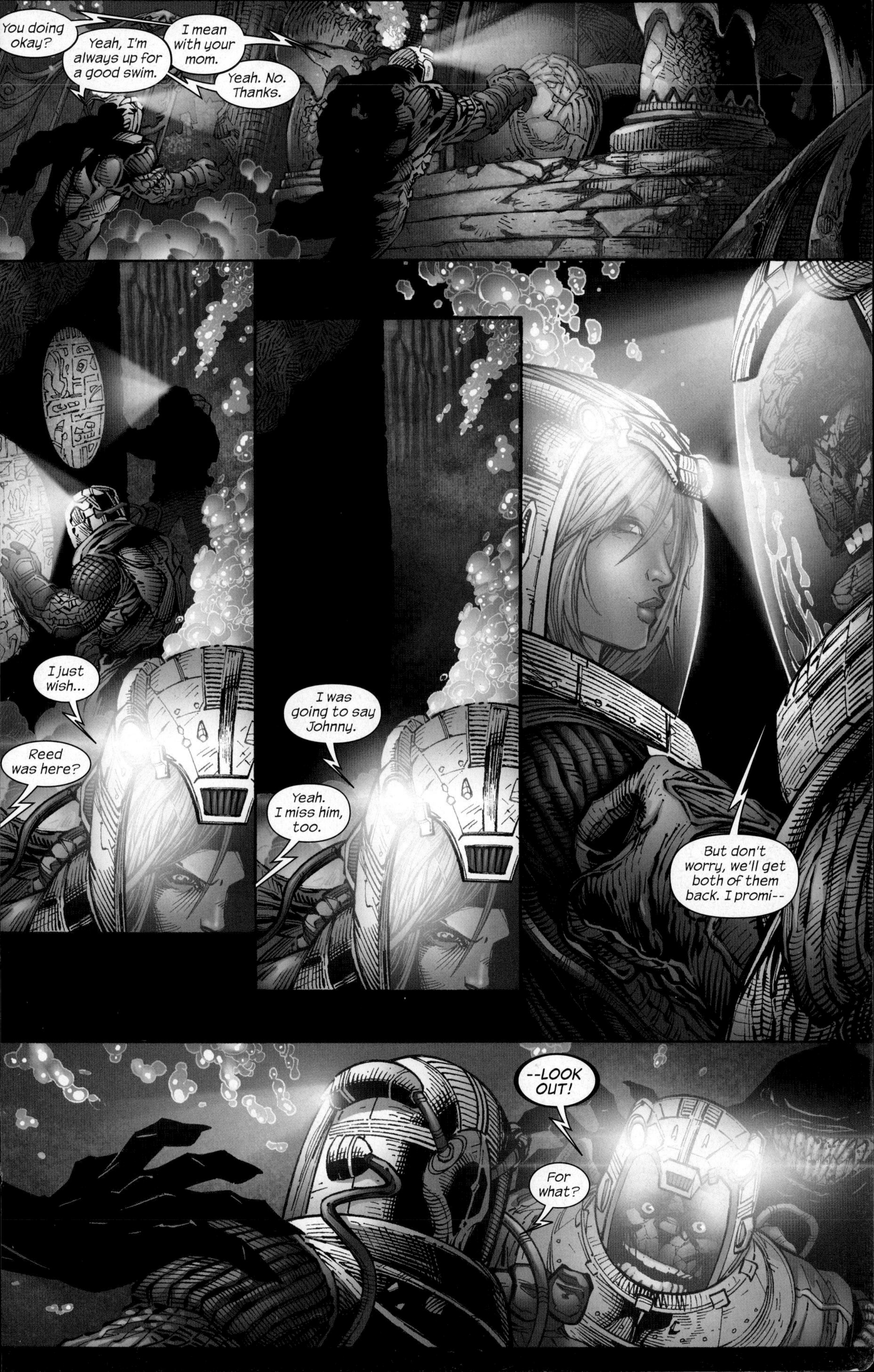
You doing okay?
Yeah, I'm always up for a good swim.
I mean with your mom.
Yeah. No. Thanks.
I just wish...
Reed was here?
I was going to say Johnny.
Yeah. I miss him, too.
But don't worry, we'll get both of them back. I promi--
--LOOK OUT!
For what?

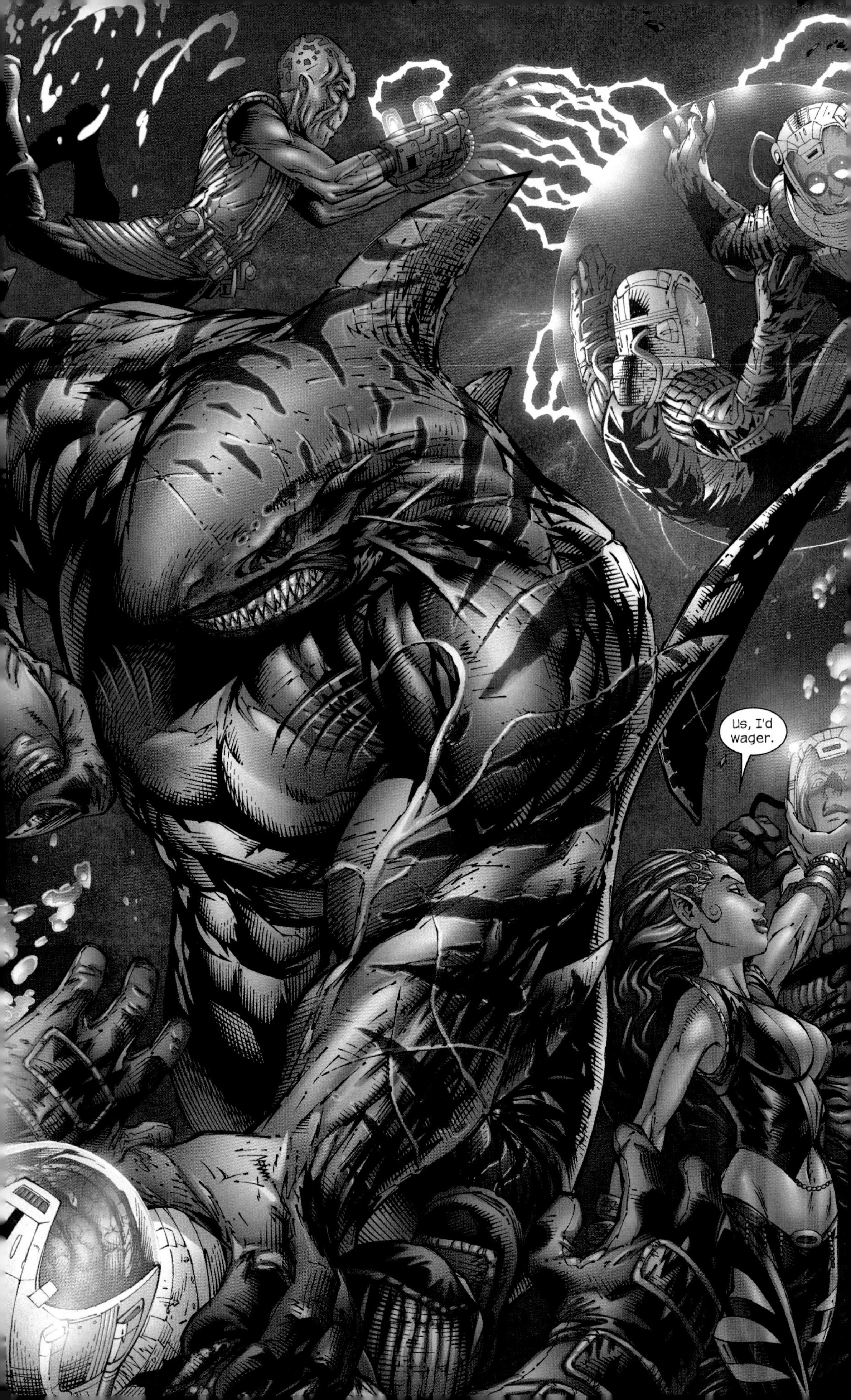
Us, I'd wager.

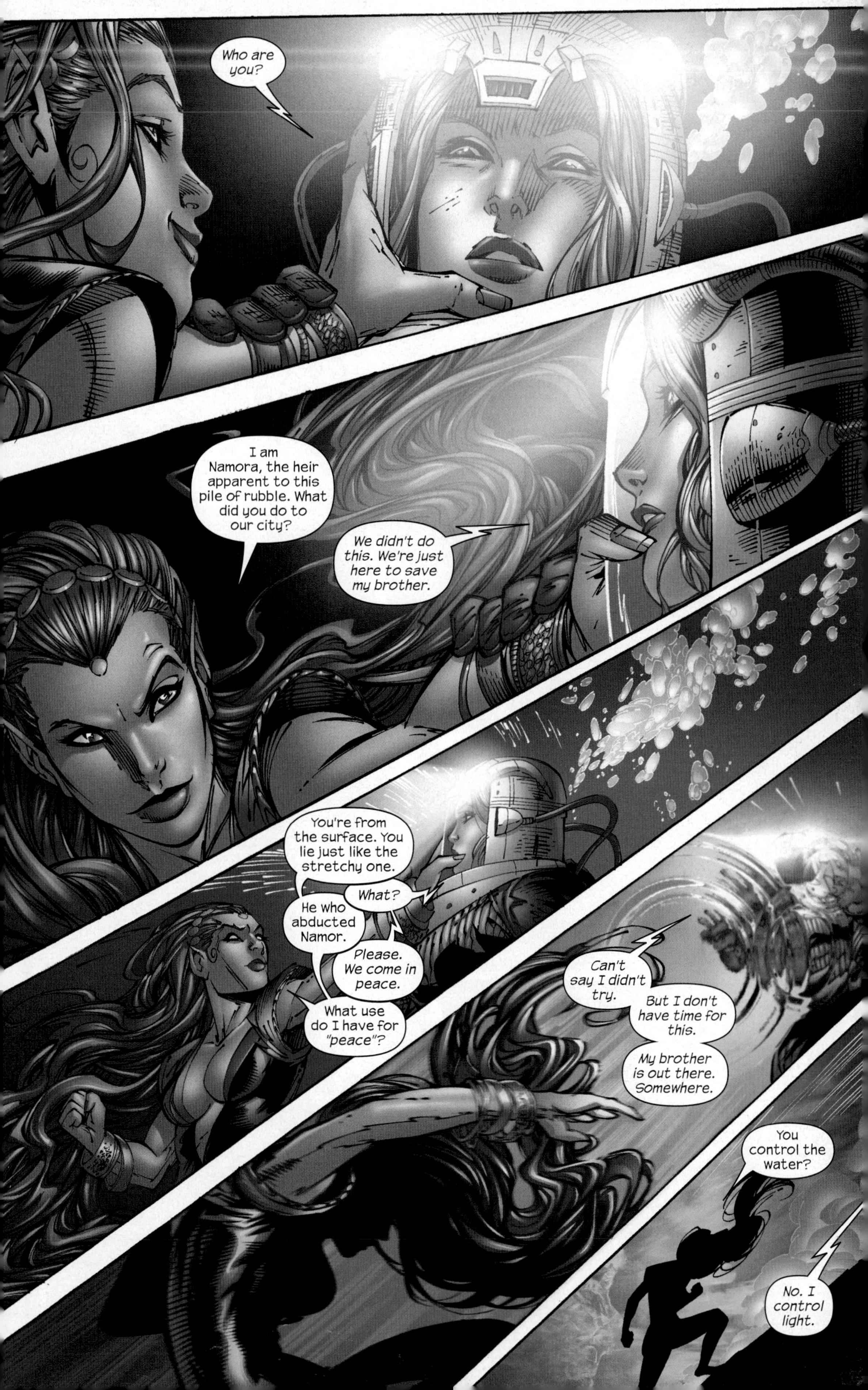

Who are you?
I am Namora, the heir apparent to this pile of rubble. What did you do to our city?
We didn't do this. We're just here to save my brother.
You're from the surface. You lie just like the stretchy one.
What?
He who abducted Namor.
Please. We come in peace.
What use do I have for "peace"?
Can't say I didn't try.
But I don't have time for this.
My brother is out there. Somewhere.
You control the water?
No. I control light.

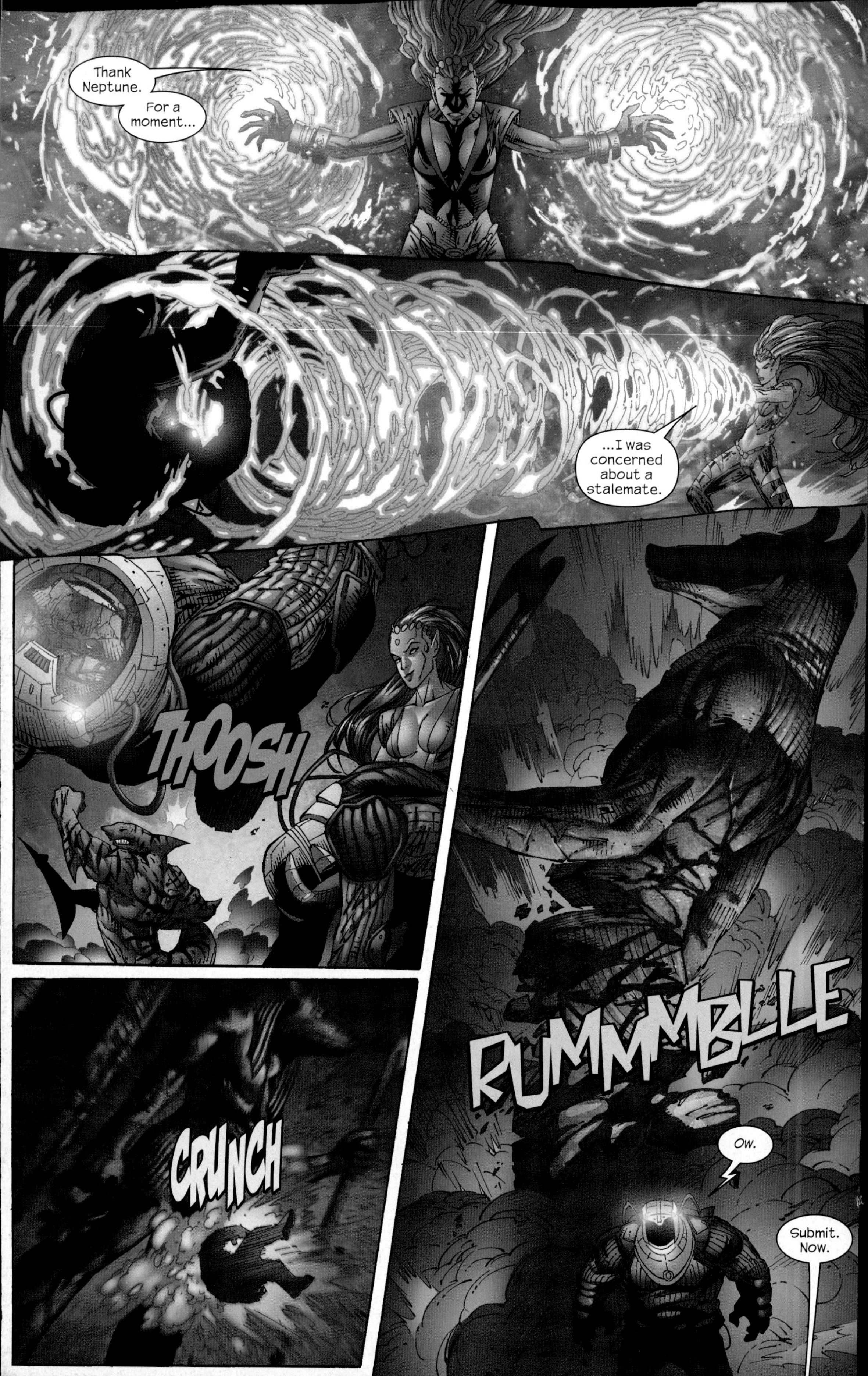
Thank Neptune.
For a moment...
...I was concerned about a stalemate.
THOOSH
CRUNCH
RUMMMBLLE
Ow.
Submit. Now.

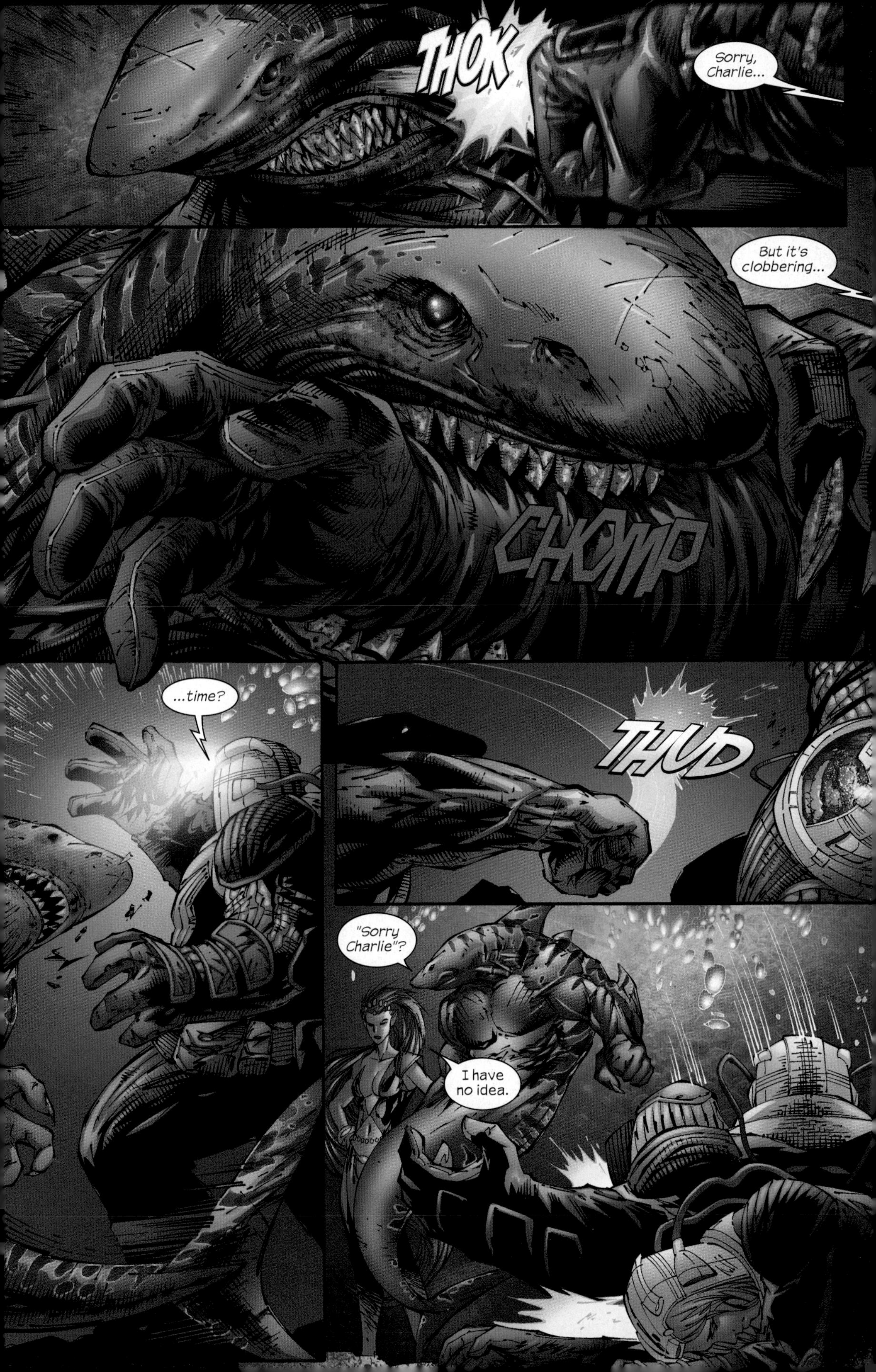
THOK
Sorry, Charlie...
But it's clobbering...
CHOMP
...time?
THUD
"Sorry Charlie"?
I have no idea.

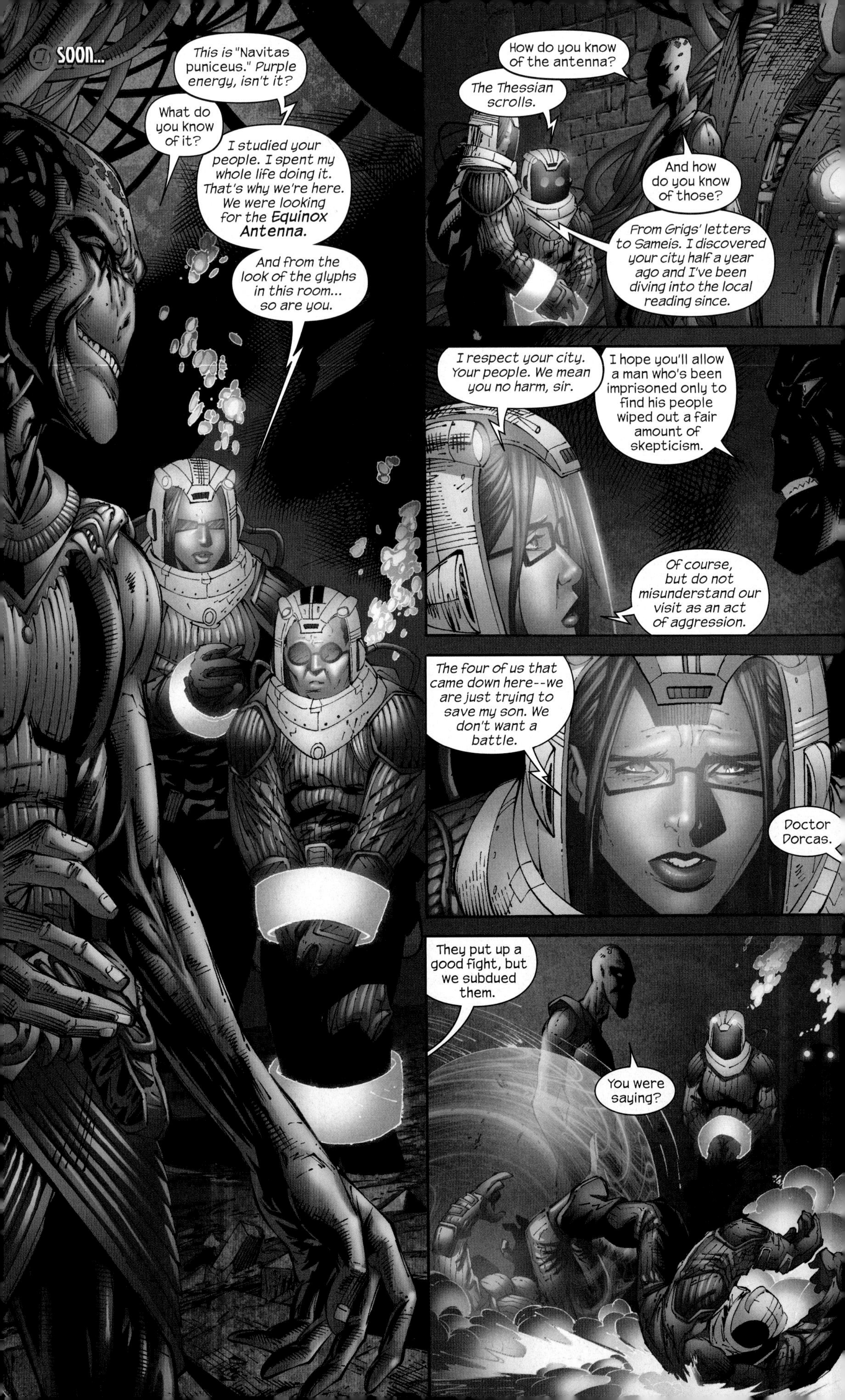
SOON...
This is "Navitas puniceus." Purple energy, isn't it?
What do you know of it?
I studied your people. I spent my whole life doing it. That's why we're here. We were looking for the Equinox Antenna.
And from the look of the glyphs in this room... so are you.
How do you know of the antenna?
The Thessian scrolls.
And how do you know of those?
From Grigs' letters to Sameis. I discovered your city half a year ago and I've been diving into the local reading since.
I respect your city. Your people. We mean you no harm, sir.
I hope you'll allow a man who's been imprisoned only to find his people wiped out a fair amount of skepticism.
Of course, but do not misunderstand our visit as an act of aggression.
The four of us that came down here--we are just trying to save my son. We don't want a battle.
Doctor Dorcas.
They put up a good fight, but we subdued them.
You were saying?

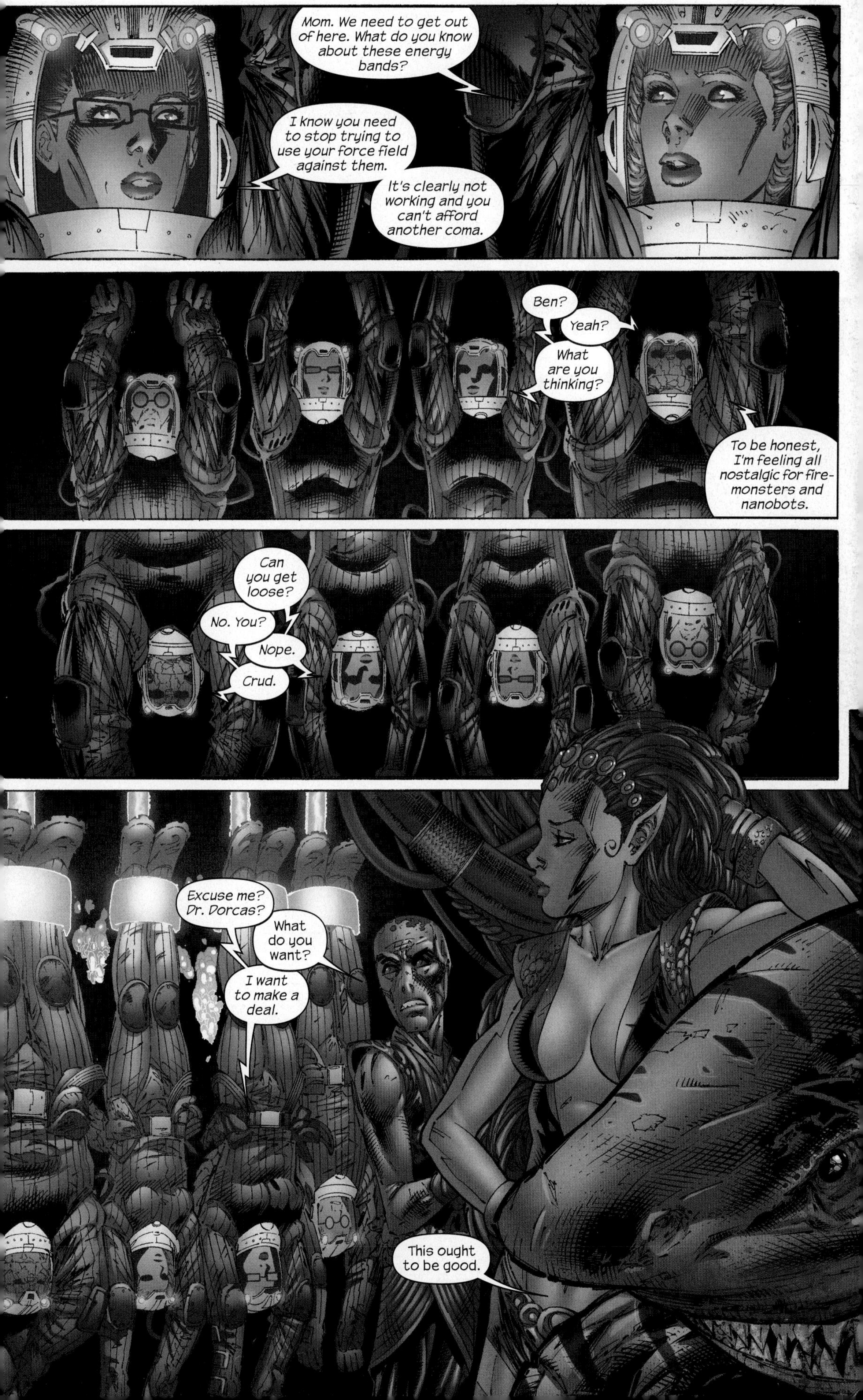

Mom. We need to get out of here. What do you know about these energy bands?
I know you need to stop trying to use your force field against them.
It's clearly not working and you can't afford another coma.
Ben?
Yeah?
What are you thinking?
To be honest, I'm feeling all nostalgic for fire-monsters and nanobots.
Can you get loose?
No. You?
Nope.
Crud.
Excuse me? Dr. Dorcas?
What do you want?
I want to make a deal.
This ought to be good.

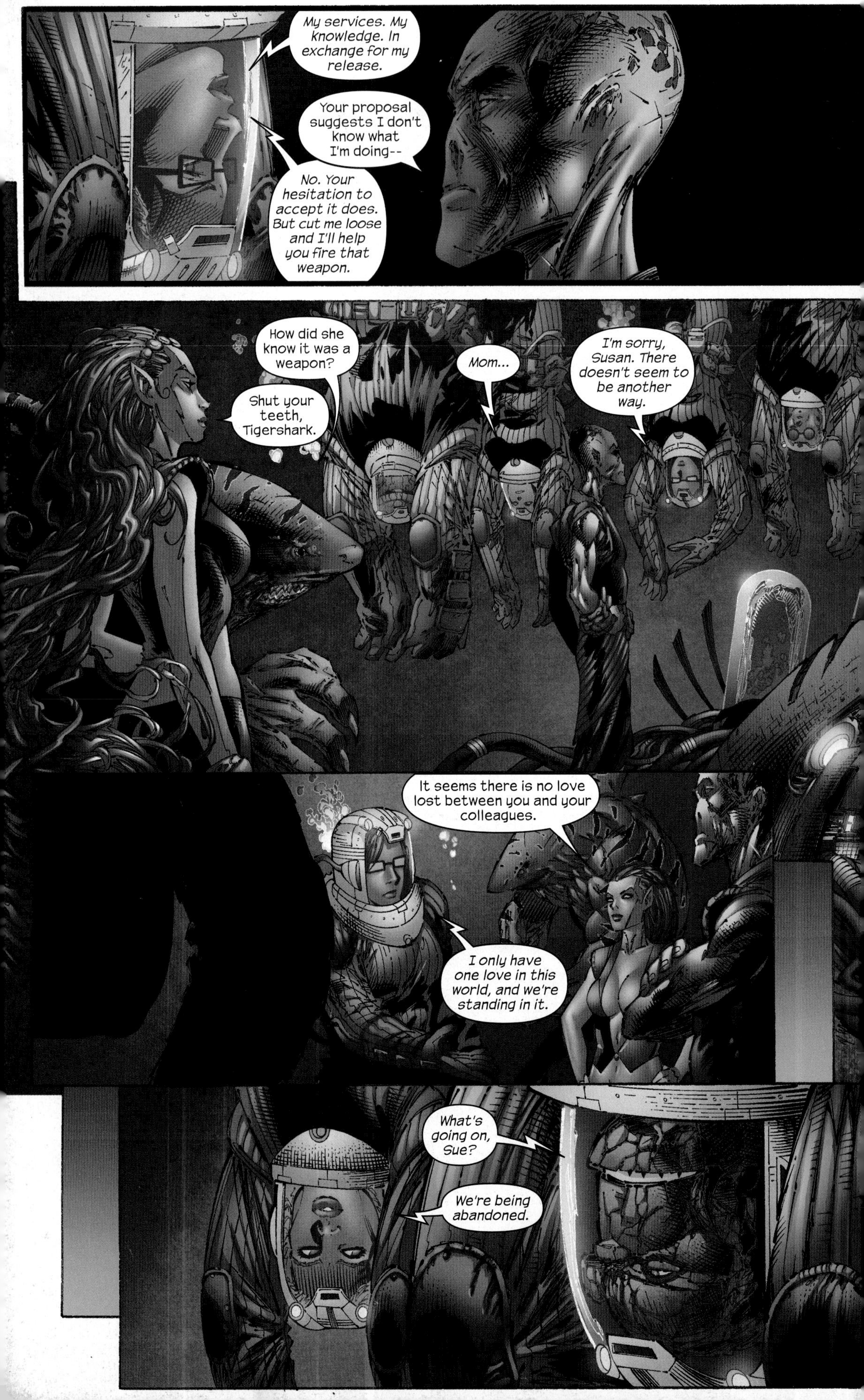

My services. My knowledge. In exchange for my release.
Your proposal suggests I don't know what I'm doing--
No. Your hesitation to accept it does. But cut me loose and I'll help you fire that weapon.
How did she know it was a weapon?
Shut your teeth, Tigershark.
Mom...
I'm sorry, Susan. There doesn't seem to be another way.
It seems there is no love lost between you and your colleagues.
I only have one love in this world, and we're standing in it.
What's going on, Sue?
We're being abandoned.

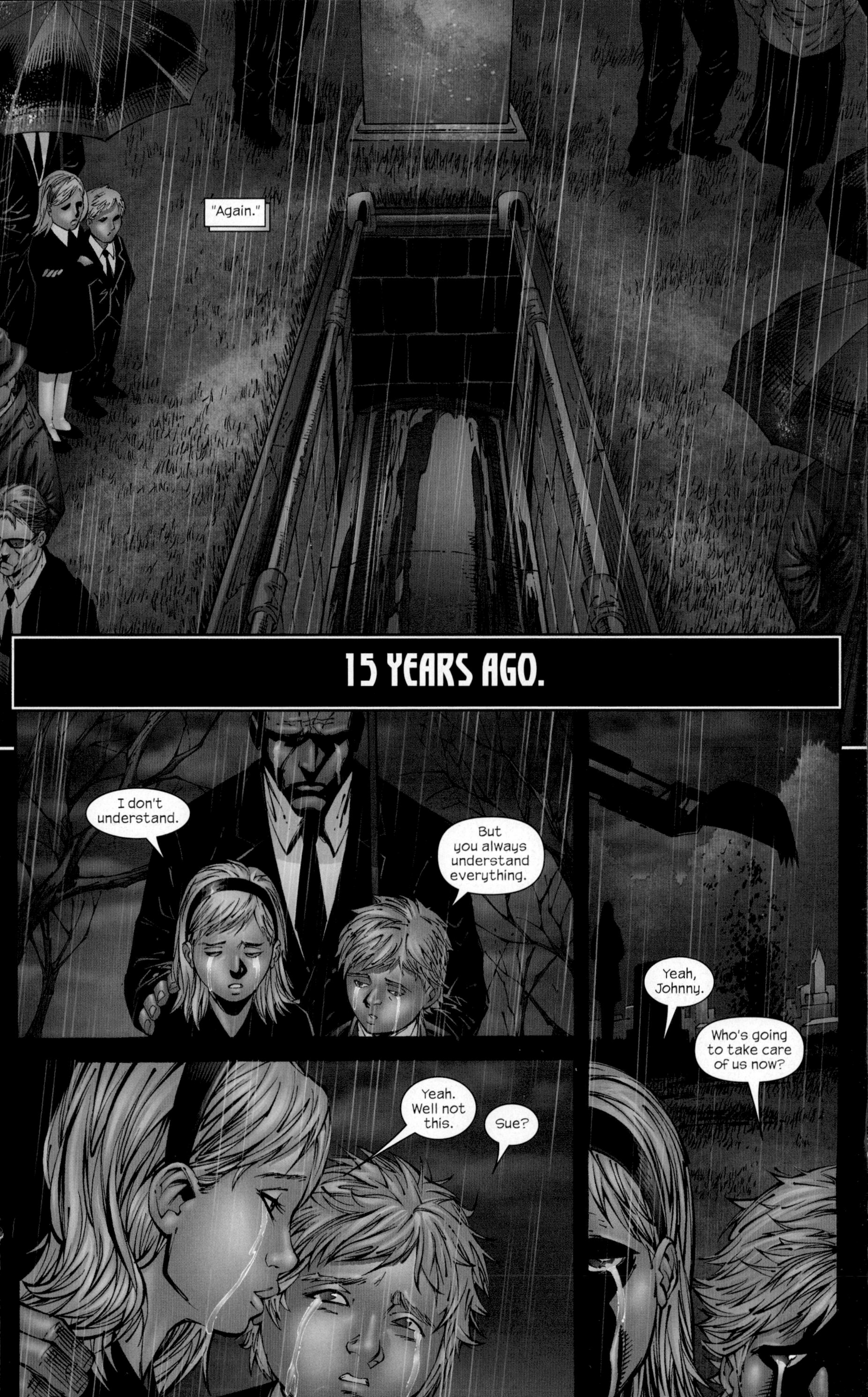
"Again."
15 YEARS AGO.
I don't understand.
But you always understand everything.
Yeah, Johnny.
Who's going to take care of us now?
Yeah. Well not this.
Sue?

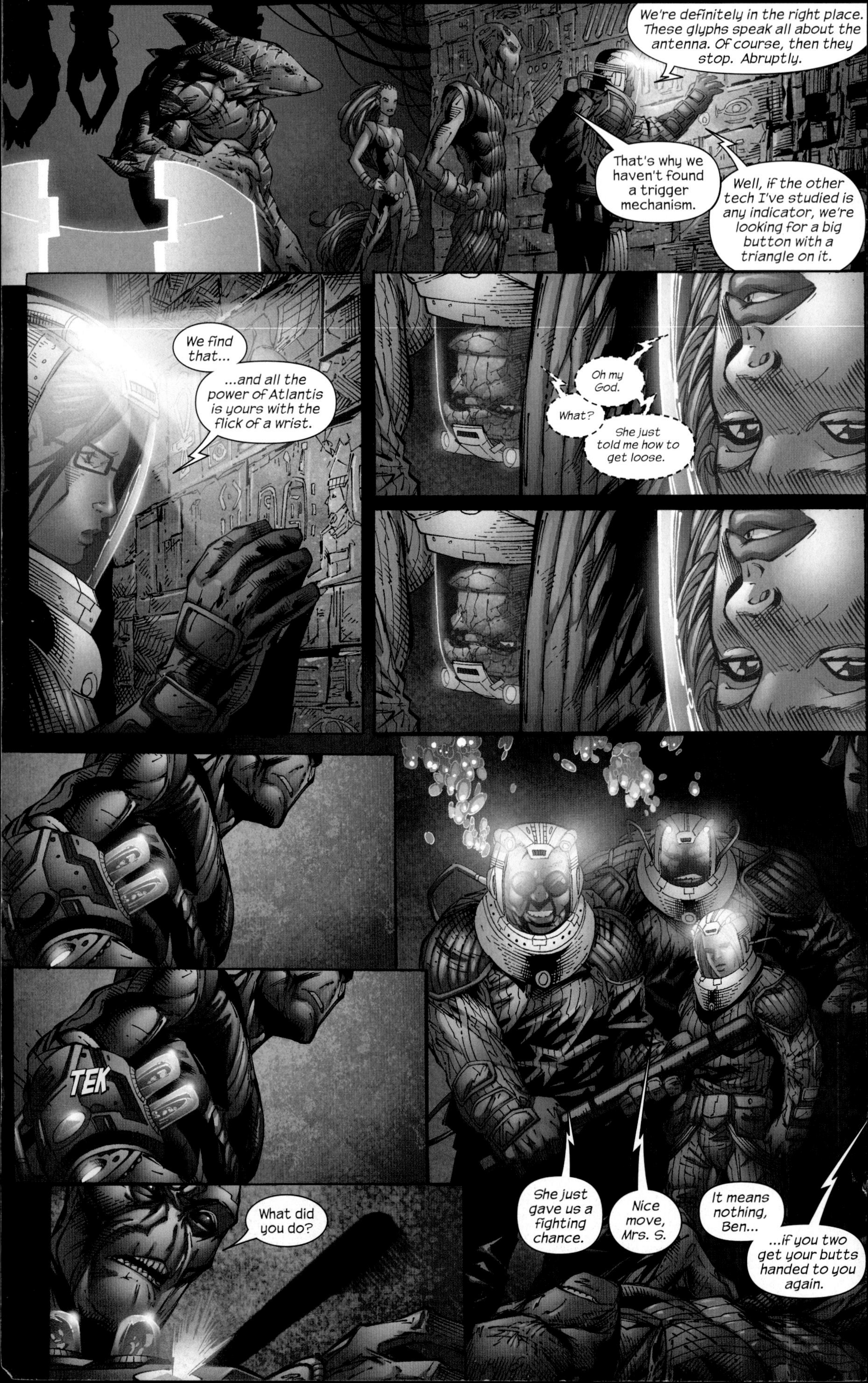
We're definitely in the right place. These glyphs speak all about the antenna. Of course, then they stop. Abruptly.
That's why we haven't found a trigger mechanism.
Well, if the other tech I've studied is any indicator, we're looking for a big button with a triangle on it.
We find that...
...and all the power of Atlantis is yours with the flick of a wrist.
Oh my God.
What?
She just told me how to get loose.
TEK
What did you do?
She just gave us a fighting chance.
Nice move, Mrs. S.
It means nothing, Ben...
...if you two get your butts handed to you again.

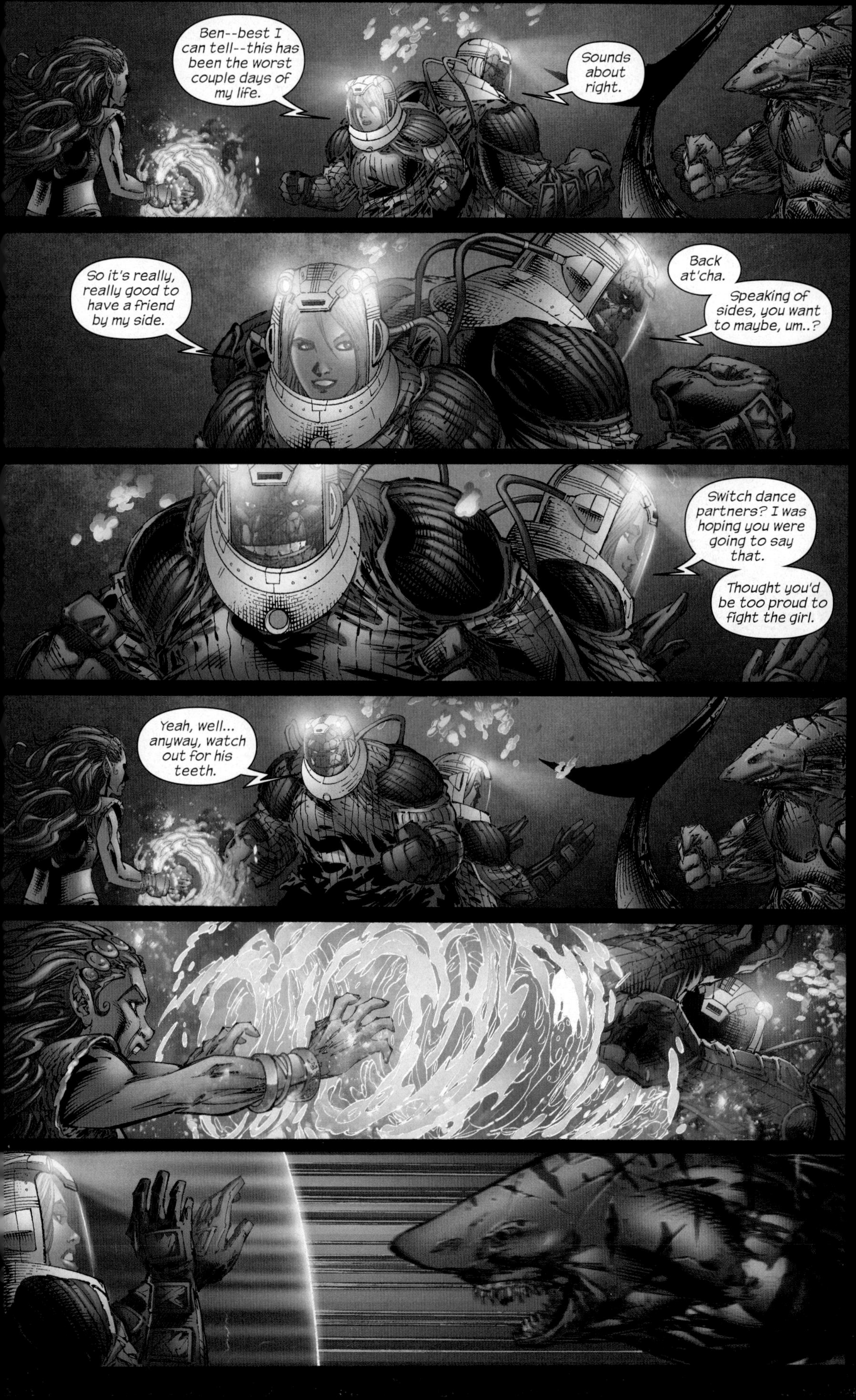
Ben--best I can tell--this has been the worst couple days of my life.
Sounds about right.
So it's really, really good to have a friend by my side.
Back at'cha.
Speaking of sides, you want to maybe, um..?
Switch dance partners? I was hoping you were going to say that.
Thought you'd be too proud to fight the girl.
Yeah, well... anyway, watch out for his teeth.

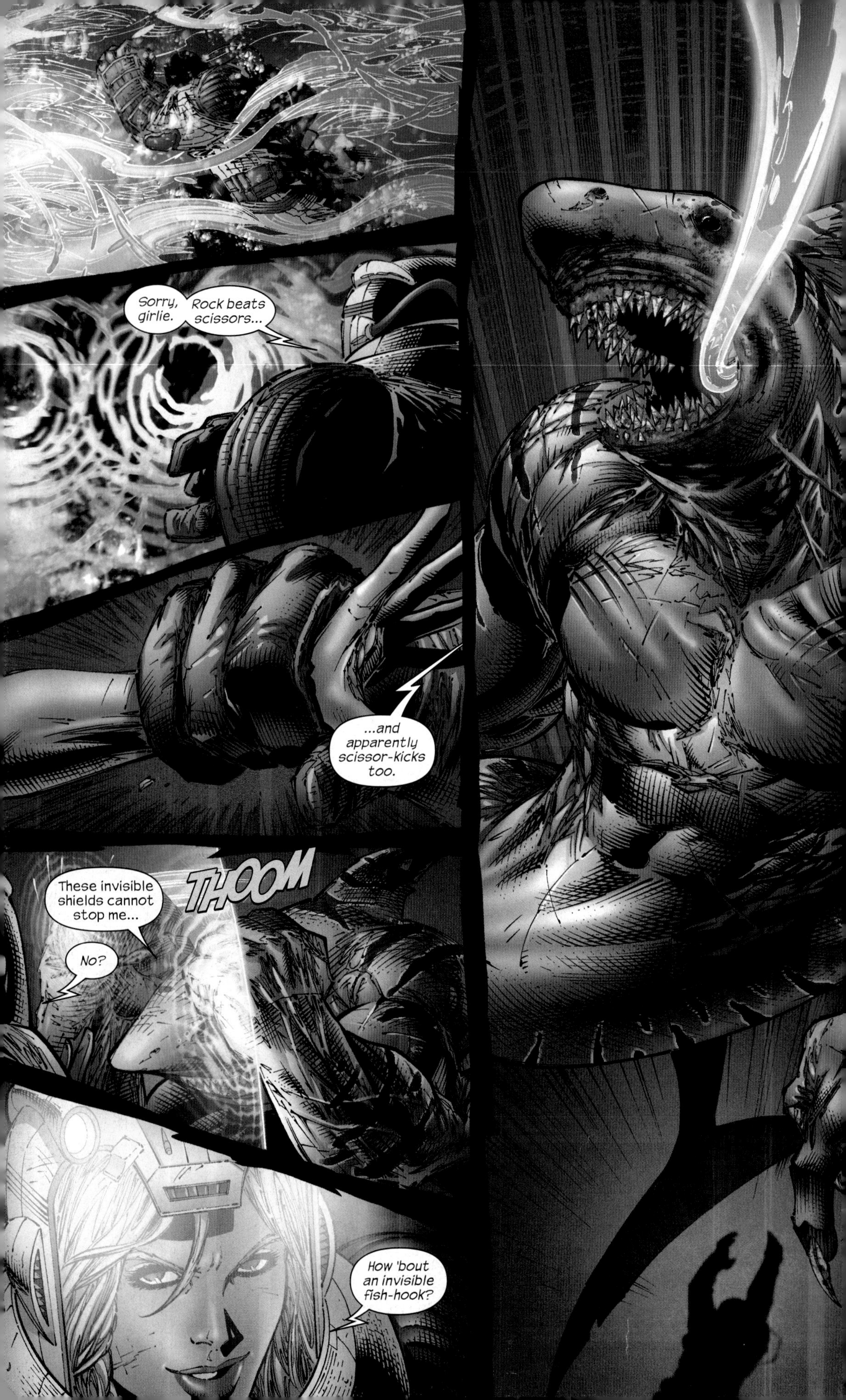
Sorry, girlie.
Rock beats scissors...
...and apparently scissor-kicks too.
THOOM
These invisible shields cannot stop me...
No?
How 'bout an invisible fish-hook?

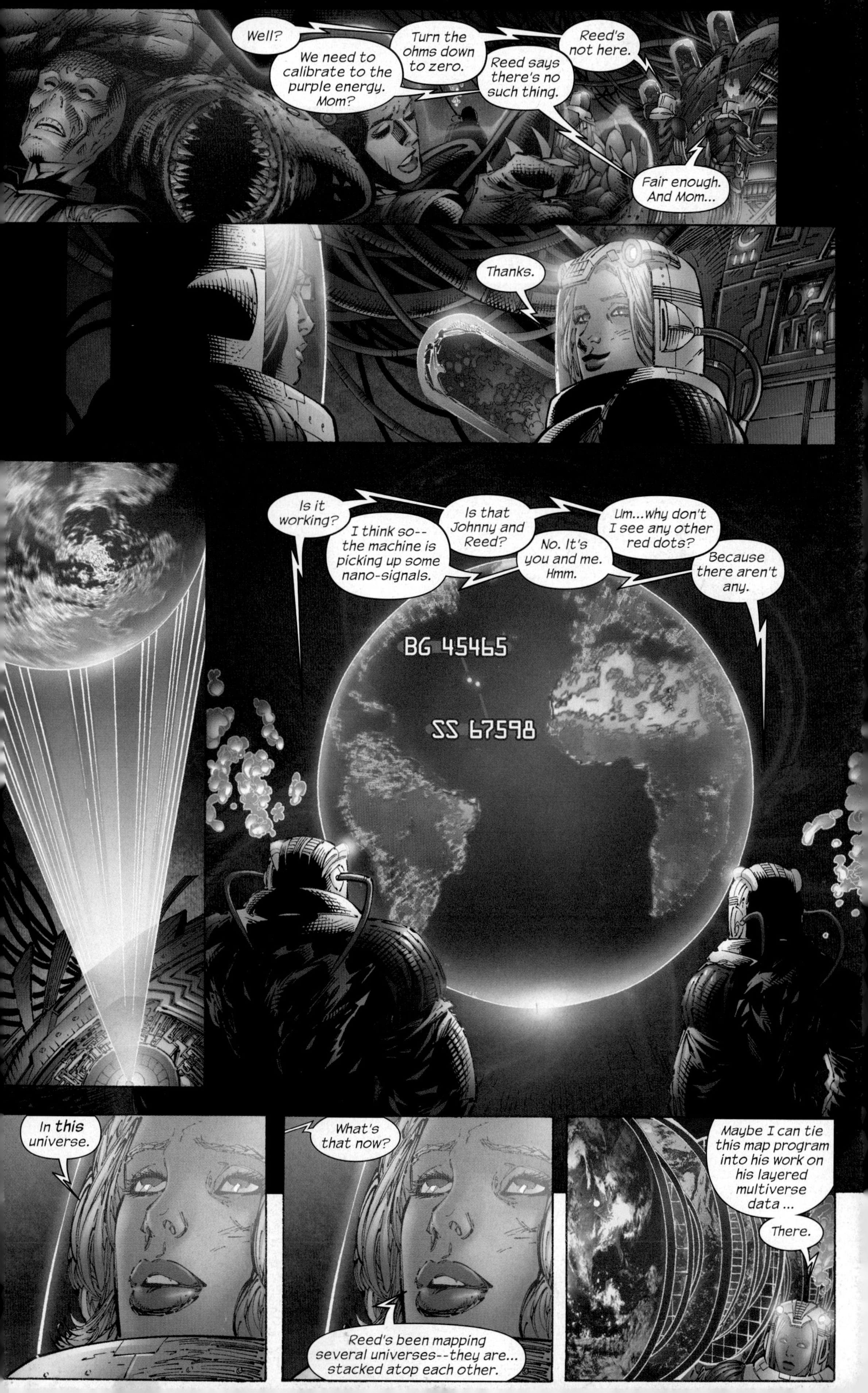
Well?
We need to calibrate to the purple energy. Mom?
Turn the ohms down to zero.
Reed says there's no such thing.
Reed's not here.
Fair enough. And Mom...
Thanks.
Is it working?
I think so-- the machine is picking up some nano-signals.
Is that Johnny and Reed?
No. It's you and me. Hmm.
Um...why don't I see any other red dots?
Because there aren't any.
BG 45465
SS 67598
In this universe.
What's that now?
Reed's been mapping several universes--they are... stacked atop each other.
Maybe I can tie this map program into his work on his layered multiverse data ...
There.

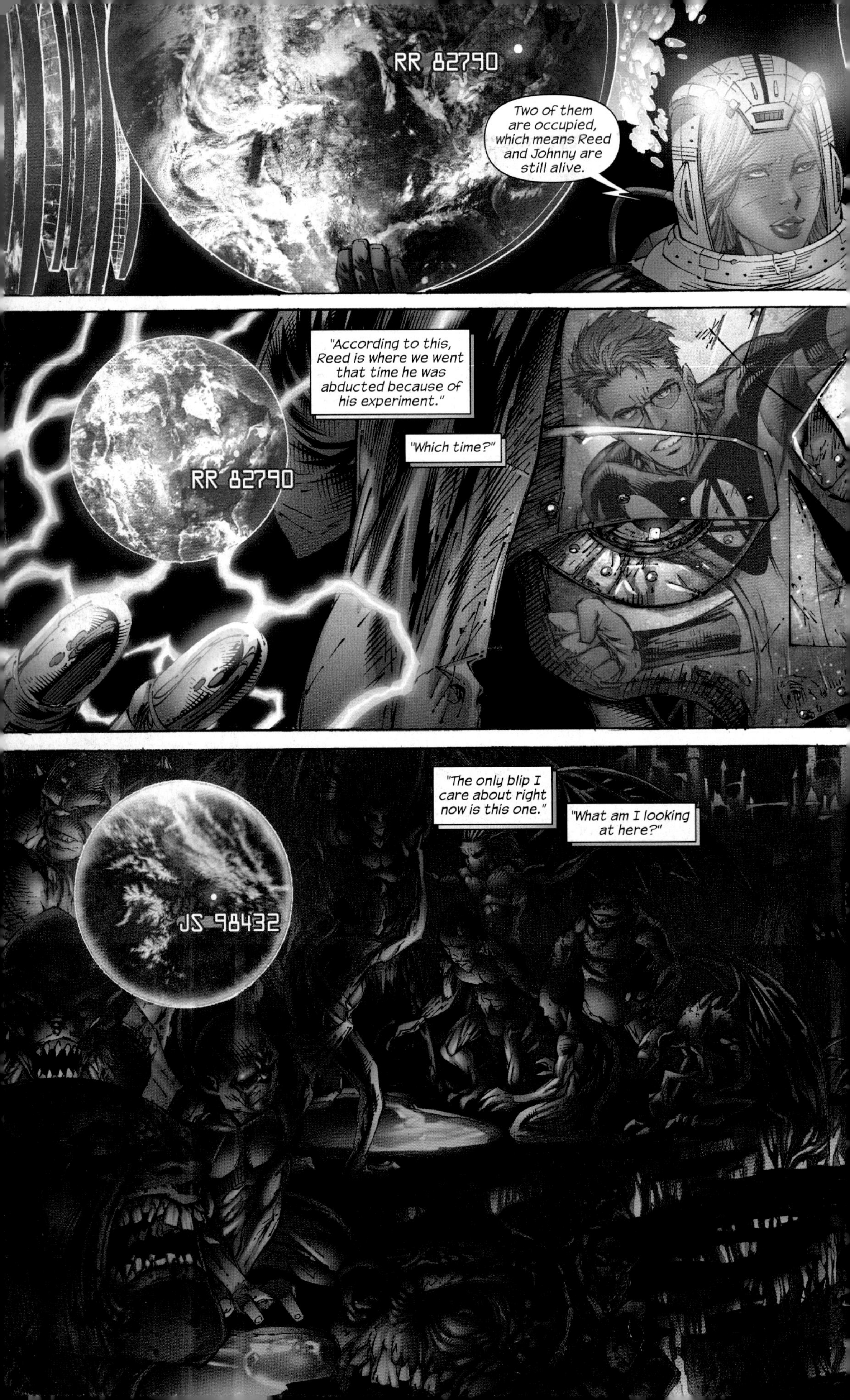
RR 82790
Two of them are occupied, which means Reed and Johnny are still alive.
"According to this, Reed is where we went that time he was abducted because of his experiment."
"Which time?"
RR 82790
"The only blip I care about right now is this one."
"What am I looking at here?"
JS 98432

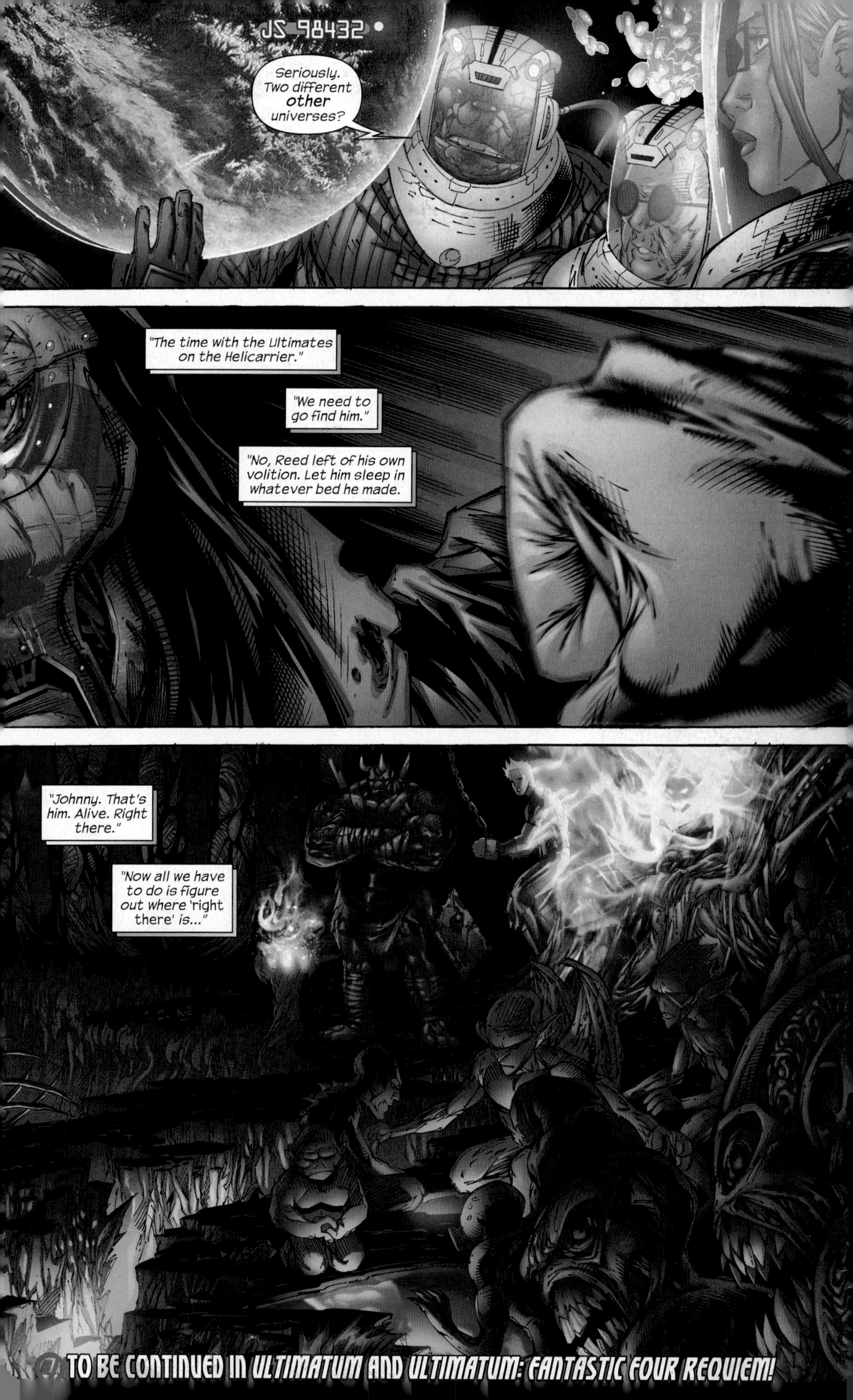

JS 98432
Seriously. Two different other universes?
"The time with the Ultimates on the Helicarrier."
"We need to go find him."
"No, Reed left of his own volition. Let him sleep in whatever bed he made.
"Johnny. That's him. Alive. Right there."
"Now all we have to do is figure out where 'right there' is..."
TO BE CONTINUED IN ULTIMATUM AND ULTIMATUM: FANTASTIC FOUR REQUIEM!